The Socially
Savvy Advisor

The Socially Savvy Advisor

Compliant Social Media for the Financial Industry

JENNIFER OPENSHAW

with
Stuart Fross and
Amy McIlwain

WILEY

Cover image: top: ©iStock.com/VLADGRIN; bottom: ©iStock.com/Alex Belomlinsky
Cover design: Wiley

Published by John Wiley & Sons, Inc., Hoboken, New Jersey.
Published simultaneously in Canada.

For general information on our other products and services or for technical support, please contact our Customer Care Department within the United States at (800) 762-2974, outside the United States at (317) 572-3993, or fax (317) 572-4002.

Wiley publishes in a variety of print and electronic formats and by print-on-demand. Some material included with standard print versions of this book may not be included in e-books or in print-on-demand. If this book refers to media such as a CD or DVD that is not included in the version you purchased, you may download this material at http://booksupport.wiley.com. For more information about Wiley products, visit www.wiley.com.

Library of Congress Cataloging-in-Publication Data:
Openshaw, Jennifer.
  The socially savvy advisor: compliant social media for the financial industry / Jennifer Openshaw, with Stuart Fross and Jerry Gleeson.
      pages cm. – (Wiley finance series)
  Includes index.
  ISBN 978-1-118-95907-7 (cloth/website); ISBN 978-1-118-95910-7 (ebk);
ISBN 978-1-118-95908-4 (ePub) 1.   Financial services industry. 2.   Investment advisors.
3.   Social media.   I. Title.
  HG173.O645 2015
  332.1068'8–dc23
                                                                              2014027686

Printed in the United States of America.

10 9 8 7 6 5 4 3 2 1

Dedicated . . .

To every investor who seeks financial security, and to every financial advisor who struggles in a rapidly changing world to make those investors' goals a reality.

Contents

Foreword

The world as you know it is being reshaped!

This statement couldn't be more descriptive of the Financial Services industry and the world of wealth management. Leadership teams around the globe are grappling with the rapid adoption of, increasing reliance on and relationship dynamics fueled by social platforms.

Facts called out in *The Socially Savvy Advisor* may have bordered on blasphemy in board rooms years ago. However, as author Jennifer Openshaw clearly points out, these behaviors are setting new rules of engagement. We live in a world where:

> *Fifty percent of investors . . . rely heavily on financial websites and blogs, ahead of financial newspapers and financial planners.*
>
> —ING Direct

> *Seventy percent of wealthy investors have restructured their investments . . . based on content found on social media.*
>
> —Cogent Mass Affluent 2014

> *Among "Under 40" HNWI, 40.5 percent cite social media as importance for accessing information and 36.3 percent for engaging with wealth managers and firms.*
>
> —RBC Wealth Management/CapGemini
> World Wealth Report 2014

And these are changes I've seen firsthand. I have spent the past 15 years focused on digital technologies that disrupt, enhance, and create value for clients as they navigate their intricate relationships with financial institutions.

Having joined LinkedIn in early 2011 as Global Head of Category Development–Financial Services, I've watched the LinkedIn network grow threefold to over 313 million members today. Within this vast network, the Financial Services industry has seen tremendous traction. In fact, the Financial Advisors Group is one of our fastest-growing communities, with more than 700,000 members globally. These members are actively leveraging LinkedIn to build their professional brands, grow their businesses, and, as a knowledge platform, to access industry news, market perspectives, and peer insights.

This rapid uptake presents financial services firms and those selling to them with tremendous opportunities to engage and interact with prospective clients. But there are right and wrong ways to go about this.

The Socially Savvy Advisor is a comprehensive guide to our social ecosystem and regulatory landscape. It provides pragmatic advice and how-to tips that can transform your social marketing efforts from being a tangential business strategy to a decisive game changer.

A concise and digestible read, this book is suitable for advisors at all stages of the "social practice" continuum. In it, you will find:

- Compelling stats and consumer insights.
- Use cases of social platforms, successful marketing practices, and a getting-started checklist.
- Overview of regulatory rules and a compliance planning guide.
- Best practices for content creation, content distribution and migrating to an "always-on" content strategy.
- Standards related to marketing and business development.

So read on for clear guidance when it comes to tapping into this new opportunity without breaking the rules.

JENNIFER GRAZEL
Global Head of Category Development
Financial Services
LinkedIn

Acknowledgments

You've heard it before: it takes a village. But you know it's true when we're talking about compliant social media for the financial industry!

Numerous industry leaders and experts shared their invaluable time and insights, and for that I'm especially grateful. They include Melissa Callison, vice president of communications compliance, Charles Schwab; Michael Kitces, author of *Nerd's Eye View*; Blane Warrene, co-founder of Arkovi; Renee Brown, senior vice president and director of social media at Wells Fargo; Edward McNicholas, partner at Sidley Austin; Dan Schreck, head of investor relations at Equinox Partners; Tina Petruzziello and David Rozenson of Boston Compliance Associates; Marie Swift, CEO of Impact Communications; Barbara Stettner, managing partner of Allen & Overy; Frank Eliason, director of global social media at Citibank; Sunayna Tuteja, director, social business & e-commerce at TD Ameritrade; Frank Gosch, senior director of search and analytics at Hearst; Lindsay Tiles, managing director of social media at Charles Schwab; Mike White, chief marketing officer at Raymond James; Melissa Sochi, SVP of brand & marketing delivery at LPL Financial; April Rudin, founder of Rudin Marketing; Brittney Castro, founder of Financially Wise Women; and Bill Winterberg, CFP® and founder of FPPad. You all bring tremendous energy and foresight.

I'm grateful to the Wiley team, especially Tula Batanchiev, for immediately seeing the tremendous need for this book. Judy Howarth, thank you for your valuable production guidance.

Stuart Fross, partner at Foley & Lardner, a gifted attorney and dear friend, and Amy McIlwain, president of Financial Social Media, were both invaluable contributors. You've enriched this guide with your expertise.

Two people—among the most dedicated I've ever met—deserve special applause. Marketing Manager Sherry Chen brought her usual perfection to the images and examples in the book, and Jerry Gleeson, one of the most gifted editors in financial journalism, imparted his years of wisdom and breathed life into my words.

Finally, to my family—husband Randy and daughters Gianna and Elizabeth—you are my village of support and sage advice on the homefront.

When I walked through the door and shared the delight at nearly completing the book, you were just as excited.

"Where's the book, Mommy?" asked 4-year-old Gianna. "Can I see it?"

"It's not ready yet, honey," I said. "But you can help me choose the cover."

"Okay!" she said with glee.

I showed her the four options that the publisher had sent over. After just a few moments, she pointed confidently at one. . . and I knew it was the right choice.

Introduction

Nicky Gumbel arrived early at his kid's soccer game. Realizing the regular referee was late and no other dads were around, he decided to step in.

Nothing was set up—no cones, no nets, no markings for the boundaries. Gumbel wasn't a soccer player himself and knew little about the rules. But he thought, *What the heck, let's get the kids on the field and start kicking the ball.*

The problems started early and quickly escalated.

"Some shouted that the ball was in. Others said it was out. I wasn't at all sure, so I let things run," Gumbel recalled. "The game soon descended into complete chaos."

Kids were getting hurt and arguing over purported fouls, but Gumbel couldn't tell who was right or how to resolve the disarray.

Then Andy, the regular referee, appeared on the scene. "The moment Andy arrived, he blew his whistle, arranged the teams, told them where the boundaries were, and had them under control," Gumbel said. "Then the boys had the time of their lives!"

What does this have to do with social media in the financial industry?

Advisors frequently chafe against the restrictions that compliance places on them. That's become more acute in recent years, as people in the industry explore the bounds of what works and what doesn't in the new world of social media.

Yet limits—whether on the soccer field or in the financial social media world—actually create a framework. They allow us to operate within the cones and spawn a game with purpose and excitement. Without limits, we're not really free to enjoy the game, or our work.

Imagine you're an asset manager or an advisor at a bank or wealth management firm. You or your colleagues are on social media, conversing about whatever comes to mind, engaging with whomever—on Twitter, LinkedIn, or Facebook.

You know how conversations can get sometimes at the office water cooler or restroom? It's easy to toss off some uncensored bon mot, share a quick laugh, and head back to your desk. Well, people are doing that on social media, and the outcomes aren't always pretty. In fact, as you'll see in this book, the professional damage can be substantial.

The point is: without structure, there's chaos. Advisors and firms, and certainly compliance officers, need a sense of orderliness and oversight. The end investor does, too, for his own protection.

Hopefully, I bring a little perspective. In the early Internet days of 1999, I left a large investment advisory firm to head up to Silicon Valley. It was there that I launched Women's Financial Network, an online brokerage, content, and advisor network venture focused on this growing market. It was the Gold Rush of online action, and we were leading the way, with 1,000 women signing up for our service *each day*. Since then, I've advised and worked for many firms and nonprofits, trying to bring a consumer-focused experience that leverages the technologies of the day.

Leap forward 10 years, and today that milieu is social media. We are in Web 3.0, where business relationships can be built—and brands ruined— with a handful of keystrokes.

There's danger for investors, too. Unscrupulous individuals can now reach thousands, if not millions, of people to tout some dangerous investment or maybe even attempt to access their personal financial information.

Do we need structure? You bet. Not just to protect our business, but to enable you—the advisor or the firm—to operate freely and successfully.

The insights and guidance you're about to glean from this book come largely from my work over the past three years with more than 300 firms—from small registered investment advisers (RIAs) and banks and wealth management divisions to hedge funds, mutual funds, and other asset managers.

Some time ago, the leaders at LinkedIn approached me about joining their Influencer program—a chance for accomplished professionals in various industries to write about issues from their perspectives. I held off at first because I was preoccupied with my job and my column at MarketWatch, but curiosity about writing on a new social media platform led me to try it out. The experience with my first column astonished me: Every hour I checked in, the views would go up by a thousand. I found myself replying to some of the comments, which produced more comments. Overall, the story generated more than 100,000 views and 400 comments— four times what many articles in traditional online channels generate.

As impressed as I was by that, I understand that many people still have questions about what social media means for them. Indeed, even as this book was going to press, a new study by Gallup questioned social media's impact— 62 percent of consumers surveyed by the firm said social media had no influence on their buying decisions.

Clearly, social media is in its infancy, especially in our industry. There's still a great deal of debate over things like return on investment (ROI), but my goal here is to at least provide you with the rules of the game and some insights as to how others—advisors, managers, and even associations in our industry—are playing on the field.

I know you don't have much time, and that's why this book is designed to answer the biggest questions you ponder over every day when it comes to using social media. You'll find lots of specific guidance and how-tos, along with compelling visuals to illustrate how you might move forward.

We are at an exciting time in our industry—where technology, regulations, and investing are creating the perfect storm for change. Sure, we may have been slow to adopt social media, but the opportunity to change the financial landscape and continue to serve as the world's pre-eminent financial center remains in our hands.

Join me in continuing the innovation on behalf of investors.

PART One

The New Business Environment

CHAPTER 1

How Is Social Media Changing Investor Behavior?

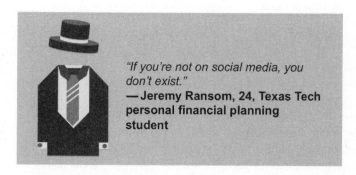

"If you're not on social media, you don't exist."
—**Jeremy Ransom, 24, Texas Tech personal financial planning student**

You remember that small innovation called e-mail? It changed everything from how we behaved to how we managed our workloads.

In e-mail's early days, many compliance officers insisted, "We'll never adopt this." But soon enough, e-mail became a part of their daily lives. Compliance officers and marketers were forced to embrace it as the rest of the world did, leading them to invent new policies and procedures in order to remain compliant with regulators.

Imagine where your business would be today if you hadn't adapted to e-mail. The service is such a part of the landscape that nobody bothers to give it much more than a second thought. That's how it is with transformative technology—it upends the market, the market adapts, and its use is taken for granted.

Now fast-forward another two decades or so, and have a look at the latest game-changer: social media. Today, it's a New Tech World Order, as I call it. Our society has never seen anything like it; information can be sent in nano-seconds and shared in ways that are empowering people and upending traditional ways of doing business. In the financial world, that can be information shared between investors, from a company to investors, or vice versa.

For you or your business, that dynamic can be both a blessing and a curse. The blessing, for those who embrace it, includes getting out of the starting gate early as the market evolves. The curse is the uncertainty of the new—Am I doing this right? How do I prepare for risks I don't fully understand right now?

One way to understand what social media means in the New Tech World Order is to look more closely at how it's affecting the lives of the clients on whom the financial industry depends.

HOW INVESTORS ARE GETTING SOCIAL

First, let's take a look at how today's investors are behaving. They are using the online, social world to engage in five key ways:

1. **Convening**—Connecting with others like them. You're familiar with online gatherings around a profession. Even the old-fashioned investment club is more active online, with greater access to tools and content for more efficient exchanges. Consumers are increasingly gathering with those like them, whether it's to engage in impact investing, to encourage more women to move into our industry, or to call for a greener world. Yes, the online world now makes niche convening with people truly "like me" more possible than ever before.
2. **Sharing**—Thanks to the new federal Jumpstart Our Business Startups Act, firms and investors are increasingly sharing information and investment opportunities. They're doing it through online investment sites that allow them to discover Warren Buffett's latest investment. Soon, they'll be accessing prospectuses of investment opportunities that previously were available only to sophisticated investors.
3. **Reacting**—You've wanted to react many times. To a bad product or service or a rude professional, or, on the flip side, a great experience. Now, imagine that reaction shared online, magnified by thousands if not millions. It's happening, especially through Facebook and Twitter, as we'll discuss in the coming pages.
4. **Opining**—Perhaps the biggest surprise to some is the new ease with which overnight investment gurus can emerge. Many are springing up either with their own blogs, on sites like SeekingAlpha where professionals can share their investment insights, or on financial news sites and networks, from Dow Jones' MarketWatch to Motif, a consumer-oriented social investing platform.
5. **Protecting**—One of the greatest empowerment moves is the ability to help consumers make better decisions—from choosing restaurants to

hiring a handyman—and protect them from bad actors. I was once asked if online networks will pose a greater threat to investors who might be prey to the next Bernie Madoff. Interestingly, in Europe, a social network for investors called Unience (sister to Finect in the U.S.) discovered that members actually acted quickly to protect fellow members from bad investment products or people. Just as one can instantly flag a spammer on Yelp, so too can they instantly call out a disreputable professional.

These behaviors aren't occurring in a vacuum. It should come as no surprise that they've helped shape the way investors approach financial advice and related services.

INVESTORS ARE DEMANDING MORE WITH TRANSPARENCY AND REAL-TIME ACCESS

Starting just a few years ago—after the financial crisis, and as social media usage picked up—investors became increasingly drawn to the Internet as a source of investment advice. This was due in large part to a massive loss of trust in major U.S. banks. Nearly 50 percent of investors now rely heavily on financial websites and blogs—ahead of financial newspapers, periodicals, and financial planners—for their investment information (see Figure 1.1).

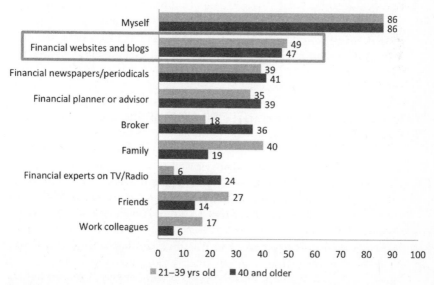

FIGURE 1.1 Sources of Investment Advice
Source: ING Direct USA's Sharebuilder Survey

It's clear that investors, especially younger ones, are actively engaged in the online world in other ways:

- **They're reallocating.** According to a survey conducted by Cogent Research of 4,000 investors with more than $100,000 in investable assets, nearly 70 percent of wealthy investors have restructured their investments, started, or altered relationships with investment providers, based on content found through social media.
- **They're researching electronically.** Just in the last few years, consumers have had more access to real-time information, from scrolling through Twitter on their smartphones to pulling out their iPad while at the gym. In fact, a Fidelity Investments survey found that two-thirds of the millionaires surveyed said they would like to use electronic media with their advisors. And young millionaires—those ages 44 and younger—are three times more likely than millionaires of all ages to select a financial professional through a website providing detailed information on advisors, according to Spectrem Group.
- **They're engaging online.** Young millionaires are four times more likely to express interest in a blog or tweets from their advisor, and nearly six times more likely to say they'd like their advisor to be on Facebook. "The overall percentages of young investors wishing to connect with advisors via social media remain small, but the differences in attitudes between young millionaires and millionaires of all ages are striking," Spectrem Group says.

Indeed, investor involvement with social media will play out profoundly in the years ahead, with serious implications for advisors who fail to take the trend seriously.

WHAT INVESTORS REALLY WANT: FIND THEIR ADVISORS ON SOCIAL MEDIA

Think about it. Suppose an investor decided the time had come to begin working with a financial advisor. It's natural to start such a search on the Web. Would the investor be able to find your business on the Web? And if so, would he find the information on your site that he really wants to know?

It turns out this may be harder for the investor than you would think. In late 2013, a survey with investors uncovered some surprising findings (Figure 1.2). Nearly half of those surveyed want to connect with their financial advisors through social media, but they either cannot find advisors or they conclude the advisors don't operate through this online channel.

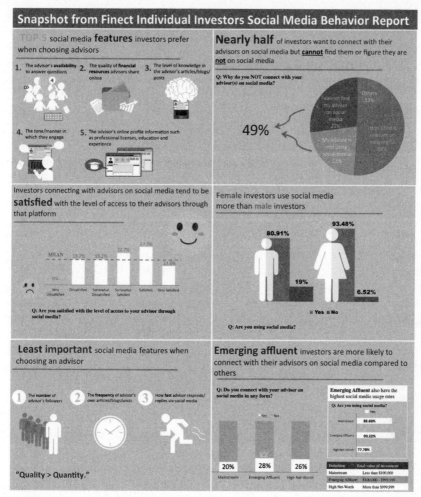

FIGURE 1.2 Investors' Preferences for Financial Advisors on Social Media
Source: Finect Inc.

The survey also found that those investors who *do* connect with their advisors through social media are generally satisfied with their interaction. Among the key findings:

- Investors age 44 or younger are more likely to connect with their advisors on social media than those over 45.
- Emerging affluent investors (more than $100,000 to under $1 million in assets) use social media more than mainstream and high net-worth investors do.

- Investors who connect with their advisors on social media tend to be satisfied with the level of access to their advisors.
- Female investors are 11.5 percent more likely than male investors to connect with their advisors on social media.
- Investors do not care about the details of their advisors' personal lives on social media—which is not to be confused with being personable.
- The *most important* social media interaction with advisors, according to investors, is sharing trending investments or personal finance news.
- The number of social media followers an advisor has is the *least important* feature for investors when choosing advisors through social media.
- An advisor's availability to answer questions is the *most important* feature for investors when choosing advisors through social media.

The message is clear. Successful American industries have adapted when consumer preferences and behaviors change. Automobiles are safer to drive, restaurants serve healthier food, and home computers operate more quickly and with more sophisticated software. The financial industry now faces new demands from investors who are more empowered via social channels. As the survey underscores, younger investors already expect their advisors to interact with them in this medium. Clearly those advisors who do so will be the ones who thrive as the future inevitably closes in. The financial industry has adapted to paradigm shifts of this sort in the past, and will continue to do so. Advisors and other professionals who adapt to the trend will have a leg up on their competitors. What are you waiting for?

CHAPTER 2

What Are Social Media's Implications for the Financial Industry?

A t the end of Chapter 1, I alluded to examples of how different industries in the United States responded to changes in behavior by their customers—new safety features in automobiles, less sugar and salt in food, and so on. It also happens that many American industries also are *au courant* with developments in social media as well.

Whether it's fashion or food, they not only have embraced social media, they've incorporated it into their businesses or built online communities around niche markets. Think of Yelp or Hotels.com for locally rated restaurants or overnight stays. Amazon.com has refashioned retail, not only by making it easier for consumers to buy what they want, but also by tracking customer interests and using that data to suggest other products their clients might enjoy. Even in our personal lives, places like Match.com have, for nearly a decade, transformed the way consumers can find their life partner.

SITTING OUT THE GAME?

And yet a good portion of the financial industry remains skeptical about this revolution. To be sure, there is a healthy and growing presence of financial advisors on professional networking site LinkedIn, yet participation in other key social media channels is still pretty thin. A 2013 survey by *InvestmentNews* showed that only one out of four advisors used Facebook, and participation in other channels was markedly lower.[1]

---

[1]"Advisers and Social Media," *InvestmentNews*, 2013, www.investmentnews.com/assets/docs/CI90361823.pdf. Accessed June 2014.

Social Media Tools Used by Advisers Professionally		
2013		**2012**
67.5%	**Linked in**	61.9%
25.3%	facebook	21.7%
23.1%	twitter	18.7%
16.3%	Blog	13.2%
11.3%	Google+	7.9%
9.7%	You Tube	7.4%
0.9%	Pinterest	1.1%
0.3%	Instagram	0.6%
13.1%	DO NOT USE	17.0%

FIGURE 2.1   LinkedIn Leads Among Advisors
Source: InvestmentNews' Advisers & Social Media Survey 2013

Industry experts say many firms are just tiptoeing into this new channel—testing tools to allow content distribution, piloting basic regulatory compliance through social media, and shaping their online voices. The goal is to build brand and awareness or increase engagement with investors, although many in the industry remain concerned about how strong the impact will be on revenue growth and the return on their investments (see Figure 2.1).

And yet the pace is picking up, says Alan Maginn, an analyst at Corporate Insight, which follows developments in the retail financial services industry and conducted one of the industry's earliest studies on social media involvement.

"In 2008, there were just a few early adopters of social [media] in the financial industry," he says. "Now, the ship has sailed: most financial firms who are going to be involved in some capacity are. . . . Those who do a good job are the ones that are able to effectively engage with their audience."

Still, the difference between social experience by investors and that of advisors is striking; it's almost like comparing a go-cart race to the Indianapolis 500. For example, the Pew Research Center found in 2011 that 70 percent of millionaires use social media; of those investors, 46 percent used

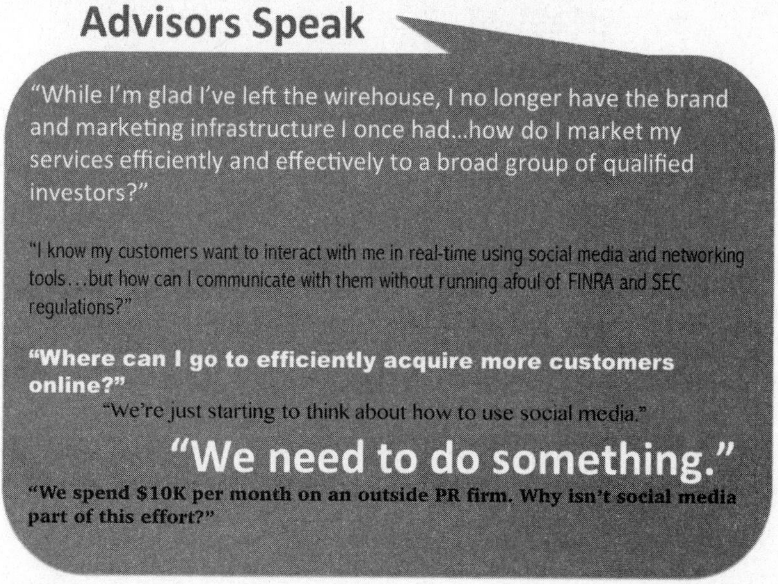

Advisors Speak

"While I'm glad I've left the wirehouse, I no longer have the brand and marketing infrastructure I once had...how do I market my services efficiently and effectively to a broad group of qualified investors?"

"I know my customers want to interact with me in real-time using social media and networking tools...but how can I communicate with them without running afoul of FINRA and SEC regulations?"

"Where can I go to efficiently acquire more customers online?"

"We're just starting to think about how to use social media."

"We need to do something."

"We spend $10K per month on an outside PR firm. Why isn't social media part of this effort?"

FIGURE 2.2   Advisor Talk as They Begin to Think Social
Source: Finect

Facebook, nearly double the 26 percent in 2010.[2] By comparison, a recent survey by TD Ameritrade found that more than 90 percent of advisors have a social media profile of some sort, but only 5 percent of their referrals come from social media.[3]

So the good news is the financial world is moving—gradually—into the social media universe. The problem is, their customers are already there in large numbers, numbers that are growing at a far greater pace than that of the financial industry itself (see Figure 2.2).

FINANCIAL ADVISORY WORLD IN FLUX

And yet, while some advisors are hesitant about going more deeply into social media, their world already is being reshaped.

---

[2]Maeve Duggan and Aaron Smith, "Social Media Update 2013," Pew Research Center, December 30, 2013, www.pewinternet.org/2013/12/30/social-media-update-2013.

[3]"Advisor Index," TD Ameritrade, March 11, 2013, www.amtd.com/files/doc_news/research/Q22013_AdvisorIndexResults_FINAL[1].pdf.

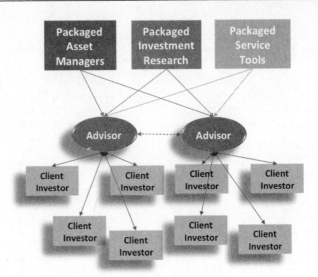

FIGURE 2.3 Traditional Wirehouse Ecosystem

Take the wirehouse channel, for example. These top-of-the-food-chain brokerages have long had established ecosystems in which information and services were organized and the roles of brokerage, advisor, and investor client were fairly clear. Wirehouses could dictate products and fee structures, and their advisors and clients would get in line (see Figure 2.3).

But advisors increasingly are finding alternatives to toiling in the wirehouse world. They're moving toward independence, bolstered in their efforts by third-party providers of every service from technology needs to asset management. Indeed, the registered investment advisory channel alone grew from 34 percent of all financial industry advisors in 2007 to an expected 47 percent in 2013, according to the industry research firm Cerulli Associates.[4]

Through technology and social media, advisors are finding new communities and capabilities to build their business—capabilities that allow them to work with open architecture brokerage platforms that don't dictate what securities they must buy, for example. And there's change occurring at the bottom of the investor market as well. So-called *robo-advisors*—firms that offer automated financial advice to low-asset investors for cut-rate fees—are growing as demands grows for advice among the mass affluent and tech solutions proliferate in response (see Figure 2.4).

---

[4]Cerulli Associates, "Advisor Metrics 2013: Understanding and Addressing a More Sophisticated Population," https://www.cerulli.com/publications/advisor-metrics-2013-understanding-and-addressing-a-more-sophisticated-population-P000101.

FIGURE 2.4 The New Ecosystem Provides Greater Access to Advisors and Investors
Source: Finect

This shift is presenting both new opportunities and challenges. Financial professionals and firms face increasing pressure to discover, market, and network more efficiently and cost-effectively. And while business growth and marketing remain top priorities, regulatory changes and compliance issues also rank among the top concerns weighing on leaders and advisors. As a result, more than half—63 percent—of all registered investment advisors say that investing in technology is far and away the top infrastructure investment they anticipate making over the next six months to accommodate business growth (see Figure 2.5).

And there's one other critical trend: the aging client base. We all talk about the generational wealth transfer—by some estimates totaling $41 trillion over 40 years—that is taking place. But have we thought about who, really, will be making those financial decisions—and how? By 2020, two-thirds of wealth is expected to be held by women. Already, the majority of women change advisors after the death of their spouses, according to LIMRA research (see Figure 2.6).

Regulatory Changes Still Weigh On Advisor's Minds

FIGURE 2.5   Top Business Concerns among RIAs
Source: TD Ameritrade

And how are these busy women juggling work, family, and elderly parents? By going online and using their mobile devices. Yes, women continue to rely on the Internet more than men—a trend we saw in the early Internet days—and with new hubs and networks now at their fingertips, social media is the way to connect and engage with them.

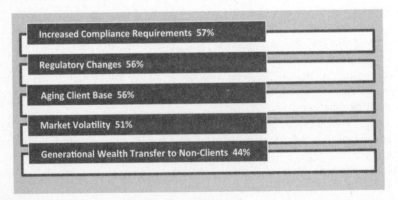

FIGURE 2.6   Top Industry Trends Pose a Challenge
Source: TD Ameritrade

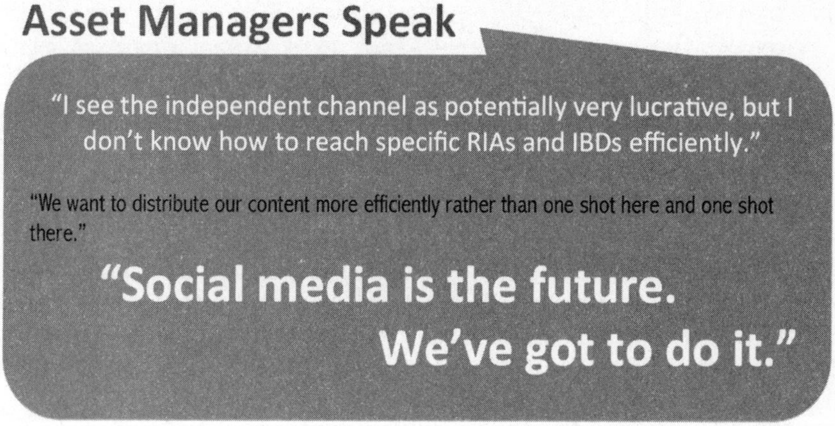

Asset Managers Speak

"I see the independent channel as potentially very lucrative, but I don't know how to reach specific RIAs and IBDs efficiently."

"We want to distribute our content more efficiently rather than one shot here and one shot there."

"Social media is the future.
We've got to do it."

FIGURE 2.7 Asset Managers Talk about Going Social
Source: Finect

So it's a changing world, both for investors and the advisors they work with. Social media clearly will accelerate the pace of that change in the years ahead. And yet, in many ways advisors feel held back in the social world (see Figure 2.7).

FOUR OBSTACLES TO GREATER SOCIAL MEDIA ENGAGEMENT

While social media use is practiced widely by Americans, many people simply avoid it. Some find the platforms unfamiliar or counterintuitive, while others see little value in sharing and engaging on the Web. Among financial professionals, however, the reasons for avoidance tend toward the technical and the specific. To look at why many in the industry feel held back in social media, let me just briefly touch on the "Four Multiples":

1. **Multiple Platforms**—Facebook, LinkedIn, and Twitter all have growing value for our industry, depending on how those platforms are used. But if marketers are just now learning how to use these platforms, how can we expect compliance officers to also understand? Moreover, focusing on any one platform could be nearly a full-time job by itself.
2. **Multiple Employees**—If you have multiple employees on multiple platforms—or even one platform—how do you track and monitor them?

It's enough to make you stop right there: Is it worth the risk to your compliance record? "Let's see how others do" is a common mode of action.

3. **Multiple Regulations**—Let's not forget the regulators. And this is problem one for many in the industry. You might be overseen by Financial Industry Regulatory Authority (FINRA), the Securities and Exchange Commission (SEC), or even the Office of the Comptroller of the Currency (OCC). How do you cope with all of those requirements for approvals, archives, recordkeeping, and more? Of course, no professional concerned about his or her job would want to do anything until they get some green light from officials that it's okay to use social media. But as we'll discuss later, that's one of the common myths. The good news is that regulators seem to be moving more quickly as they, too, embrace social media for their own purposes.

4. **Multiple Internal Layers**—Thanks to regulations and legacy bureaucracy, particularly at large firms, many organizations have multiple approval layers. It takes time to work through those layers, not to mention instituting new policies to abide by regulatory requirements.

WHAT DOES THIS MEAN FOR THE INDUSTRY, CEOs, CCOs, AND MARKETERS?

Obstacles to social media adoption are real in the financial industry, but that hasn't frozen its professionals in their tracks. In the last year alone, we've seen major brokerages like Raymond James and Morgan Stanley, top asset management firms like BlackRock and Putnam Investments, and one-man financial advisors and everything in between begin to adopt social media in some way.

It's a channel that can't be ignored. Whether your clients are retail investors or financial advisors, firms are recognizing they have to figure out social media. Marketers are partnering with compliance officers to increase their understanding and ensure the right processes are in place. Many firms are using social media at two levels: the corporate level, for building the company's brand and leveraging content; and the individual employee or advisor level, helping them build their individual brand and customer base.

Here's how it breaks down across the different advisory channels:

■ **Broker/Dealers**—Many brokerage firms have taken some initial steps toward embracing social media. For example, Cambridge Investment Research, with some 2,400 advisors on social media, permits them to post on Twitter, LinkedIn, and Facebook, subject to a post-use review. Others, such as Commonwealth Financial, prohibit product recommendations. The majority of Commonwealth's 1,400 advisors operate on at least one social media platform. At LPL Financial, more than 5,000 of their advisors operate on some platform: 36 percent on LinkedIn, 10 percent on Facebook, and about 6 percent on Twitter, former Chief Marketing Officer Joan Koury says. LPL advisors are required to get pre-approval for YouTube videos but, other than that, only static content needs to be approved.

- **Asset Managers**—Asset managers' use of social media truly depends on their audience. I recall meeting with a top consultant to the John Paulsons of the world who said: "They'll never be on social media. They prefer to keep private and operate with their own closed networks." But other asset managers are embracing social media—indeed, they view it as a more efficient way to distribute education, research, and other content more efficiently. "It's easier than going here to Schwab and there to Fidelity to post our content," one CMO told me. For now, CMOs and even CEOs at asset management firms tend to view it as an opportunity to build their brand and compete, for the first time ever, against larger, more established firms. As new consumer-oriented hedge funds are developed, we expect that they, too, will embrace social media.

- **Independent Financial Advisors**—Independent financial advisors have an easier time: Many are essentially their own compliance officers. That means no approvals and a more timely ability to get in on trending news or react to a client or prospect. Take financial advisor Jim Ludwick, CFP, formerly with Bank of America and now running Mainstreet Financial Planning. He's tweeting regularly and sending summaries of his top personal finance tweets to his followers. Or Winnie Sun, of Sun Group Wealth Partners, who reports how she's strongly built her client base through social media and snagged a $31 million client through LinkedIn. Indeed, Putnam found that some 29 percent of advisors had acquired a client with more than $1 million in assets via social media.

WHAT THE FUTURE HOLDS

Clearly, different segments of the financial industry demonstrate wide differences in the degree to which they are embracing social media. But the involvement of individual advisors or firms will depend to a great extent on their ability to adapt to some of the changes already under way. As you or your firm look to use social media, what are some of the key things to watch for?

- **More communications to record**—Whether you're a compliance officer or technology leader, you'll have to address the massive amounts of content that may require approval and will certainly require archiving.
- **More internal partnering**—Firms that are successful work hand-in-hand with their compliance officers. Today's CCOs recognize they can't be gatelockers when the world is quickly moving ahead. Successful firms are working together to build a mutual understanding of the business case.
- **Increase in data collection**—As new laws open up the doors to product marketing online and as investors adopt social interactions for decision-making, we can expect a greater opportunity to capture data. This could be data at the government level or even firm level—data that can be used to detect the next Bernie Madoff or ensure that investors are matched up with suitable products.
- **More regulatory direction**—Reed Hastings, the CEO of Netflix, drew the SEC's attention in 2012 when he put up a Facebook post that referenced a big increase in the firm's streaming hours—an announcement that was promptly followed by a sharp jump in the stock's price. In the end, the SEC opted not to file charges against Hastings; instead, it said that disclosures on social media were appropriate as long as investors were alerted in advance to which channels on which they could expect to receive such information. We continue to see more timely comments from nearly all key agencies, and we also see their presence at industry events, providing more proactive guidance perhaps than ever before. The SEC also made it plain that CEOs are always speaking for the firm when they speak about the firm. Hastings' tweets were attributable to his firm.

The financial industry has often felt hogtied and handcuffed by compliance issues in the past. The arrival of social media on the landscape—a game-changing dynamic that both regulators and financial professionals are still getting their arms around—in many ways has exacerbated the tension wealth managers feel as they plan for business in the twenty-first century. And yet the history of the industry shows that it can, and does, adapt. The tools exist for the advisor who wants to move forward.

CHAPTER **3**

What Are the Tensions Between Social Media and Regulation?

When considering the use of social media in the financial advisory space, it's hard not to think about what an odd couple they make. Social platforms allow people to share any thought that comes into their heads with an audience that numbers typically in the hundreds or thousands of people. By comparison, the financial industry is heavily regulated, particularly where communication is concerned. Advisors and their firms are held to account for the way they present themselves on social media, since investors on the Web can be as easily misled as those of 30 or 40 years ago who read bogus investment pitches in newspaper or magazine ads.

Indeed, nearly 75 percent of financial advisors report working for a firm with a written social media policy, and 82 percent of these advisors say the policy restricts social media use or bars it outright. Advisors who want to use social media more actively in their businesses could be excused if they felt a chill in the room.

And yet, consider the odd couple metaphor a little more. At the end of the day, two people with intrinsically different world philosophies and lifestyles still manage to live together. Likewise, financial advisors and regulatory constraints can co-exist in the social media universe.

Are you an advisor who worries about getting flagged in an audit for stepping outside the bounds? Take a page from the advice you offer clients who struggle with reaching their financial goals: Have a plan.

Regulators like firms that lay out their plans for using social media compliantly; indeed, regulators insist on it. Attorney Stuart Fross, former senior vice president of compliance and general counsel at Fidelity International who now works with firms globally, puts it this way: "Having a system to manage social media is a defense."

THREE REASONS WHY ADVISORS FEEL REGULATORS MAKE SOCIAL MEDIA DIFFICULT

So, do regulators make social media difficult for financial professionals to use? Many advisors certainly believe so, even if it's their own compliance officers who are raising the bar through restrictive in-house rules. Charles Schwab's vice president of compliance communications Melissa Callison said in an interview for this book that regulators have "tried to make expectations clear, but it's extremely complex because you're dealing with third-party sites, and they aren't always cooperating."

Consider some of the issues that make it hard for the industry to view regulators as friendly to social media in general, and to the way financial professionals use it in particular:

- **Old Rules for New Media**—Many of the existing rules go back to the 1930s and 1940s, an age where social media was a fit subject for science fiction. The SEC's latest pronouncements for advisors on testimonials and social media were more enlightened than many expected.[1] But many industry pros feel they have to manage a modern approach to communication with many old rules.
- **Regulatory Reputation**—Some industry leaders believe regulators are concerned about how they look in the new social media world order as they work their way through investor protection. As a result, "They're unwilling to give anyone a sort of pass for anything that happens on social media," says Theresa Hamacher, CEO of NICSA, a sponsor of online forums for the global investment management community.
- **Layer upon Layer**—Adding to the complexity of rules and guidelines that have existed for decades are new rules and oversight activities, such as spot-checks of advisor activity on social websites. Some advisors feel it only compounds the difficulty of having simple-to-use systems in place.

Faced with the challenges of serving client interests in the wake of the 2008 financial crisis, advisors often see compliance as one more obstacle to overcome.

---

[1]SEC, Guidance on the Testimonial Rule and Social Media, March 2014, www.sec .gov/investment/im-guidance-2014-04.pdf. Accessed May 15, 2014.

WHAT REGULATORS *COULD* DO TO MAKE SOCIAL MEDIA EASIER

Absent an entire rewrite of arcane rules, managers in the financial industry have told me there are a few things regulators like FINRA could do to simplify investor protections.

For example, some have suggested moving to a more principles-based approach for rulemaking. Callison points out that the SEC employs this philosophy, which essentially lays out a rule and then leaves it up to the firms to outline the best course of supervision.

In comparison, FINRA's prescriptive approach to rulemaking lays out specific rules for firms to follow. It requires firms to know—and implement— a great deal: static versus interactive content on the Web; pre-approval versus post-approval of content; content standards such as fair and balanced, and no false or exaggerated content; no predictions . . . the list goes on.

And while users of social media are on their sites to absorb quick, digestible pieces of information, the necessity of disclosures surrounding most financial conversations makes having a social venue for those discussions a real problem.

So a regimen that sets goals and allows some flexibility for reaching them offers advisors some options for serving clients responsibly while staying within regulatory boundaries

A DEFENSE: POLICIES IN PLACE

The temptation among many advisors is to just stay on the sidelines while the regulatory issues surrounding social media work themselves out. You may well say to yourself, "Why not let others mess up their reputations? We'll get started later, when we're ready and the system has ironed out the kinks."

The obvious problem with that approach is that it means sitting out a dynamic market and ceding leadership to others. It may sound obvious, but in order to learn how to manage social media, you have to *use* social media. But the bigger problem with staying on the side in this industry is that it's unnecessary. A firm has a defense when something goes awry as long as it has policies and procedures in place to address what regulators expect.

Hamacher likens it to a sexual harassment policy: If a company has established rules explicitly restricting inappropriate behaviors, it provides the firm with greater protection, except in the most egregious instances.

The problem, she points out, is that "there isn't that clear statement in the social media world." That's precisely why the industry remains so confused.

THE REAL BARRIER: REGULATORS OR INDUSTRY?

Who's to blame for this interpretational mess? Hamacher suggests the industry should look toward itself rather than at Washington rule-makers. The industry, she says, doesn't want to get caught with its social media pants down.

Remember, regulators' concerns are about *preventing* certain behaviors. But too many firms are saying: *We don't want to do this because we don't want to get caught.* In their view, if you post a bad tweet and it goes viral, you're in trouble.

In other words, while the industry should be focused on how to prevent underlying bad behavior—such as saying something they shouldn't on social media—they are more focused on a different issue: the concern that mistakes made on social media carry greater and more permanent exposure and damage. It's the consequences of the behavior and not the behavior itself.

Let me take this a step further. A broker might say something foolish in a phone call: "Mrs. James, I've got an investment that will double your retirement portfolio in three years." But the odds of that broker getting caught are slim. "The industry has done a wink and a nod to that for many years," Hamacher notes.

What if the broker behaved that way in the social media world? The behavior is easier to target. The penalties to his career are easy to imagine, to say nothing of what could happen to his firm. The industry has a clear opportunity for using social media to change firm behavior for the better, but many firms may choose to not change. "It's like sexual harassment: We instruct employees not to tell horrible jokes or touch people," Hamacher says. "When the industry talks about social media, it's more focused on the fear of getting caught by the inappropriate behavior rather than using social [media] as a way to reinforce the right behaviors."

SOME FINAL THOUGHTS

So what should firms do in the light of what's happening? First, they have to view social media as part of their entire compliance effort. Chief compliance officers (CCOs) are expected to prevent misbehavior on websites, but many in the industry would agree that part of their job is to take greater care that such misbehavior doesn't leave a trail that regulators can pick up. The alternative? CCOs could use social media as an opportunity to train employees on how to sell appropriately. You may not get extra credit from regulators, but you will be able to more comfortably and quickly leverage this critical channel.

Enlightened firms don't fear being toast with a badly crafted Web message that goes viral. They would tell you that you just have to be thoughtful about how you approach social media. These firms are open to social media because they *aren't* afraid of conducting their business in the light of day. They've trained their employees, and they know that anything their employees say can be repeated in public because it's the right message. They also know that every compliance program turns up mistakes, fixes them, and gets a bit better. Perfection is not the regulatory standard; active supervision is the standard.

In today's transparent day and age, that approach carries the day.

CHAPTER 4

Are the Risks of Using Social Media Worth the Benefits?

The risk of not using social media is greater.
—Melissa Callison, Charles Schwab's vice president
of compliance communications

Some time ago I had a conversation with a twenty-something young man about a job offer he'd received from an investment advisory firm. The company wasn't active on social media at the time and had some misgivings about embracing a quickly evolving communications technology within a regulated—some might say hidebound—industry. Still, they understood the world was changing.

The sense that the future was upon them only grew during their conversation with the young man. "I wanted to know if I could use LinkedIn and other social media. This was essential to my success on the job, and if I couldn't use social media, then I wasn't going to take the job," he recalled.

The idea that a talented job prospect would pass up a career with their company over its resistance to social media led the managers to rethink their views.

In the end, the firm changed course—permitting not only their new hire to use social media, but also other professionals there as well.

SOCIAL MEDIA'S SHIFTING WINDS IN FINANCIAL ADVISORY

The tensions that the use of social media is producing in the financial industry are palpable. The vast majority of financial professionals still feel that social media is a quagmire of potential risks: costs, technology, compliance, reputation, and perhaps even the loss of their own jobs.

And yet if you're an investment advisor or other professional, you're probably already using social media in some manner—to communicate with friends, family, and colleagues or simply to maintain your professional profile. You're not alone: Even lawyers helping clients in the regulatory, brokerage, and financial advisory world are actively using this media. They're embracing social media for the same reasons you're reading this book: to learn how to build their brand, develop new relationships, and simply be current.

Are the risks of using social media worth the benefits? Another way to ask this question is whether an advisor or other professional *can not* or *should not* use social media.

In this day and age, most investment advisors are sensing the growing necessity of using social media. The issue really is how to go about it and how to ensure compliance with regulatory requirements. One solution is to hire talented people, the next generation of financial industry employees who are savvier than most with technology and social media.

But a firm has to open the door to social media first before it can bring others on board. Toward that end, it helps to evaluate what the real challenges are in using social media and the ways of coming to terms with them.

FOUR SOCIAL MEDIA RISKS AND SOLUTIONS

Set aside for the moment the concerns about getting dinged during a regulatory audit over a mismanaged tweet. When we talk about risks, we're talking about broad issues with deep implications: social endurance, reputation impact, recordkeeping and advertising, and millennial hiring risk. Let's have a closer look at each.

Social Endurance

We all know that our digital footprints remain permanent. Tweets, blog posts, and other social communication can have a life on the Web that's stubbornly resistant to deletion. The United Kingdom's High Court announced in 2014 that it is requiring Google to grant users of its search engine a "right to be forgotten" and erase links to things like embarrassing legal records.[1]

---

[1]*New York Times*, "E.U. Court Orders Google to Grant 'Right to Be Forgotten,'" *Bits* (blog), May 13, 2014, http://bits.blogs.nytimes.com/2014/05/13/daily-report-e-u-court-orders-google-to-grant-right-to-be-forgotten.

It remains to be seen whether this will be an issue someday for users in North America as well.

What is clear is that the content that advisors and other financial professionals share in social media can have great reach and a long lifespan. How can firms address this?

- **Shadowing employee activity**—Some firms shadow employees as they begin to use social media, making sure that their responses are in line with policies. In other words, someone will review their articles, tweets, and other posts that same day, perhaps in an artificial environment, before going live, so that a correction can be made and the employee can build his communication skills.
- **Careful monitoring**—Internal spot checks, rather than editing content before it is posted online, are common both to monitor issues or trends and to correct behavior.
- **Training**—Firms must provide instruction to staff that's commensurate with the companies' presence on social media, anything from monthly activity reviews of blogs or posts that were problems to an annual workshop on how to do things better.

Reputation Impact

There is an enduring fear in the financial industry that clients and others will say terrible things about you, your firm, or your products and services—a condition that has only been exacerbated by the 2008 financial crisis.

I remember a meeting in 2012 at a major Boston-based asset management firm, with the head of its advisor network, the chief marketing officer, the head of social media, and the head of customer service. As we were talking about the pros and cons of using social media, the head of customer service piped up, "Why would we want to be on social media when people can say things that hurt your brand?"

The CMO instantly chimed in, "It's happening anyway. This is a way to *manage* our brand."

She hit the nail on the head: Failure to use social media in some way poses a greater risk—a risk that your reputation will be shaped by the conversations happening out there, conversations that are led by others, not by you. The new online world presents an opportunity to know what's being said and to manage it. How you respond says a great deal about your firm and its leaders.

Other fears include customer grievances being aired online. That's a real issue, since some 70 percent of customer complaints on Twitter go unanswered, according to social media researcher Maritz Research.[2]

Whether it's the airline customer who's upset about lost suitcases and bad follow through, or someone like myself who could have turned to Twitter to share a major trade mix-up between accounts, grievances can and do happen online. These are situations that can be broadcast instantly, not only to friends and family, but back through the company's own Twitter handle, now making the bad news accessible to prized clients. See Figure 4.1.

All companies with a social media presence need to manage their online reputations, a process whose importance grows exponentially when online anger erupts over a particular failure in products or services. Wise managers have already put plans in place to handle such outbreaks, so when trouble brews, the firm isn't scrambling to improvise.

This practice can actually work for a firm in the middle of a public relations disaster. Companies that respond to viral denunciations with sophistication can emerge from the crisis with heightened credibility among followers for demonstrating their expertise in managing the problem; even angry followers will respect that the company was engaged in their complaints and made efforts to reach out. See Figure 4.2.

Recordkeeping and Advertising

Two of the biggest challenges to get right are recordkeeping and advertising. It is no small feat to do so.

All advisors must keep records of their communications. In a way, social media makes that difficult because *every* communication by an investment advisor is an open record—whether a tweet, a post, a recommendation, a "like," or some other form of agreement with someone else's recommendation.

Further, investment advisors need to make sure any content that might be construed as advertising has been pre-reviewed and complies with securities laws. Communications with prospective clients might contain information about performance or other advertising, including the effectiveness of past recommendations, and are governed by specific rules.

---

[2]"Maritz Research Company & evolve24 Twitter Study," September 2011, www .maritzresearch.com/~/media/Files/MaritzResearch/e24/ExecutiveSummaryTwitter Poll.ashx.

FIGURE 4.1 Twitter Backlash: Consumer Complaints Go Viral

In order to make social media use compliant, the investment advisor and chief compliance officer must cover these bases. The advisor and firm will have to meet the recordkeeping requirements, which may even include the preservation of screen shots. Now, that's possible for an advisor or firm to do in any social media context, but it's not easy.

Another approach is to employ a third-party platform to channel their communications and keep proper records. The SEC has said that a third-party provider can be appointed by an advisor as the company's record-keeping source. For example, if a site or service keeps records and preserves your screenshots for you, that could be quite handy.

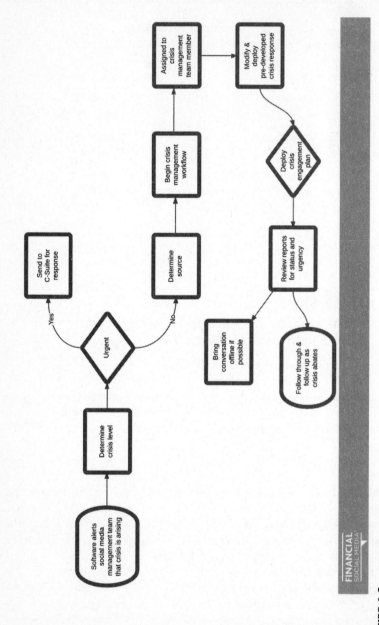

FIGURE 4.2 Crisis Management Process

Source: Financial Social Media

FIGURE 4.3 Students of Texas Tech's Personal Financial Planning Program
Source: TTU's PFP website

Social media can be a gift if the right tools are deployed—tools that make it possible and practical to track communications and even to pre-review postings for advertising content.

Millennial Hiring Risk

I touched on this at the start of this chapter, but let me use another example. It highlights both the expectations of the next generation of employees you might hire and the needs that your firm might have.

I had an opportunity to talk some time ago with students and professors of Texas Tech University's personal financial planning program—the largest degree program of its kind in the United States. The students were at varying stages of their careers (see Figure 4.3):

- Heather Ford, 26, plans to grow her financial planning practice by working with her mother's accounting business.
- Jeremy Ransom, 24, a military vet who returned to college to get a degree.
- Phanay Binford, 37, an undergraduate pursuing a dual MBA and PFP.
- Dustin Parks, 43, a career changer from the information tech industry.

Their professor, Barry Mulholland, stressed the importance of preparing them to use and understand social media's use while remaining compliant.

"We have a divergent group of people in the industry, including established advisors looking at who will take over their business and move it forward," he said. "They're turning to young people who look very different from the industry. We're preparing our students to use social media so that they're ready to enter a very dynamic industry."

Student Heather Ford pointed out that having a strong social media skill set is "something we can offer our employers."

Dina Katz, CFP and assistant professor at Texas Tech, adds that the program is looking at trying to get more aspects of technology into the financial planning business. "Whether our students become entrepreneurs, marketers, or financial advisors, social media is a vital part of their business—or should be," she says.

It's no secret that recruiting young talent is a challenge. The average age of a financial advisor hovers around the mid-50s in the United States. We're not seeing the same flows of talent into the financial profession as we once did. If we don't recruit this innovative talent, we risk losing the next generation of advisors—a disservice both to them and to the industry.

So, if you consider young people emerging from America's colleges to be an asset, then you won't want to undervalue their knowledge of social media—and you may even want to leverage it.

The bottom line: Top leaders and big-brand companies are moving forward swiftly. Sure, firms are asking themselves if the risks of social media are worth the benefits. But as Callison, Schwab's vice president of communications compliance, put it to me: "We're doing it because we hear from our reps and advisors that that's where they want to be: They're missing part of the discussion or missing opportunities if they're not on social media. If we don't, others will have an advantage."

CHAPTER 5

How Will Social Media Change Our Industry in 10 Years?

What was life like for you 10 years ago? Can you recall those early experiences with the Internet? I can.

Some 12 years ago, after working in southern California and studying for an MBA, I decided to start a financial company in the heart of where it was all happening: Silicon Valley. We were assembling websites, producing digital content, and creating new ways to help consumers find the right financial advisors. In short, we were empowering investors and leveling the playing field.

Looking back, in some ways the evolution hasn't been that radical: We still have content, only it's more visual and less wordy; we can still connect with people, but on a more individualized level and with deeper analytics.

Yet in other ways, the jump from the Web 1.0 to Web 3.0—in a span of about 15 years—has been significant indeed.

As a reminder:

- Business models that refused to adapt went bust. Many of those that survived are still playing catchup. Think of your local newspaper competing with the *Huffington Post*. Target still hasn't gotten online purchasing down the way Amazon has, and now its business has been shaken following a major breach in the security of customer credit card data.
- Borrowers can now bypass lenders, banks, and middlemen and go straight to other consumers for a $10,000 loan to start successful businesses.
- Your smartphone has more capabilities than devices carried by the men who first went on the moon.

It's useful to ponder such rapid transformation, because even industry leaders can find themselves in last place. Eastman Kodak was a giant in the retail photography industry in the twentieth century until digital cameras toppled the company, which emerged from a bankruptcy filing in 2013 as a far smaller enterprise. Motorola invented the mobile phone, but developments in smartphone technology left it in the dust; it said in 2014 that it would sell its cellphone business. Clearly, managing change is an increasingly important skillset for the years ahead.

GET READY: MORE CHANGE IS COMING

What are some of the key drivers of change that we need to be aware of? Let's look at the big ones:

- **Demographic Shifts**—The nation's baby boomer population—those 65 and older—will grow to a whopping 83.7 million by 2050, nearly double the number in 2012, according to the U.S. Census.[1]
- **Women's Wealth**—As women outlive men, they will control 70 percent of the $41 trillion in intergenerational wealth that is expected to transfer over the next 40 years, says Boston College's Center on Wealth Philanthropy. In 2013, women represented nearly 40 percent of the high-net-worth segment. These are significant trends, yet many financial advisory companies have not really planned for it in a meaningful way. Heads up, advisors: Recently widowed women frequently change wealth managers after their husbands die.
- **Mobile Devices**—Forrester's highlights these trends: In America, 50 percent of online adults who use a mobile phone use their devices to check sports, weather, or news at least weekly, 45 percent access social networks on their phones at least weekly, and 22 percent research physical products for purchase.[2]
- **Use of Social Media**—Pew Internet recently reported that 73 percent of online adults now use social networking sites; 42 percent use multiple sites. And seniors continue to deepen their online engagement, with 59 percent now using the Internet, a 6 percent increase in a year,[3]

---

[1]U.S. Census Bureau, www.census.gov/newsroom/releases/archives/aging_population/cb14-84.html, June 3, 2014.
[2]Pew Social Media Update 2013, www.pewinternet.org/2013/12/30/social-media-update-2013/, June 3, 2014.
[3]Pew Research, "Adults and Technology Use," www.pewinternet.org/2014/04/03/older-adults-and-technology-use/, June 5, 2014.

although many still lag younger consumers in their adoption of technology. Facebook remains the dominant social media network with 1.3 billion users, although some surveys show slipping usage among younger people.

■ **Niche Investing: Impact Investing**—As technology has enabled specialization, buzz has been growing about impact investing opportunities for mainstream investors, investing that provides both a financial return and measurable social or environmental impacts. According to U.S. Trust's 2013 Insights on Wealth and Worth, about half of affluent women are interested in environmentally or socially responsible investments, compared to only about one-third of men.[4] See Figure 5.1.

A 10-YEAR LOOK: HOW THE FINANCIAL INDUSTRY WILL CHANGE

So our lives and the ways we make choices—from picking hotels and dining spots to dentists and attorneys—have changed.

Want to find the restaurant serving the best steak or the clothing shop with the best-fitting jeans? It's all online, as open and transparent as you'd ever imagined, with ratings, reviews, and the ability to engage with like-minded consumers.

And yet, these changes haven't yet happened in the financial industry. Rest assured: They will. Regulators already have made efforts to define what financial professionals and others in the industry can do with social media. The gates are opening, and the financial world is starting to pass through. First, a trickle, then most of the herd.

The pace is already quickening; nearly 70 percent of wealthy investors have reallocated investments or began or altered relationships with investment providers based on content found through social media, according to a survey conducted by Cogent Research of 4,000 investors with more than $100,000 in investable assets.[5] See Figure 5.2.

Some advisors are sensing that the social universe has made reviews and ratings critical. In the brokerage industry, someone's reputation is their

---

[4]"U.S. Trust 2013 Insights on Wealth & Worth," www.ustrust.com/publish/content/application/pdf/GWMOL/UST-Fact-Sheet-Insights-on-Wealth-and-Worth-2013.pdf, June 5, 2014.
[5]"Cogent Research: Now Trending—Social Media Fuels Investor Decision Making," www.businesswire.com/news/home/20130222005037/en#.U6O4Y41kEnI, June 3, 2014.

	% Who use social networking sites
All internet users 18+	**73%**
Men	69
Women	78
Race/ethnicity	
White, Non-Hispanic	72
Black, Non-Hispanic	73
Hispanic	79
Age	
18-29	90
30-49	78
50-64	65
65+	46
Education attainment	
No high school diploma	74
High school grad	69
Some college	75
College+	75
Household income	
Less than $30,000/yr	77
$30,000 -$49,999	73
$50,000-$74,999	73
$75,000+	75
Urbanity	
Urban	76
Suburban	72
Rural	70

FIGURE 5.1 Who Uses Social Networking Sites?
Source: Pew Research Center's Internet Project Library Survey 2013

hallmark; how well someone behaves in meeting a customer's needs and meeting their best interests is critical.

What are the implications of empowered investors? For one, it means that they'll become even less attentive to those multimillion-dollar ad campaigns and more attentive to their social networks. Just as we've been able to aggregate the opinions about restaurants and hotels, so, too, will we be aggregating opinions about financial professionals and products.

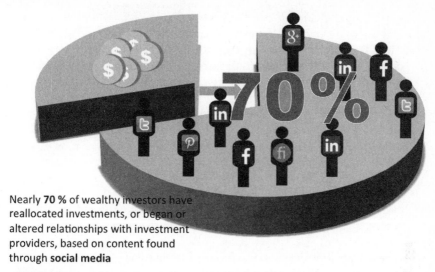

Nearly **70 %** of wealthy investors have reallocated investments, or began or altered relationships with investment providers, based on content found through **social media**

FIGURE 5.2   Content Found on Social Media Impacts Investors' Decisions
Source: Cogent Research

EIGHT PREDICTIONS FOR THE NEXT DECADE

Ten years from now, here's what financial professionals will see:

- **More Communication, More Places**—This one's obvious: More communication will occur online between financial advisors and clients. Part of this will stem from the boomer generation's increased usage of social media and the even-greater adoption of the next generations.

    But social media is also changing *how* we communicate. In the past, conversations happened with the client sitting across at your desk, on the Web, or through e-mail. Increasingly those conversations will happen on third-party sites—sites that are outside your control. The change will lead firms and advisors to adapt to new devices: mobile and tablets and perhaps even Google Glass and technologies we can't yet conceive.

    This will also spark new ways of managing compliance, as Melissa Callison, Charles Schwab's vice president of compliance communications, points out. "This will necessitate a change in how we supervise our brokers, because today it's a lot of e-mail or over-the-shoulder supervision because they're in our office. In 10 years, we'll need ways to supervise them when they're not close to home, and that'll take new ways to manage compliance and infrastructure investment."

- **The Chief Digital Officer Replaces the CMO**—Related information will be formatted first for online purposes. That means—as we are just now starting to see—a shift to more visuals such as graphics and far fewer words. Content will be made digital first—from brochures to annual reports. This, in turn, is already leading companies to hire leaders with digital experience, oftentimes replacing the traditional chief marketing officer.
- **Social Media Trumps Mainstream Media**—You've worried about how traditional public relations might harm you or your firm's reputation. What about social media? If you look out 10 years, social media might even take over traditional PR as the primary reputation channel you'll need to address. If that's not reason enough to get social, we're not sure what is.
- **Crowd-Sourced Advisors, Products**—Transparency in the online world empowers a broader range of public opinion, not just media pundits. The thumbs-up/thumbs-down reviews you've seen at your favorite hotel or restaurant review site may eventually apply to advisors, money management firms, portfolio managers, and investment products. In essence, you'll get crowdsourced opinions on financial advisors and products—not a bad thing at all. Crowds are generally honest, although you must be careful not to put too much credence into any single source.
- **Peer Reviews of Advisors**—Imagine you're a retail investor looking for good financial advice. In the past, you might have chatted with a friend over coffee. Or you might have forgone the discussion entirely, not feeling comfortable about raising the subject of money. To find a professional advisor, you'd probably do a search online or even in the Yellow Pages. And you'd be hard pressed to know anything about the advisor aside from what they say about themselves.

  Today's advisors increasingly understand that investors are able to easily and privately view a pro's biographical and professional info online, everything from licenses to certifications. And increasingly, they'll be able to find an advisor through their social networks. Their advisor might connect with them through Facebook to invite the investor to view his or her video on retiring successfully. Investors might engage in a private online chat. They'll also be able to seek online opinions about advisors from other investors who have worked with them. See Figure 5.4.
- **Trading through Social Networks**—We're already seeing social networking sites built for investing—sites that allow investors to form

FIGURE 5.3   The Evolution of News Distribution

groups around common themes and invest in baskets of stocks they create or to follow and invest in others' portfolios. But might we even see people placing trades through Facebook? I recall the app we developed several years ago that showed consumers on Facebook how they could instantly have a basket of mock stocks based on their interests. You couldn't make a trade through Facebook, but you certainly could get introduced to the idea in a personalized and compelling way. And that will likely pose new challenges for regulators: How do you supervise that?

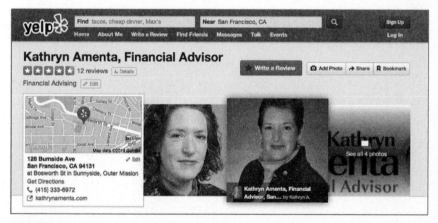

FIGURE 5.4   Yelp Reviews of Advisors

■ **More Access to Financial Education and Viewpoints**—Puzzled over how a particular security works? When you have financial questions, you can peruse online libraries to track down information and research on the topic. You'll be able to get opinions on the research from others exploring the same topics. And you'll be able to get regular feeds to such content and engage with its creators in ways that, in recent years, were available only to the rich or connected.

■ **Less Insider Trading**—Recent SEC interpretations involving Regulation FD have allowed publicly traded firms to disclose financial information on social media within certain guidelines. This transparency of information will deter corporate insiders from trading illegally on what they know. Insider fear of being exposed will serve to self-police the online world, a trend that Unience, an investor social media platform in Europe, has already seen. And regulators will have developed better online tracking systems to collect and report data on emerging issues. Ideally, technology will help them more quickly detect fraud and prevent investors from losing their nest eggs.

The financial industry knows it needs to improve its reputation following the damage wrought by the 2008 financial crisis and the multi-billion dollar fraud of Bernie Madoff. Technology is a tool that can transfer power to the hands of individual investors who are looking for more transparent ways of working with wealth managers.

Technology first, then transparency. We've seen this movie before. Now we'll all watch as it comes to a financial theater near you.

CHAPTER 6

What Are the Biggest Social Media Myths?

I t's happening all around you—in every demographic in every nation, people are using social media. And despite what you may assume, they're not just using it to stay in touch with friends, play games, and post silly videos. While these pastimes do represent one aspect of social media, you'd be wise to remember that the overwhelming majority of Americans have also come to count on social media for many of the more important things in life—from making strategic business contacts and following the companies and organizations they're interested in, to researching products and services and adding their two cents to national or even global conversations.

So it's hard to figure out why, when millions of people are engaged in countless social media exchanges every day that are shaping both the business and consumer marketplaces, any reasonable businessperson would ignore it. These days, you almost have to go out of your way *not* to engage in social media. The advisors who want to thrive now and well into the future already know this and are immune to the many myths. But it's still surprising that so many of their colleagues keep missing the boat, citing any number of excuses why social media, investors, and advisors don't mix.

Here we'll not only debunk 10 of the most common social media myths, but we'll also unravel the secrets to turning these myths into actionable realities.

1. Social media is just for kids, and they're not my target audience.

You could just as easily argue that not long ago, cell phones were just for adults, but now they're ubiquitous, even among kids. The same is true of social media—it graduated from the kiddie table to the grown-up table years ago. In fact, AARP found that 85 percent of the 50 or older population uses one or more social networks. The networks most commonly used—Facebook, LinkedIn, and Twitter—are cost-free channels that allow you to make an impression on your target audience, so it's natural for your clients to expect to find you there. In fact, if you're not on social media, then you just don't exist to your next generation of clients. To a great number of investors, a healthy social media presence engenders brand recognition, trust, and confidence in your abilities. Still skeptical? Yet another study, this one by BRANDFog, revealed that a full 82 percent of consumers will trust a company more if its leadership team and CEO are active in social media.[1]

2. Even if investors and clients do use social media, it's not to find a financial advisor.

Wrong. A recent survey from Cogent Research found that millions of high-net-worth investors actively use social media to help make informed financial decisions.[2] That's because today's consumers do more research across a broader spectrum of media than ever before, and they do it for virtually every service (think of Angie's List and Yelp), every product (there are innumerable sites, blogs, ranking organizations, podcasts, etc., to help inform their choices), and any issues they feel pertain to them. Consider how many investors follow individual advisors or companies like *The Wall Street Journal* on Twitter. The heart of the matter is social media works because you get direct access to literally thousands of engaged consumers in your specific market without having to shell out a single dollar. If you generate the content they're looking for, you can't miss them.

3. There really aren't that many benefits to using social media.

This is perhaps one of the most bewildering social media myths. As mentioned above, in addition to being a cost-free method to get your message

---

[1]"The Global Social CEO Survey," brandFOG, 2014, http://brandfog.com/CEO SocialMediaSurvey/BRANDfog_2014_CEO_Survey.pdf. Accessed June 15, 2014.

[2]Chris Savio and Jake Raroque, "Social Media's Growing Influence Among High Net Worth Investors," LinkedIn and Cogent Research, May 2012, available at http://marketing.linkedin.com/sites/default/files/pdfs/LinkedIn_HNWInvestorResearch_2012.pdf. Accessed June 4, 2014.

in front of thousands of investors who are actually looking to do business with you, social media also strengthens your brand recognition and exposure and increases traffic to your website. Other clear benefits include very low marketing expenses, higher search engine rankings, and, of course, lead generation.

4. I can't use social media due to compliance issues.

While it's true that financial advisors have more concerns to address when crafting social media campaigns than professionals in other industries do, there nevertheless are countless ways to benefit from incorporating this medium into your marketing efforts while remaining in full compliance. That's what your compliance officer or broker is there for; he or she can provide you with details regarding what you can and cannot do in the social media world. FINRA and the SEC are disseminating more specific guidelines for helping advisors compliantly engage in social media, and this information is readily available on their websites.

5. There's no way for me to track social media's return on investment (ROI).

Sure, it may be harder to quantify how many leads you get from your social media efforts, but that doesn't mean there aren't other ways to measure your success. There are several tools you can employ to help measure your social media marketing's return on investment. For example, all of the top social media platforms provide tools aimed at revealing your key performance metrics, including your audience reach and engagement. (This includes things such as the number of followers you have, any other Internet mentions or comments about you, how often your content is shared, or how many tweets get retweeted, etc.) You can also use Google Analytics to gauge your website's traffic.

And don't forget the immeasurable benefits of even the most passive of campaigns. If a potential investor goes online to read a certain article and you just happen to be quoted in it, you'll get immediate recognition as an authority with whom they'd be interested in working. Or let's say someone is looking for tips on the best ways to manage their 401(k) and come across your expertly written blog; you can count that as another win. Remember, no medium can give you exact information on impressions or leads, but that doesn't mean it's not occurring regularly.

6. I should ignore or just delete any negative comments.

Deleting or simply ignoring a negative post is the worst possible way you can react. It's impossible to make everyone happy all the time, so expect at least a few unpleasant comments to crop up during your career. And while it may seem unpleasant on the surface, these occasions are also an opportunity to demonstrate that you really care about your clients and are actively listening to what they have to say. Respond to every single one of these comments publicly and do so with class. Don't become confrontational or defensive. If need be, post any policies that may address the complaint, and then extend an offer for them to contact you personally to discuss the matter further. You may consider drawing the line at material that is patently offensive, not because it paints you in a bad light, but because it is hate speech. But, while deleting offensive material is one thing, if you are the target of criticism you do well to leave the post as is.

7. Social media is only good for prospecting; it's worthless to existing clients.

While it's true that social media can be a tremendous opportunity to market to prospective clients, it's equally valuable to your existing clients. You can bet that many of your current clients are already following you on Twitter, reading and commenting on your blogs, and even "liking" you on Facebook. This is because all the work you've done to position yourself as the expert in your market is working, and your clientele will want to know what you're discussing now or if you have any new products that may suit them. Yes, social media is a great tool for attracting new clients, but it's just as effective for maintaining and keeping your current clients satisfied.

8. Social media only works for B2B marketing, not B2C.

Many advisors seem to think social media can only be effective in the B2B space, since many of its marketing and sales practices differ from B2C industries. Granted, the content itself is different when dealing with consumers than with other businesses, but it serves the same primary functions: You use social media to be, well, social, and to position yourself as a helpful and caring individual with all the right information. All you have to do is ensure your content is audience appropriate; it can be wildly effective in boosting both your B2B and B2C connections.

9. A social media campaign will diminish the impact of traditional marketing methods.

This is simply not so. Did VCRs kill the movie theaters? Did the Kindle replace all paper books? The answer is obvious, as these new ways to access content only enhance a business's marketing efforts rather than destroy them. Your e-mail or direct marketing channels won't suffer from introducing social media into your plan; they'll only serve you better (especially if you include links to your social media content in these more traditional methods).

10. Using social media is too hard and too time consuming.

This is perhaps the worst and most destructive myth of them all. The great thing about social media is its innate economies of scale. You can easily post one of your relevant articles to all of these platforms and be done in a half-hour or so. That alone should be enough to disabuse you of the level of effort needed to operate a successful social media campaign, but if you're uber-busy, why not turn to some of your younger support staff? Chances are they'll be intimately familiar with how best to leverage social media, so consider entrusting maintenance of your social campaign to them. And if you're really hard up for resources, you can also consider hiring a professional social media campaign manager to do everything for you.

The point is, social media complements the way we as a society now live our lives and do business, and it certainly won't be going away. Forget these myths and step into reality: Either got on board and get social, or step out of the way.

PART TWO

The Regulatory Environment

CHAPTER 7

What Are the Top Challenges Compliance Officers Face?

"*O*h *no! New technology is on hand that is destined to change the way my financial advisory practice does business! I'm the chief compliance officer, and the buck stops with me—how am I going to get my arms around this in a way that ensures I don't run afoul of dreaded regulators?*"

If you're a chief compliance officer (CCO) who's reading this book, you may have had that very conversation with yourself—perhaps 20 years ago. Yes, when e-mail first arrived on the scene, many advisors fretted that this new way of doing business would carry regulatory pitfalls that could lead to their undoing. It's natural to fear the unknown, and advisors are loath to serve as test cases for oversight agencies that are getting their arms around the implications of technology. Yet ask yourself this question: When was the last time an advisor stumbled seriously during a regulator's audit over an e-mail issue?

"*Plus ça change, plus c'est la même chose,*" as the French put it—the more things change, the more they remain the same. CCOs who are concerned that the emerging universe of social media could trip up their practices should consider that advisors have been down this road before, and the results weren't disastrous. Indeed, the basic rules that govern compliance—rules that exist to protect investors from harm—do not represent a sea change from the principles that have steered advisors for decades, as we shall see.

WHAT CCOs SHOULD KNOW

If you manage compliance, know this—your advisors are using social media. Be sure of it. Their clients are on sites such as Facebook and Twitter, and it only stands to reason that this reality is driving advisors down the same path, even if it's just posting a brief bio on LinkedIn. Indeed, many financial practice employees have access to multiple social media venues, and may be using personal accounts. That can lead to problems for the compliance environment, since CCOs need to be vigilant about their advisors' and other employees' behavior.

So what kinds of things do you, as CCO, need to think about?

CCOs should consider evaluating both the likelihood and impact of various risk scenarios, such as the ones outlined below by Financial Social Media, a digital marketing firm for financial services companies:

- Reputation and Brand
  - Negative reviews or comments
  - Negative posts, including sharing negative press
  - Brand inconsistency
  - Viral negative sentiment
- Regulatory and Compliance
  - Violation of advertising or e-communications regulations
  - Failure to archive
- Legal and Privacy
  - Leaks of confidential information
  - Unauthorized use of copyright works
  - HR employee rights issues
  - HR hiring issues
  - E-discovery issues
- Operational
  - Decrease in employee productivity
  - Cybersecurity risks/Technology system security breaches

The good news is, the rules haven't changed dramatically. To this day, the major body of compliance rules continues to come from the Investment Advisers Act of 1940[1]. Most of its rules are designed around the use of U.S. mail and telephones, although they did expand this a bit to include "any means or instrumentality of interstate commerce, directly or indirectly."

The rules are pretty clear about what advisors can say, how they can say it, and what records must be kept. With the traditional means of mail and telephone everyone became used to the protocols, and they continue to this day.

---

[1]"Investment Advisers Act of 1940," SEC, https://www.sec.gov/about/laws/iaa40 .pdf. Accessed June 13, 2014.

Now along comes social media. It presents some new challenges, particularly for compliance to advertising, recommendation, and record-keeping rules. If you "like" someone's post about an investment, is that a recommendation? If you post or tweet a news item, how do you keep a record of that?

In early 2012, the SEC made its first formal attempt to clarify social media responsibility for investment advisors. (See this four-page Office of Compliance, Inspections and Examinations National Examination Risk Alert in the Addendum and companion website.[2]) Bottom line: They reminded us all that the old rules applicable to investment advisors apply to social media, too.

The SEC is adapting to social media; for example, it has recognized the concept of Internet investment advisors interacting through social media. They now offer special registration rules allowing such advisors who interact with all of their clients (and a maximum of 15 non-interactive clients) through a website to register only with the SEC, avoiding cumbersome state registration.

The investment advisory world got even more nervous about compliance in June 2013 when FINRA announced spot checks for compliance in the social media space. The spot checks basically require you to say what you're going to do, then do what you say in the social media space. To deal with these spot checks, you should specifically document your social media policies and their use, and have measures in place to assure your team's compliance with your policies.

FIVE KEY CCO CHALLENGES

In the wake of these new guidelines and spot checks, we recommend that you take special care to address the following five trouble spots:

1. **Unsupervised Content**—There are many social media platforms out there that employees can use at any given time, and the opportunities for poorly written or non-compliant content to make its way into the world are numerous. Any CCO should have the ability to supervise and review content before it is posted. Now, it would be difficult to review every single post, but it makes sense to spot check your own team's content, and by doing so, make sure they are fully up to speed on the rules. As

---

[2]SEC Office of Compliance Inspections and Examinations, "Investment Adviser Use of Social Media," *National Examination Risk Alert*, January 4, 2012, www.sec.gov/about/offices/ocie/riskalert-socialmedia.pdf.

FIGURE 7.1   Monitor Online Content

CCO, you should be able to review, approve, or reject a post before it is put up on a site. See Figure 7.1.

2. **Poor or Nonexistent Processes**—The novelty of social media often means firms haven't yet developed a game plan for dealing with all the contingencies that go along with its use. CCOs need to document their firms' review process and be able to present it to regulators. These should include policies and procedures that include guidance about:
   - Who has access to social media
   - How those employees are trained
   - How those employees are supervised

   For example, you may want to put rules in place to (1) review content before posting, and (2) train employees who are posting on the site. You may want to give special attention to any performance information, past specific recommendations, or success stories. There are specific requirements that must be considered before posting this type of information, and your review process should catch those issues.

3. **Where's That Post?**—Depending on how large your firm's presence becomes on social media, it may be difficult to track down the many blogs, tweets, and other content that are produced on a weekly or even daily basis. Proper recordkeeping has been a hallmark of the Advisers Act, and it continues in this day and age even as social media presents

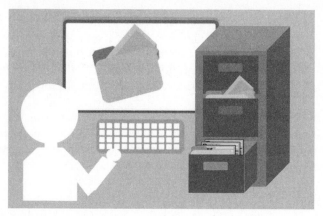

FIGURE 7.2   Mind Your Recordkeeping

some special challenges. Good records cover what web content was posted and when; it must be indexed and easily accessible if it's in electronic format. Ideally, time-stamped screenshots should be taken of any post. Records should be kept for a minimum of five years, the first two in an advisor's office. As with content review, CCOs should test recordkeeping protocols among individual advisors periodically, and take corrective and training actions as needed. See Figure 7.2.

4. **Unwanted Third-Party Posts**—There are risks associated with third parties posting information or testimonials on your website, company page or profile, or blog (a "like" of your social media profile, for instance, may be considered a prohibited testimonial). Use of, linkage to, "liking," sharing, or referring to third-party sites can cause problems, as *they* may not be compliant, depending on the context. The SEC has said, for example, that if the public is invited to "like" an advisor's biography on a social media site, it could be considered a testimonial disallowed by law. Don't assume that disclaimers will cover you in every contingency. We address this in greater detail in the chapters that follow.

   Compliance officers absolutely must possess the ability to scrub non-compliant content posted to a firm's website by someone else. If it's your site, it's your compliance issue—even if someone else posted it! Advisors should be vigilant about such bad content, and compliance officers should have the ability to remove the offending content/comments immediately. As CCO, you should set the rules on who can post what content to your sites—and have the ability to block such postings altogether. Keep in mind the distinction between third-party posts on your site that you may view as your own, and third-party posts on third-party sites that you may link to or allow to be visible on your site. We cover this in greater detail later. As to the former, it is right that you might screen them for inappropriate content. As to third-party sites, as we will see, if you link to them, you have to leave them be.

5. **Unschooled Staff**—With the broad range of platforms available in social media and the continuous evolution in what each platform offers, it's no surprise that people who work in financial practices can find it difficult to get their arms around everything. Ignorance of the social universe, of course, is no defense as far as regulators are concerned. As FINRA puts it, "A firm must conduct appropriate training and education concerning its policies, including those relating to social media" (*Regulator Notice 11-39*). Choose a learning regimen that's commensurate with the depth of your involvement in social media, formalize it as policy, and review it annually.

WHEN TO CALL FOR HELP

Do these social media compliance requirements make you feel queasy? Are you worried about spending all of your time managing posts, taking screen shots, and keeping other records? There's good news. Per the SEC, it is okay to bring in a third party to help out. A growing number of firms are offering financial practices one-stop compliance platforms, with dashboards that can monitor social media activity and track detailed history across multiple social media networks.

Bottom line: Social media compliance is a challenge, but it's a manageable one. Say what you do, do what you say, keep track of it all, and you'll come out fine. And don't forget—having the right tools can also help.

Remember that we live in a real-time world, and we don't want to let that compromise us by trying to rush something into the social media world before its approved by compliance.

CHAPTER 8

What Does FINRA Say about Social Media?

The twin goals of protecting investors and overseeing registered representatives in the broker/dealer channel has been the responsibility of the Financial Industry Regulatory Authority (FINRA). The self-regulating arm of the brokerage industry, FINRA is no stranger to interpreting technological change to its member advisors.

As long ago as 1999, the agency specifically likened a registered representative's participation in Internet chat rooms to making in-person presentations to investors, subject to the same rules governing such presentations. (For example, a firm's registered principal does not have to approve extemporaneous comments in advance that are made at such events.) Four years later FINRA codified the phrase *public appearance* to include participating in interactive electronic forums.

The environment continues to evolve as social media use in the business and personal world grows exponentially. In 2009, FINRA formed a committee of agency staff and industry reps to examine the implications of social media. The goal, the agency said, was "to ensure that—as the use of social media sites increases over time—investors are protected from false or misleading claims and representations, and firms are able to effectively and appropriately supervise their associated persons' participation in these sites."[1] FINRA added that it wanted a flexible approach that would allow firms to communicate with clients and investors using the new methods afforded by social media.

---

[1] "Regulatory Notice 10-06: Social Media Web Sites," FINRA, January 2010, www .finra.org/web/groups/industry/@ip/@reg/@notice/documents/notices/p120779.pdf. Accessed June 8, 2014.

THREE NEW AREAS OF FINRA GUIDANCE

A year later, FINRA released new guidance on social media use for business purposes.[2] It had specific things to say about certain aspects of the business:

- **Suitability Responsibilities**—Representatives who recommend securities via social media are still subject to the requirement that such investments be suitable to their clients, FINRA said. Whether a particular communication constitutes a recommendation depends on the circumstances of the communication, the agency added.

  FINRA took into account that fact that social media can cast an enormous net. It told reps to keep in mind that, when they make recommendations on different social platforms, such recommendations would need to be suitable for every investor to whom they are made. That could mean hundreds or even thousands of people, depending on how the rep is using the platform.

  So there was no ambiguity, FINRA noted that it has disciplined firms and reps over interactive electronic communications that contained misleading statements about products in recommendations.

- **Static Content versus Interactive Content**—FINRA went into detail on how to compliantly use blogs. It drew a distinction between two types of content. Static content is just that—content that remains the same until it is changed by a firm or individual. It can include blog posts by an advisor, for example, or newsletters, photos, advisor websites, or social media profiles. All of these are considered advertising for the purpose of compliance and must be approved by a firm's principal before they go up.

  Interactive content that allows real-time back-and-forth communication between reps and investors does not require pre-approval, but is still subject to supervision, the agency said. Interactive can include updates on LinkedIn and Facebook, tweets, and blog comments.

- **Recordkeeping**—Firms that use social media for business must ensure that they can retain records of such business, FINRA held. The agency observed that some tech companies were providing systems that would allow broker/dealers to record social media-related communications both on and off the main website of the firm; it didn't have opinions on how valid such services might be, but said advisors would have to ensure that whatever services were being provided dovetailed with industry requirements. FINRA subsequently held that broker-dealers

---

[2]FINRA, "Regulatory Notice 10-06: Social Media Web Sites."

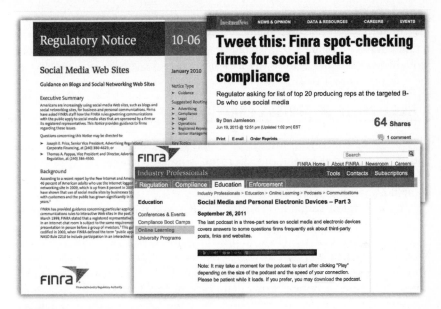

FIGURE 8.1 FINRA on Social Media
FINRA is a trademark of the Financial Industry Regulatory Authority Inc. FINRA is not affiliated with the author or publisher of this work and does not endorse it.

must keep certain records for a period of at least three years, with the first two years in an easily accessible place.

CHOOSING YOUR CONTENT: STATIC VERSUS INTERACTIVE

Which is better, static content or interactive content? This depends on your goals. Interactive content—comment sections of a blog, tweets, and live chats, for example—keeps clients and potential investors engaged and may be useful in client servicing, a topic discussed later. And if reps are creating or sharing posts about useful or interesting subjects, their followers are more likely to share that content themselves. In addition to spreading the rep's name and presence around the social media universe, it could possibly increase search engine rankings—making it easier for a potential client to find the rep during an Internet search.

It helps to remember that when it comes to static content versus Interactive content, anti-fraud rules and the standard for negligent misstatements and omissions apply to both. Advisors need to think carefully about what they're putting out on social media—even tweets, which are short and to the point, carry compliance responsibilities. Always keep in mind that if you wouldn't say it offline, don't say it online.

A FINRA SWEEP OF ADVISOR PRACTICES

Following the enactment of new rules related to electronic communications and boosting social media and electronic communications as a priority in exams, FINRA then took another step: conducting a sweep to determine compliance with its social media rules.

In the Target Examination Letter, FINRA said that firms will be subject to periodic spot-checks.[3]

Charles Schwab's Melissa Callison, who serves on FINRA's Social Media Task Force, says the sweeps were part of a gut check to see if firms were applying the guidance from FINRA RN 10-06 (2010) and RN 11-39[4] (2011) and to determine if firms had implemented reasonable supervisory processes (for example, are they performing the same procedures in light of the guidance) and recordkeeping practices. The spot-check results indicated that recordkeeping continues to be a pain point for firms, and there will continue to be dialog and follow-up calls with the industry, which may lead to additional regulatory guidance on the topic.

Most interestingly among the list of items FINRA reviewed was a firm's top 20 producing advisors—based on commissions—who have used social media for business purposes. One theory for the focus may have been to see if top producers were using social media and how that correlated to commissions earned on those activities. This target is less an issue for firms that do not employ commission-based advisors than for those that do.

Should advisors be concerned? In our interview, Callison, like others, says "social media for advisors is a great opportunity to connect with clients and get their name out." But still, many are discouraged by FINRA regulations, which they feel make it difficult to be able to communicate as freely as they want. What can advisors do?

---

[3]"Re: Spot-Check of Social Media Communications," FINRA Targeted Examination Letters, June 2013, www.finra.org/Industry/Regulation/Guidance/Targeted ExaminationLetters/P282569. Accessed June 8, 2014.
[4]"Regulatory Notice 11-39: Social Media Web Sites and the Use of Personal Devices for Business Communications," FINRA, August 2011, www.finra.org/web/groups/industry/@ip/@reg/@notice/documents/notices/p124186.pdf. Accessed June 8, 2014.

Here are a few tips:

- **Conduct Your Own Spot Checks**—As a best practice for your own firm, use an examination or sweep—whether it's a spot check or an examiner visit—to move proactively to review your policies and procedures. Make sure they're updated.

    Schwab, for instance, has implemented its own spot-check process because it found its own internal inconsistencies. "Because this space is so interactive and dynamic, it's tough to follow a process with social media. You need to be constantly checking in, updating your procedures, making sure your supervision is working, and seeing if your needs have changed," Callison says.
- **Watch Your Third-Party Providers**—On the record-keeping front, a lot of firms use third-party providers who say they'll handle all your supervision and archiving. So, as part of a spot check, FINRA could look at what they're actually archiving. Make sure you've conducted a thorough check yourself to avoid a third-party provider saying they're doing one thing—like maintaining posts on Facebook, tweets on Twitter, or shares on LinkedIn—but actually not.
- **Be Aware of Ownership**—In some cases, the third-party social media site may actually own the information on that site—such as a tweet. Moreover, sites like Facebook may change their APIs—the code allowing a firm to interface and capture information nightly—which could suddenly shut a firm out. Options for this, suggests Callison, include having a close relationship with these platforms and/or having paper backups.

If FINRA decides to conduct another spot check related to social media, it's expected to be looking more for violations or for firms that failed to put into place the right mechanisms, rather than simply looking for levels of consistency across firms and business models.

FINRA told the brokerages it wanted:

- An explanation of how each firm was using social media (e.g., Facebook, Twitter, LinkedIn, blogs) at the corporate level in the conduct of its business. It also sought:
    - The URL for each of the social media sites used by the firm at the corporate level.
    - The date the firm began using each of the sites identified.
    - The identity of all individuals who posted and/or updated content of the sites.
- An explanation of how the firm's registered representatives and associated persons generally used social media in the conduct of the firm's

business, including the date(s) the firm began allowing the use of each social media platform and whether the usage continued.

- The portion of the firm's written supervisory procedures concerning the production, approval, and distribution of social media communications in effect during February 4, 2013 through May 4, 2013.
- An explanation of the measures that the firm adopted to monitor compliance with the firm's social media policies (e.g., training meetings, annual certification, technology).
- A list of the firm's top 20 producing registered representatives (based on commissioned sales) who used social media for business purposes to interact with retail investors as defined in FINRA Rule 2210(a)(6) during the specified time period. It also wanted to know the type of social media used by each rep for business purposes during this time period, as well as the dollar amount of sales made and commissions earned during the period.

NEW CYBERSECURITY INITIATIVE

As advisors slowly expand their involvement in social media, their greater presence on the Web can lead to other risks of a more technological sort. We know, from following the Target credit card data breach of some 40 million customers, that hackers can be very quick. Following similar action by the Securities and Exchange Commission (SEC), FINRA announced in early 2014 that it would be conducting assessments of firms' approaches to managing cybersecurity threats.[5]

FINRA said it launched the initiative because firms rank cybersecurity among their top five risks. FINRA said it would begin by surveying 20 firms across different business models

FINRA said it's "conducting this assessment in light of the critical role information technology (IT) plays in the securities industry, the increasing threat to firms' IT systems from a variety of sources, and the potential harm to investors, firms, and the financial system as a whole that these threats pose."

FINRA has four broad goals with the effort:

1. To understand better the types of threats that firms face.
2. To increase its understanding of firms' risk appetite, exposure, and major areas of vulnerabilities in their IT systems.

---

[5] "Re: Cybersecurity," FINRA Target Examination Letters, January 2014, www.finra .org/Industry/Regulation/Guidance/TargetedExaminationLetters/P443219. Accessed June 8, 2014.

3. To better understand firms' approaches to managing these threats, including through risk-assessment processes, IT protocols, application management practices, and supervision.
4. As appropriate, to share observations and findings with firms.

The assessment addresses a number of areas related to cybersecurity, including firms':

- Approaches to information technology risk assessment.
- Business continuity plans in case of an online attack.
- Organizational structures and reporting lines.
- Processes for sharing and obtaining information about cybersecurity threats.
- Understanding of concerns and threats faced by the industry.
- Assessment of the impact of attacks on the firm over the preceding 12 months.
- Approaches to handling distributed denial of service attacks.
- Training programs.
- Insurance coverage for cybersecurity-related events.
- Contractual arrangements with third-party service providers.

In many ways, FINRA appears to be moving more quickly to address emerging issues from technology and social media than in years past. The good news is that they are recognizing that social media is a communications medium that is here to stay.

CHAPTER 9

What Does the SEC Say about Social Media?

The Investment Advisers Act of 1940 obviously predates the arrival of the Internet and social media. The leading communication technology of the time was the postal service and telephones, and most of the law's rules were written to address them accordingly. (Perhaps anticipating further developments in communication, the government broadened the rules somewhat to include "any means or instrumentality of interstate commerce, directly or indirectly"—leaving the door open for fresh-in technology.)

Indeed, when the U.S. Securities and Exchange Commission rolled out new guidance in January 2012[1] concerning compliance and social media, it

---

[1]SEC Office of Compliance Inspections and Examinations, "Investment Adviser Use of Social Media," National Examination Risk Alert, January 4, 2012, www.sec.gov/about/offices/ocie/riskalert-socialmedia.pdf.

observed that the use of social media in the financial advisory industry was fundamentally altering the business, and at an accelerating pace.

"Social media is landscape-shifting," the SEC said. "It converts the traditional two-party, adviser-to-client communication into an interactive, multi-party dialogue among advisers, clients, and prospects, within an open architecture accessible to third-party observers. It also converts a static medium, such as a website, where viewers passively receive content, into a medium where users actively create content."

SEVEN NEW GUIDELINES THAT CCOs SHOULD KNOW

Toward that end, the SEC provided advisors with a broad range of things to consider for compliance purposes as they integrated social media into their practices. They include:

- **Usage Guidelines**—Firms, the SEC said, may consider ground rules for how its investment advisor reps and solicitors could use social media— outlining a series of approved social media networking sites, for example, or barring particular functions on a specific site.
- **Content Standards**—Firms should think about what risks, if any, its content on social media poses to its fiduciary duty or other compliance matters. Does content recommend certain investments or services? Does it offer information on investment performances? Clear guidelines may be needed on whether to restrict certain content.
- **Monitoring of Social Media Use**—Firms should consider their own social media sites as well as those of any third-party sites it uses. The frequency of monitoring—intermittently? every day? real time?—depends on the firm's own assessment of its risks in this area. How often do advisors post content? What are the risks of misleading content? After-the-fact reviews of content that breaks the rules may be unreasonable, the SEC believes, given the broad reach that such content has with investors.
- **Resources**—Has the firm committed enough to meet its compliance needs? Regulators expect the level of resources to be commensurate with social media activity—in other words, the more engaged you are on LinkedIn or Facebook, the more resources regulators will expect you to have in place to support that engagement. If a firm's social media involvement is large enough, bringing in an outside vendor to oversee social media use by its reps may make sense.
- **Training and Certification**—Firms may consider setting up appropriate social media instruction, as well as the means of ensuring that their reps and solicitors understand their policies.

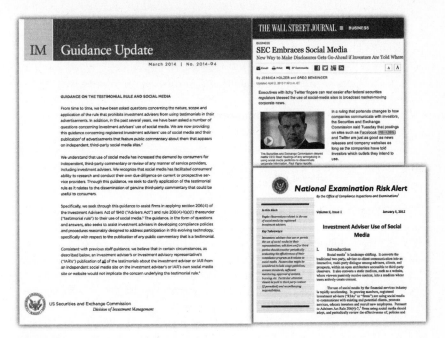

FIGURE 9.1 SEC on Social Media

- **Functionality**—Firms need to consider whether the social media sites they approve for use by their advisors are staying current with industry standards. For example, does a site have a function that endangers a client's privacy and lacks a means of disabling or modifying such a function? Rapid tech evolution makes this consideration especially significant, the SEC says.
- **Personal/Professional Sites**—Firms should consider whether its advisors should conduct business on personal or third-party social media sites. They also should evaluate whether access to such sites poses security risks. See Figure 9.1.

TESTING FOR TESTIMONIALS

The SEC has also thought carefully about the implications that social media holds for the use of testimonials. Even before the age of social media, financial advisors and managers have been pressed to adhere to this portion of compliance, which aims to protect investors from fraudulent claims of advisor expertise.

Section 206(4) of the Investment Advisers Act of 1940 generally bars these financial professionals from deceptive or manipulative practices. The law specifies:

> [i]t shall constitute a fraudulent, deceptive, or manipulative act, practice, or course of business . . . for any investment adviser registered or required to be registered under [the Advisers Act], directly or indirectly, to publish, circulate, or distribute any advertisement which refers, directly or indirectly, to any testimonial of any kind concerning the investment adviser or concerning any advice, analysis, report or other service rendered by such investment adviser.

Using such testimonials in ads is inherently misleading, the agency says, since they tend to emphasize favorable opinions and ignore unfavorable ones. In its 2012 guidance, the SEC extended this thinking to social media. Depending on circumstances, it said, the use of "like" buttons on social sites could be deemed to be a testimonial as defined under the Advisers Act "if it is an explicit or implicit statement of a client's or clients' experience with an investment advisor or IAR.

"If, for example, the public is invited to 'like' an IAR's biography posted on a social media site, that election could be viewed as a type of testimonial prohibited" under the law, the agency said.

The SEC has left some wiggle room for interpretation here, with its use of language like "could be a testimonial" and "depends on all the facts and circumstances." Clearly, using "like" in a way that speaks to a person's experience with the advisor is something the agency wants to prevent.

Some in the industry, however, are not letting the SEC's antipathy toward "like" prevent them from using such functions within their own web presence, albeit in ways that accord with their view of what's compliant. Major registered investment advisors (RIAs) and broker/dealers have Facebook pages with "like" buttons, as do individual advisors. They don't see "like" as a comment on their abilities as a financial professional.

Brittney Castro, owner of the Financially Wise Women practice, uses a "like" button on her business' Facebook page. You have to "like" someone to follow their posts on their site, she notes, so people who "like" her have a desire to know what she's saying rather than testifying to what she can do as an advisor.

Michael Kitces, financial planner and author of the industry blog *Nerd's Eye View*, observes that the SEC has never explicitly banned the use of "likes." "It's worth noting that ultimately, all the SEC ever said in their 2012 guidance is that a 'Like' *could* constitute a testimonial given certain facts and circumstances, if it violates the principles of being a client testimonial," he says. "Welcome to principles-based regulation."

New guidance issued by the SEC in March 2014[2] sought to refine some distinctions on testimonials, although not specifically regarding "like" buttons.

A LOOSER INTERPRETATION

The SEC said that client reviews do *not* violate its ban on testimonials as long as they appear on independent social media or review sites. There's an important proviso: *all* public comments about the advisor, regardless of whether they are positive or negative, must be available for the public to see. It's also important that advisors themselves have no means of controlling how the comments appear on the sites (see Figure 9.2). For example:

- **Permitted**—Testimonials on Yelp, Google, or any so-called advisor review site (such sites deemed as objective).
- **Not permitted**—Testimonials written on an advisor's Facebook fan page (because the advisor controls the page) and LinkedIn recommendations.

It's a good idea for advisors to use social media to direct prospective clients to reviews on objective third-party sites. But advisors need to take care that they direct viewers to pages that display *all* reviews, both pro and con, and not just a single review.

THREE CLARIFICATIONS ON EARLIER GUIDANCE

The 2014 guidance also sought to reduce ambiguity in a few other areas concerning social media compliance.

- **"Friending" and Connecting**—The SEC has made it clear that "friending" someone on Facebook or connecting with someone on LinkedIn is not considered a testimonial or endorsement.
- **Testimonials on Outside Subjects**—Direct testimonials are now permitted if they relate to an advisor's community involvement and not the advisor's financial expertise.

---

[2]SEC Division of Investment Management, "Guidance on the Testimonial Rule and Social Media," *IM Guidance Update*, March 2014, www.sec.gov/investment/im-guidance-2014-04.pdf. Accessed June 8, 2014.

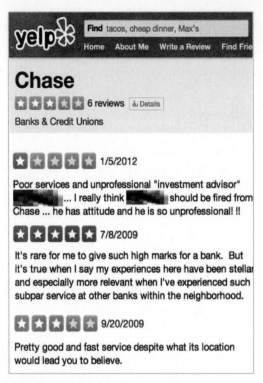

FIGURE 9.2   Both Positive and Negatives Reviews on Chase's Yelp Profile

- The SEC wrote that it "no longer take(s) the position, as [it] did a number of years ago, that an advertisement that contains non-investment related commentary regarding an IAR, such as regarding an IAR's religious affiliation or community service, may be deemed a testimonial" that violates the rules. It means that advisors may now include their membership in charitable activities, their knowledge about coaching youth soccer teams, and their interest in bicycling as skills that members may endorse on social sites.
- The SEC guidance aims to allow advisors to connect with clients and prospects more closely by permitting advisors to present a deeper portrait of who they are.
- **Directing Traffic to Social Sites**—Advisors may acknowledge their presence on social media channels in various media.
- The SEC says, "An investment adviser or IAR could reference the fact that public commentary regarding the investment adviser or IAR may be found on an independent social media site, and may include the logo of

the independent social media site on its non-social media advertisements, without implicating the testimonial rule."

Here's what this means for advisors:

- **Do** tell listeners to "Check us out on Facebook" in a radio spot or interview.
- **Do** print "Follow us on Twitter to get up-to-date information and learn more about our company" in a direct mail piece.
- **Do not** print a specific testimonial in an advertisement or read one particular (and clearly positive) review in an interview.

CHAPTER 10

What Gets Financial Professionals into Trouble with Social Media?

> "Another idiotic article on ARNA from someone who has no clue what she's talking about . . . 'a reputedly safer and more effective competitor drug' WUS or OREX? LMAO. Brooke do your due dili. There's no safer weight loss drug than ARNA."
>
> —A post by a financial advisor who subsequently was sanctioned by FINRA

Sometimes it seems as if social media has just created a universe of new ways for financial advisors to run afoul of regulators.

Consider the following stories.

- A New York-based money manager paid a $100,000 penalty in 2014 and was censured after he used Twitter and other media to disseminate misleading statements about business performance, the Securities and Exchange Commission (SEC) said. Among other things, regulators charged that the manager tweeted that he was responsible for model portfolios in his newsletters that "doubled the S&P 500 the last 10 years," even though he had no involvement in the model portfolio performance for the first three years.
- The Financial Industry Regulatory Authority (FINRA) fined a Hauppauge, New York, broker $5,000 and suspended him for 10 days in 2013 after he

posted unwise remarks on his Facebook account about a pharmaceutical company whose weight-loss drug he was promoting. In disputing a comment about Arena Pharmaceuticals' (ARNA) stock price, the broker wrote: "Another idiotic article on ARNA from someone who has no clue what she's talking about . . . LMAO. Brooke do your due dili. There's no safer weight loss drug than ARNA." FINRA said the post made exaggerated claims, was neither fair nor balanced, and neglected to mention that the broker owned 10,000 shares of the stock.

- An Owens Mills, Maryland, broker was fined $10,000 in 2013 and suspended for 2 months after FINRA found that he had put up unapproved websites, including a LinkedIn profile, that violated rules requiring balanced presentations of investment content. Among other things, FINRA said, the LinkedIn profile declared that the broker worked "to create tax-advantaged, wealth building and protection plans," without identifying the strategies or products covered in such plans.

The three incidents offer important lessons. Disciplinary cases of these types don't happen very often but are likely to come up more frequently, as both FINRA and the SEC pick up the pace in reviewing social media communications. What's striking about these three stories is the fact that all three brokers would have gotten into trouble if social media had never existed and they had simply carried on with their behavior using older forms of communication. The rules for presenting advertising in a complete and balanced fashion, for example, have existed for decades. Social media hasn't changed that.

With that in mind, let's turn to some of the regulatory issues that advisors need to keep in mind if they want to avoid social media mishaps. Among other things, we will look at ways of managing risk, dealing with problematic content that finds its way onto websites, and sharing some big-picture tips.

REMEMBER THE GROUND RULES

Here are some of the things that financial advisors need to keep uppermost in their mind if they want to avoid getting into trouble on social media:

- **Fiduciary Duty**—Fiduciary standards still apply—including, of course, the duty of care. Advice must be prudent and suitable to the client. Hasty or flippant comments on social media are no more appropriate than they would be using any other form of communication.

- **Use of Third-Party Sites**—Using or linking to third-party sites—including "liking" or sharing content on those sites—can cause problems since the sites themselves may not be compliant. For example, FINRA bars links to third-party sites that contain false or misleading content.
- **Third Parties Posting on Your Site**—Similarly, there are risks associated with third parties posting information or testimonials (if you are an investment advisor) on your site. (A "like" of your site may be considered a prohibited testimonial by the SEC.) Disclaimers are a minimum remedy; many sites restrict or prohibit third-party posting altogether, others allow you to turn off the "like" or endorsement feature. On the other hand, the SEC has taken an open-minded view on third-party ratings and rankings, if handled correctly. Typically, most sites can be made to work with some advance planning.
- **Compliance with Advertising Standards**—More generally, the rules from the Investment Advisers Act of 1940 are fairly specific about the content of advertisements. Advisors who are regulated under the SEC and are using social media might find it difficult to avoid posting something that could be construed as an advertisement. Brokers who are regulated under FINRA have more leeway in certain areas; for example, the agency has held that social media fits its definition of public appearances, a distinction that relieves registered principals at a firm from having to approve in advance extemporaneous comments by brokers at public events.
- **Paper Trails**—The Advisers Act requires investment advisors to maintain certain books and records relating to their advisory business (required records) for a specified period of time. "Records" in this case cover most aspects of an advisor's interaction with clients, and are interpreted by regulators to include social media interactions.

REMEMBER: THERE'S RISK

One of the things that gets financial pros into trouble with social media is the same thing that has gotten some of them in trouble for years: failing to convey the element of risk in investing and being overly enthusiastic about investment prospects, says Stuart Fross, partner at Foley & Lardner LLC.

For example, if you post a Tweet that says, "Learn about our favorite fund returning 96%!" you have created a series of violations just from being excessively enthusiastic—even if it's true. Whenever you quote performance information, you must follow rules aimed at helping investors evaluate the claims; these include showing performance over relevant time periods and noting any special circumstances that gave rise to the particularly good performance environment.

Fross says the difference with social media is that the securities laws penalize misstatements and omissions of material fact. Material omissions (or even the risk of material omissions) "are what bury people with social media," he says.

So how can you convey the potential for risk in social media? Fross suggests including footnotes in static content online; blog postings can include disclaimers that say, "Remember that all investing brings with it risks." Platforms with limited space for such techniques, such as Twitter, require different approaches. Authors must take care that tweets aren't promissory; you can't link from a tweet to a disclaimer, he says, because a warning requires equal prominence with an investment idea. You can, however, link to a piece that tells more, and have the tweet be an invitation to learn more about the subject of the tweet, so long as the tweet is not promissory. You may also include a link to a disclosure in your profile as seen in Figure 10.1 by BlackRock.

FIGURE 10.1   Disclosure link on BlackRock's Twitter Profile

DRAWING LINES BETWEEN BUSINESS AND PERSONAL

When it comes to social media and online communication, the distinction between business and personal accounts has blurred—with troubling consequences.

The social universe is rife with examples of executives who overshare in ways that reflect badly on their companies: racist or sexist comments, for example. Some say it's not a problem as long as their accounts are personal and their postings reflect just their own thoughts.

Do the shareholders care? Yes. If you can tie an inappropriate tweet from an executive back to his company's brand, it matters. Just by using Twitter, for example, the executive has already broadened his public presence. A "my tweets are my own" disclaimer will do no good.

If you want to tweet in a thoroughly candid fashion on a personal basis, consider these precautions:

- **Don't** display your company title (such as SVP).
- **Don't** use the same headshot for personal and business social media profiles/accounts.
- **Don't** include your work e-mail on the account.
- **Don't** say where you work, so your tweets are truly personal.
- **Do** use privacy settings, if you want your social profile strictly personal or you want to control who actually accesses your social communications. For example, you can control which of your followers on Twitter may actually view your tweets.

FOUR WAYS TO MANAGE SOCIAL MEDIA RISK

The first step in managing risk, of course, is to be aware of, and understand, the risks mentioned above. Then advisors need to establish standards, document them, and monitor the way they comply.

Let's look at these more closely:

1. **Understand the risks**—Investment advisors are specifically charged with the responsibility of knowing the risks in their business—for example, they must avoid creating an advertisement or miscommunication with the public. Investment advisors should identify risk exposure given their operations, and must implement and supervise compliance procedures reasonably designed to assure compliance with the Advisers Act advertising rules.

2. **Document policies and procedures**—The expectation nowadays is that a social media presence will be accompanied by policies and procedures designed to assure compliance with securities laws. For example, you may want to put rules in place to review content before posting, and train employees who are posting on the site. You may want to give special attention to any investment performance information, past specific recommendations, or success stories. There are specific requirements that must be considered before posting this type of information, and your review process should be sensitive to those issues.
3. **Test and monitor**—Investment advisors should test their compliance procedures to see how well they address risks, and set up a system of regular monitoring.
4. **Pay close attention to third parties**—Investment advisors may be responsible for third-party content, and you may have to take some third-party content down from your site.

KEYS TO HANDLING BAD CONTENT

You've been told to remove bad content from your website or social media, but what exactly does that mean? When it comes to staying compliant on social media, it's actually pretty straightforward.

Bad content would include a recommendation, especially given the fact that such recommendations on social media are publicly available and would not go through the typical know-your-customer process. A simple test for deciding if content is acceptable is to determine if it is educational or if it offers advice. Be wary of calls to action; those statements that encourage people to buy or act.

While social media typically is not an appropriate place for recommendations, there is an exception: a user group that is prescreened. If advisors know who the population of the group is and have a defined universe, so to speak, they can have conversations and include recommendations that are appropriate for the group's members.

Finally, three more things to keep in mind when posting on social media:

1. **Company Policy**—It's not enough to put up posts that pass muster with regulators; they also have to comply with the internal guidelines of the advisor's employer as well. Know what your boss expects of you online.
2. **Avoid Social Media Fights**—Sometimes it seems as if the new technology lends itself to fiery personalities, and it's tempting to lash out at remarks on a website with which you disagree. But even if you're not violating federal or state regulations, it's best not to pick quarrels using

intemperate language. Remember that many posts have a long shelf life on the Internet, and your investor clients and supervisors will judge you on how you present yourself.

3. **You're Leaving a Trail**—Quite a few message boards now require posters to include links to their Facebook or LinkedIn pages, partly to keep inflammatory rhetoric to a minimum. Often they even have the pictures from those websites. It's like leaving your business card at the end of a discussion.

CHAPTER 11

How Do We Create a Social Media Policy?

Regulators expect financial firms with a presence on social media to document the strategies and policies that govern their social media interactions in the same manner that firms must document many other operations within their business, such as training and recordkeeping. This practice is particularly helpful when applied to social media, because it forces the firm to think through the implications of using a new technology—one that can have surprising and sometimes disconcerting effects on operations.

In the appendix to this book, as well as in the companion website (www .wiley.com/go/financialsocial), you can access a model social media policy for your use.

There are a number of different approaches that financial professionals can take when preparing a social media policy. What regulators want to see, and what actually is most helpful to the firm, is a policy that is specific and relevant to the firm itself. It also must dovetail with the firm's own compliance rules.

FIVE STEPS TO STARTING YOUR POLICY

Here are five good ways to get started with your policy:

1. **Address the purpose of social media**—Here is where strategy ought to be scrutinized, with a clear description for the firm's employees. Why is your business using social media? What should the reader/user take away after reading the policy? These are all important questions that need to be addressed in the introduction of your policy. In essence, you need to set the stage and make sure everyone is clear on the whys.

2. **Define** *social media*—After the why comes the what. What is social media? And with what social media platforms does your business participate? Again, this is important for building the foundation of your social media policy. Don't assume that the employees at your firm who need to know your policy are well-versed in social media.

3. **Personal accounts on social sites**—Employees are assumed to be representatives of their organization, so it's wise to set up guidelines for how they should conduct and present themselves on their personal social media presence—their Facebook page, their Twitter account, and so on. Ensure that their communications are transparent, ethical, and accurate, and establish guidelines for how employees should engage with clients on their websites.

4. **Establish best practices for the various platforms**—How should your associates conduct themselves on social media? What are the compliance regulations set forth by the Financial Industry Regulatory Authority (FINRA) and the Securities and Exchange Commission (SEC)? Topics that should be addressed here can include commenting, posting, handling controversial issues, managing confidential information responsibly, and exercising best judgment and ethics.

5. **Protocols for crises**—Many companies fail to include this element in their social media policy. Let's face it: people are fallible—and it's better to prepare for a crisis than get caught with your pants down when one shows up on your doorstep. Consider the example of NatWest, the bank owned by the Royal Bank of Scotland, which faced a barrage of criticism in 2012 after hundreds of thousands of depositors were unable to withdraw funds due to computer malfunctions.

One related bit of advice: When it comes to crafting a sound social media policy, consider the philosophy espoused by Sharlyn Lauby of Mashable. She suggests "focusing on things that employees can do rather than what they can't do." Why? Because a social media policy succeeds best when it seeks to leverage the positive.

Michael White, chief marketing officer at Raymond James Financial Inc., notes that social media is an evolving technology—one that calls for a flexible approach to compliance. Social media policies should be "principle-based," he says, to accommodate dynamic platforms.

For example, LinkedIn developed an endorsement feature subsequent to Raymond James' policy, but the policy already had principles related to testimonials that applied in the new case, White says. Financial professionals should expect the compliance landscape to continue to change where social is concerned.

FIGURE 11.1   Social Media Policy

"If your policy is six months old and hasn't been touched, that's not good," he says. "It needs to be a living document."

FIVE POLICY ELEMENTS THE SEC LIKES TO SEE

The SEC has urged industry leaders to avoid weaving social media compliance into their firm's existing compliance policies and procedures. Social media policies, the regulators say, should stand on their own.

In preparing such a policy, there are a number of issues that its authors need to address, including the following:

1. **Who's On First?**—The policy should define *who* among the firm's investment advisor representatives and solicitors can use social media and which forms of social media can be used. Remember that the policy should encompass *personal* use of social media. Advisors cannot be barred from using social media in their personal lives, but firms must set guidelines for how they use it. Moreover, in all cases, personal use will have to be scrutinized systematically with respect to firm- or product-related information.

2. **What's Okay to Say?**—Define content standards that apply to any investment recommendations, investment service, or investment performance. One of the decisions that a social media policy author must make is whether to prevent recommendations. If so, be sure to include rules to avoid so-called calls to action. If not, then the standards should assure suitability of the advice given to all of its recipients. Consider requiring pre-approval of all postings, or of some categories of postings (blog posts versus comments in chat rooms, for example).

3. **How Much Effort Do I Need?**—The level of conversation monitoring should be proportional to the number of users in the firm. The more activity you expect to have on social media, the more oversight you will be expected to perform. The firm's monitoring resources have to be proportionate to social media usage, and vice versa.

4. **Who's On Third?**—In addition to monitoring its own social media sites, a firm needs to consider those third-party sites—media sites like SeekingAlpha or advisor review sites like Yelp—that employees and clients may use, and consider the level of participation—if any—that seems appropriate.

5. **Is My Data Overexposed?**—A firm should consider if use of a social media site presents information security risks to the firm.

Recordkeeping rules also belong in a firm's social media policy. Your social media content has to be recorded, in effect, to include all postings, e-mail, and chats. You will have to be able to produce all of your historical content upon inspection, and you will need to confirm that you are meeting your retention requirements. Plainly, your standalone social media policy will be supplemented by cross-references to other policies, such as recordkeeping and retention in other aspects of the business. You might consider test driving a third-party record-keeping business to whom you can outsource some of these responsibilities.

THE THREE "Ss" OF A SOCIAL MEDIA POLICY

Finally, here are a few general principles for creating a social media policy:

1. **Simple**—Be a Hemingway. Use plain grammar and easily accessible language. If you use heavy jargon and technical terms, your readers at the office are more likely to misunderstand things.

2. **Short**—Your policy need not be a novel. Keep it short and to the point. Also make it easily navigable for readers by using headers, bullet points, and other formatting tools.

3. **Specific**—Overly broad policies can create confusion and attract unwanted regulatory attention. In 2012, the National Labor Relations Board accused General Motors of developing unlawful social media policies. The NLRB said the automaker's policies infringed on workers' rights by establishing vague rules, including a prohibition against misleading posts. This outcome serves as an object lesson for financial firms looking to set up boundaries of their own for social media. Be sure to be detailed when you do so.

Creating a social media policy need not be difficult. Indeed, policies from some of the largest companies have been as brief as two pages. They are living documents that evolve, as do the firm's social media initiatives. If you need help, you can get started by using the social media template provided in the book and companion website, www.wiley.com/go/financialsocial (password: savvy123).

Key Playing Fields in Social Media

CHAPTER 12

How Can We Use LinkedIn?

There's a reason LinkedIn is one of the top talked-about social networks for connecting with investors and growing relationships. LinkedIn is a virtual tradeshow. It's a place where you can mingle among others in your industry, build your brand, distribute relevant content, join specific groups and conversations, and build beneficial relationships.

When optimized and used efficiently, LinkedIn can be used to bring in more client relationships and job opportunities, to network with peers and industry leaders, to engage with existing clients, to add a more personal face to your business, and to offer a valuable offshoot to your website.

So, how do you filter through the fray of people and profiles to find those strategic connections and build your brand? That's what we'll be talking about in this chapter.

FIRST, WHAT EXACTLY IS LINKEDIN?

LinkedIn is a business-oriented, profile-based social networking site connecting millions of people worldwide. Profiles are filled with job histories, educational backgrounds, recommendations, referrals, and even resumes. Your ability to network with relevant associates, clients, and leads is almost endless.

In February 2014, the platform reported more than 270 million registered users in more than 200 countries and territories (and more than 19 languages around the world). The financial services industry was reported as the second largest industry, with more than 2 million members in 2013. Statistics show that two people sign up for a LinkedIn account *every second*. There is no doubt it's one of the most important social networks.

WHY IS LINKEDIN DIFFERENT FROM OTHER SOCIAL NETWORKS?

LinkedIn is different from other networks because of its high degree of professionalism and business networking-focused culture. This isn't Facebook, Twitter, or Instagram. You won't see posts of your friend's vacation photos, cat videos, or food pictures. You will, however, see millions of conversations pertaining to your local network and industry. People are using LinkedIn in many ways:

- To prospect and generate leads
- To discover valuable connections
- To network with others in your industry
- To increase brand exposure and to position your business as a leader
- To establish credibility as a business and/or individual
- To seek employees and/or employment
- To gain insights from discussions with experts in group

THREE STEPS TO GETTING STARTED ON LINKEDIN

Okay, so advisors, asset managers, and hedge fund executives are on LinkedIn, but is it making a difference? The answer is a resounding yes. Many advisors using social media are seeing real business results from it, in terms of both clients and assets. Now that you know why you should be on LinkedIn, let's discuss how you can get started.

1. Optimize Your LinkedIn Profile

With more than 270 million professionals on LinkedIn, how are you going to stand out and increase the awareness of your brand? As we've stated, there are a myriad of reasons to make your presence known on the LinkedIn network. When you set up your profile, you want it optimized and filled out properly so you can leverage those relationships and increase your connections and brand awareness.

Here are some important aspects of the LinkedIn profile for you to develop once you've clicked the sign up button:

Use Keywords   A keyword is a term that people use when trying to find you. On LinkedIn, it's essential that you optimize your profile around keywords you want to be found by. For example, if you're a retirement planner, you'd

FIGURE 12.1 Use Appropriate Keywords

want to optimize your profile so that when people search for *retirement*, your profile is first—or at least on the first page. To do this, you need to make sure key terms recur multiple times in your headline, current job titles, past job titles, personal summary, and skills (see Figure 12.1). Here is what you can do to achieve the best results:

- **Use long-tail keywords**—For example, instead of using *financial advisor* as your primary keyword, use something more narrow and specific like *financial and retirement advisor.*
- **Use keywords generously throughout your profile**—Once you have a list of keywords that are the most pertinent to you and your business, use them recurrently throughout your profile, in your headline, current job titles, past job titles, summary, and skills.

Create Descriptive Headlines The headline of your LinkedIn page is extremely important. It's the first impression, and we all know that first impressions create lasting impressions. Next are a few strategies for creating good headlines.

FIGURE 12.2   Powerful LinkedIn Headline

- Use your headline to describe what you do. Rather than just stating your current title, try something descriptive, like "Experienced Financial Advisor in the Denver Area Specializing in Wealth Transfer."
- Avoid filler words. For example, use & instead of writing out *and*. It saves space.
- Use keywords frequently, include the location, and make the headlines encompass the services you offer.

Figure 12.2 is an example of a powerful LinkedIn headline.

Complete Your Summary   When filling out your summary, first include a personal summary followed by an overview of your business. If you have a company biography or mission statement on your website that you feel is strong, use it. For larger firms, craft an "about the company" message that is approved for all advisors to share in their LinkedIn summaries. Here are some basic suggestions for a standout summary:

- This should be personal. Speak about yourself in the first person.
- Include a brief introduction about yourself, how you got into the industry, your education/designations, and a little information about your personal interests.
- Use strong language. For example, don't just say, "I help people plan for retirement," say "I am passionate about preparing clients for a comfortable retirement."
- Use keywords and be sure to include any specialties or areas of focus.
- Embed interactive media. Include videos and links to your blog and SlideShares to help visualize your story and expertise.

Edit Your Contact Information   Make sure that people can contact you. Take advantage of the online real estate available and fill in your work e-mail, phone number, Twitter handle, links to any websites, and even your birthday. (See Figure 12.3.)

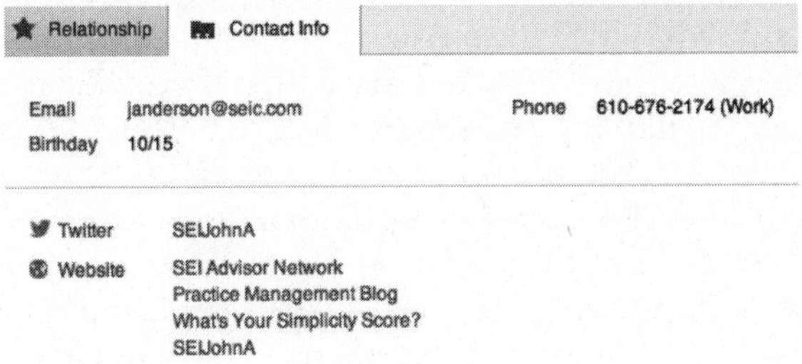

Relationship ★   Contact Info ✉

| Email | janderson@seic.com | Phone | 610-676-2174 (Work) |

Birthday   10/15

🐦 Twitter   SEIJohnA

🌐 Website   SEI Advisor Network
              Practice Management Blog
              What's Your Simplicity Score?
              SEIJohnA

FIGURE 12.3   Leverage Your Contact Info

NOTE: LinkedIn gives you the ability to add up to three websites to your profile. Take advantage of this feature. Utilize all three options with your website, your blog site, your Facebook link, links to external associations you are part of, or other relevant options. Not only do these provide an easy outlet for your connections to view your information, but it also can aid in driving traffic to your website. Whenever you include links to external sites, consider using a call to action. For example, instead of saying "Smith Financial Website," say "Visit Smith Financial."

2. Build Your Network

Once you have your profile set up, there are many ways to approach connecting on LinkedIn. While we strongly suggest you connect with a broad range of professionals—who might also become future clients or business partners—there are multiple approaches you can take. *Social Media Sonar* has four encompassing connection strategies:

1. **The Lion**—Lions are completely open connectors. They seek to increase their connections through actively sending out and accepting connection invitations. While I'm sure there are a few who take pride in touting the specific number, the majority believe that large networks lead to more opportunity.
2. **The Turtle**—Turtles are the opposite of lions. Turtles primarily connect with those they know well. They see value in having a tight network made up of individuals they completely trust. Their networks tend to be highly selective and can be counted on to pass on introductions, much like a private networking group.

3. **The Hound Dog**—A Hound Dog is someone who uses LinkedIn to connect to those they know and those they would like to know. They also accept invitations from those that would be beneficial to be connected to.

4. **The Alley Cat**—Alley cats only send invitations to people they know or people they have a specific reason for connecting to, but they accept invitations from just about anyone. They believe there is value in knowing your connections, but there are also unexpected opportunities that develop from establishing new connections—known and unknown.

There is value in utilizing all of these strategies, and we suggest you use your best judgment.

Who to Connect With?   Who should you connect with on LinkedIn?

- People in your industry
- Possible new clients
- Present and past colleagues
- People you meet at conferences
- Professional friends
- Marketing experts
- Industry and media influencers

Integration with Your Other Networks   Often times, your connections on LinkedIn will differ from your fans and followers on your other social media sites. It's important to use LinkedIn to build your audience on your other sites, if they're relevant. You can easily send a message to your connections inviting them to check out your Facebook fan page or follow you on Twitter. We already discussed how you can target specific demographics with your connections; now that you have captured them, you can invite them to engage further through your other platforms as well. We call this *cross-pollination*, and it's a great way to build each of your social networks.

3. Create a LinkedIn Company Page for Your Business

Company Pages are one of the hallmark features of LinkedIn. They consist of a company profile, newsfeed, and aggregated statistics about employees. The utilization of Company Pages can drive traffic, increase revenue, and get your brand seen by more prospective clients, partners, and influencers. It's not only a great way to track and monitor your past, present, and future employees,

Recent Updates

OppenheimerFunds CIO Krishna Memani sat down with Wall Street Journal columnist Veronica Dagher to share his views about the role emerging markets will play in the long term. The interview touches upon the valuations of emerging markets and the current state of ... more

Playing the Emerging Markets

on.wsj.com · Here's what emerging market investors might expect for the second half of the year with OppenheimerFund's Krishna Memani.

Like (6) · Comment · Share · 1 day ago

Andrew Doyle, James Waldrop +4

Add a comment...

FIGURE 12.4 Oppenheimer Funds on LinkedIn

but it's also a way to amplify your corporate communication. As seen in Figure 12.4, Oppenheimer Funds utilizes LinkedIn updates to share company news and press mentions.

Company Pages are the best forum to advertise your brand and its products or services on LinkedIn. It is the perfect opportunity for promotions because of its layout and scope within LinkedIn. You can add your Company Page to your current (or past) job title. You can also add links to your company page outside of LinkedIn. Driving traffic to your Company Page will in turn drive traffic to your company website, increasing your client traffic as well as potential new business.

Five Ways Advisors Use LinkedIn to Grow   Advisors use LinkedIn to grow in five main ways.

1. **Targeted Searches**—LinkedIn gives you the ability to target your searches to a very specific demographic, which can be incredibly valuable in terms of connecting and sending messages. A financial advisor in Cincinnati, Ohio, utilizes this feature to strategically invite prospects to his quarterly wine and financial education seminars. As seen in Figure 12.5, an advanced LinkedIn search for people near the 45255 ZIP code with the keyword "wine" in their profile brings up more than 3,000 people. From here, advisors can qualify potential clients based on profile data and invite select individuals to events. On average, the advisor mentioned above generates 25 percent of his event attendance from LinkedIn.

FIGURE 12.5 LinkedIn Target Search

2. **Warm Introductions**—LinkedIn has second-degree connections that are in your web of professional contacts but may not be linked directly to you. So not only is it "who you know," but with LinkedIn it's "who you know, and who *they* know."

   Next time you have an appointment with a client or a prospect, look them up on LinkedIn and see who they are connected with that may be a good referral. After your meeting, mention those people by name and ask for the introduction. You might see your referrals double.

   Not comfortable asking your clients for introductions? Ask other business owners. After becoming frustrated with a lack of referrals from his local business mastermind group, one advisor utilized this strategy to ask for introductions based on LinkedIn connections. First he connected with everyone in his group on LinkedIn. Next, he browsed through their connections to see who may be a good prospect and wrote down three to five names per person. At the next mastermind meeting, he asked for introductions to specific people, mentioning why he selected each individual. All of the members were open to making introductions—so much so that one drove with him after the meeting to make a face-to-face introduction to one of his connections. The lesson here? Make it easy for people to refer business your way by telling them specifically whom you'd like to meet.

3. **LinkedIn Company Directory**—The company directory offers a list of all employees at that company who are members of LinkedIn. Connect with them. Send them a message. Let them know that you work with some of their co-workers. Or, better yet, ask your clients (who are hopefully a connection already) to send you an introduction through LinkedIn. This is an incredibly powerful benefit of company pages that will really help with referrals and reaching targeted prospects.

4. **LinkedIn Groups**—Groups are gold mines in the LinkedIn world. Whether you're seeking to find valuable connections, increase brand exposure, or simply be aware of industry trends, groups will help you achieve all of these objectives. When connecting with groups, try to aim for 75 percent potential client and 25 percent industry connection to learn from your peers. Also seek out local and personal interest groups—such as St. Louis Business Exchange, Ski Club, or Golf and Business Networking.

   As one example, let's say you live in Denver and joined "Linked to Denver," a group that has more than 30,000 members in the local area, including several small business owners who are always looking for help and connections. Want to be more strategic? The "Denver Business Owners" group has more than 1,000 members in the local area, which may be a great source if you work with small businesses.

Think: Of the audiences I care about, what groups allow me to connect to them? What interests do they have in common? What groups offer valuable business exposure? Where are the industry leaders?

HOW ELSE CAN YOU USE GROUPS?

Here are a few other ways to use groups:

- To post blogs, surveys, discussions, and articles—some groups have upward of 10,000 members. That's a ton of potential exposure for you and your content.
- To start and engage in conversations about pertinent industry topics.
- To seek potential clients and/or business connections.
- To observe and learn from industry leaders.

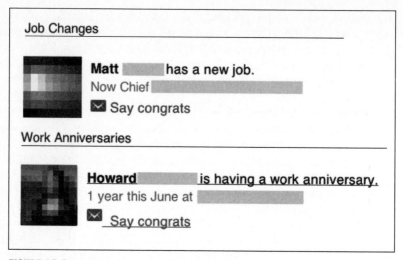

FIGURE 12.6   Take Advantage of LinkedIn Notifications

5. **Job Change Notifications**—We all know that when people change jobs, 401(k) rollovers or other financial needs often arise. With LinkedIn, you can actually be notified when any of those money-in-motion events occur. Make it a habit to click on your Network tab daily and see who in your network has been promoted or is changing jobs. Take the time to congratulate them or simply like their status to stay top of mind and remind them that you are there to help during the transition. See Figure 12.6.

THE PROBLEMATIC ENDORSE FUNCTION

As is the case with many social media endeavors, advisors need to take care that they remain compliant with the platforms they use. Unfortunately, one of LinkedIn's key features, endorsements, are a red flag to regulators since they run afoul of prohibitions against testimonials.

The LinkedIn platform makes it simple for users to endorse each other's skills: The large blue box at the head of everyone's profile asks if someone in their network has a particular skill or expertise. But according to FINRA and SEC rules, you can allow people in your LinkedIn network to endorse you only as long as the skills or expertise cited are not related to financial services and an advisor's ability to manage money (although skills such as public speaking are permitted).

If you receive an offer for a red-flag endorsement, you can always decline it right off the bat by choosing the Skip button. There also are other controls on the site that allow you further control of constraining endorsements:

1. Turn endorsement visibility completely off.
   - Click the "Edit" button at the top of your profile.
   - Click the "Edit" link in the Skills & Expertise section.
   - In the upper-right-hand corner, click on the drop-down menu next to the green check mark.
   - Select "No, do not show my endorsements."
   - Click the "Save" button.
2. Hide endorsements for specific skills.
   - Click the "Edit" button at the top of your profile.
   - Click the "Edit" link in the Skills & Expertise section.
   - Click on the "Manage Endorsements" option above the text box.
   - Select the skill or skills you want to hide.
   - In the box showing all of your endorsements for that skill, un-check the first box that says, "Show all endorsements for this skill." If all the check marks next to the individual endorsements don't automatically uncheck, go ahead and uncheck each endorsement.
   - Click the "Save" button.

Fortunately, taken in the aggregate, LinkedIn's functions can be a powerful tool to build your brand and business and develop strategic relationships. The key is to optimize it and use it correctly. LinkedIn will do you no good if you have an empty, underutilized profile and all kinds of meaningless connections, but it can be very valuable if your contacts are strategic and genuine.

CHAPTER 13

How Can We Use Facebook?

When you hear the words "social network," Facebook is most likely the first thing that pops into your head.

Facebook is more than just a social network. Nowadays, it's everything. People use Facebook to connect with family, friends, colleagues, network with people in their fields, keep up with prospective clients and employees, post pictures, update life statuses, network with peers, and so much more. All day long, people check their phones, computers, iPads, and various devices to log in and review their accounts.

Facebook is quite literally the face of social media. With more than 1.3 billion users active *monthly*, if Facebook were a country, it would be the second largest, in front of India and right behind China. And how about your target audience? Studies have found that 47 percent of Americans say Facebook is their number-one influencer of purchases, 57 percent of all American adults use Facebook, 60 percent of Internet users age 50 to 64 use Facebook regularly, and some 45 percent of Internet users age 65 or older now use Facebook, up from 35 percent who did so in late 2012. Facebook is where your target demographic lives, connects, and builds relationships. It's not only simple and user-friendly, but it's the best, most inexpensive vehicle for promoting your brand to millions of people.

Let's face it, your current and potential clients are here, and your business needs to be here as well. Ultimately, people want to do business with other people with whom they can relate and feel comfortable working. Facebook gives you the opportunity to share who you are and what makes your business tick. Ask yourself, *why would someone want to be a fan of my business or cause?*

Let's discuss the possible answers to this million-dollar question that will help you manage a successful Facebook page.

- **To receive valuable industry information**—Many fans of Facebook pages use their "likes" as a way to load their newsfeeds with valuable information about a specific industry. Think of it as another version of an RSS feed; an investor will become a fan of multiple financial publications and organizations in order to receive up-to-date news and information about the financial industry. This means that your page needs to be pushing top-notch information that's relevant to your followers and your industry. However, be careful how frequently you post to your page—you do not want to overload your fans' newsfeeds, so think quality over quantity. As a rule of thumb, try not to post more than once or twice a day.

- **To receive company news and updates**—Some Facebook users have become fans of your page because they want to follow your business and receive company news and updates. These are the kinds of fans that either already have brand loyalty or are simply looking to learn more about your company. To fulfill your duties to these types of fans, make sure you're posting relevant and up-to-date company news, such as upcoming events, promotions, and media appearances.

- **To become a brand ambassador**—These are the fans that business owners love. These types of fans already have loyalty to your brand and are looking to become a brand ambassador to help you spread the word. You're probably asking yourself, "Do I have this type of fans?" Of course you do! These fans are your employees, friends, family members, and current clients. They already know your business and are representing it in some way or another. The key is to push them to market your brand even more. Ask them to send out page invites to their friends. Ask them to post information on their personal profiles. Brand ambassadors are there to represent your business and attract new fans.

SEVEN WAYS TO START ON FACEBOOK

So, now that you know the what and the why, here are the seven best moves to help you get started on Facebook:

1. **Create a Facebook Page for Your Business**—Nowadays, when people go to check out a business, one of the first places they visit is Facebook. Believe it or not, if you don't have a page established, it causes your business to lose credibility.

   One of the biggest questions advisors have when it comes to social media and Facebook in particular is how to draw the line between business and personal. When it comes to Facebook, there are actually two types of accounts: Facebook profiles and Facebook pages. So, what's the difference between the two and how can you utilize them?

Think of Facebook like a giant shopping mall with more than 1 billion people. You, as an individual, are represented by a profile, while your page is your business' storefront in this mall. Let's face it: Your clients are there, your friends and family are there, and your business needs to be there as well.

Pages allow you to keep your business and personal life separate inside the Facebook realm, because your profile and your business' page are two completely different entities. Someone who "likes" your page doesn't gain access to your profile, and anything that you post to your personal profile doesn't get updated to all the followers of your business. Facebook also provides in-depth privacy options for personal pages, so you can control exactly what friends and the public (your future customers) can see. This setup gives users the separation they want between their personal lives and their business lives on Facebook by giving them the best of both worlds. See Figure 13.1.

2. **Establish Your Brand**—Brand consistency is extremely important, especially when you're dealing with multiple social networks. Graphics, colors, voice, verbiage, and overall feel should be parallel across all online channels. Just think: Who are you? What do you stand for? What makes you different from every other advisor out there? What message do you want to be sending to your clients and prospects?

Also, make sure that you fill in all the key areas, as a complete profile increases your searchability. Here are some tips on how to flesh out your page and keep your brand current:

- **Keep Company Info Updated**—You want to be sure all of the information on your profile is up to date. You can view this information in the *About* section. Your *About* section is indexed by search engines, such as Google and Bing, and it's also indexed by Facebook for Graph Search. Are your keywords included in both the *Short* and *Long Descriptions*? Have you filled in *Dates*, *Awards*, *Mission*, and *Products*? Are all of your website links correctly displayed? This is a great time to freshen up this information and be sure it is complete. Also, don't forget to add in your location; it will show up on an integrated map feature of Facebook.
- **Utilize Visual Space**—Visuals are very important in our fast-paced world. Make sure your visuals can pass the two-second rule. (Convey a message in the blink of an eye.)
  - The *Timeline Cover Photo* is the first thing people will see. We recommend changing it regularly to keep things interesting. While you cannot have it directly link to an external page, you can add a link in the description of the image. Use this space to announce special opportunities or events.

FIGURE 13.1 Facebook Profile and Page

- Your *Profile Image* is the image that will show up next to all of your posts and represent your company. Make sure it is similar to your *Cover Photo* and fits well in the space. Consider using a company logo or a headshot of someone representing the face of the company. See Figure 13.2.
- **Always Be Aware of New Features**—As with all technology, Facebook is constantly changing, and it will continue to evolve quickly.

FIGURE 13.2 Facebook's Cover and Profile Photo

Generally, the updates are for the benefit of the user, so pay attention because there are probably ways you can simplify or improve your marketing with each of these. For example, in late 2013, Facebook added a *Pages to Watch* section to your Business Page. This allows you to stay on top of marketing efforts by competitors and industry leaders, and possibly replicate tactics that are successful in connecting with your shared audience. See Figure 13.3.

3. **Determine your Audience and Connect With Them**—In order to promote your brand to the right people, you need to determine who your audience is. Think of the 80/20 rule. What 20 percent of your clients make up 80 percent of your business? What do they have in common? What are their ages, occupations, genders, hobbies, and so on? What are they already buying? What value can you offer them? What is their online behavior and tone? How do they like to be engaged? If you don't know to

FIGURE 13.3 Facebook's New Feature—Pages to Watch

whom you are talking, you won't know what to say. You want your message to be relevant every time you post, share, and comment.

4. **Build Your Audience**—Now that you have your foundations in place, you can begin the best part: building your audience. There's really nothing better than seeing the notification when someone "likes" your page. (Someone who "likes" your Facebook page isn't necessarily putting the advisor in a compliance bind as long as it isn't deemed to be commenting on what the advisor has done for that person. See Chapter 10.) Here are some ways to boost your following:

   ■ **Cross-promote across networks**—This is such a simple and beneficial practice. If you acquire a following on Twitter or LinkedIn (or even if you're just beginning), ask your community to check out and like your Facebook page, too.

   ■ **Widgets**—Widgets are those cool pictures you can embed on your website, blog, and newsletters that prompt people to "like" you or visit your Facebook page. You can access these directly from your Facebook page. See Figure 13.4.

   ■ **Invite your Facebook friends**—You have the option to invite all of your personal friends to "like" your business page. This is an effective kick-starter for getting more fans.

   ■ **Import contact lists**—Facebook provides you with an option to import contacts from a spreadsheet and connect with individuals based on their e-mail address. This is a great way to kick-start your fan base: by connecting with those who are already clients and contacts.

   ■ **Use Facebook Ads**—Facebook Ads are a useful feature on Facebook. For a minimal price, you can develop advertisements that target specific audiences, such as 50 to 65 year-old males who like golf that live in Wausau, Wisconsin or 50-plus single women who may be recently divorced or widowed. With Facebook Ads, businesses typically have a logo and a call to action, such as "Like" us or "Download our free investment guide." You also have the option to pay per click or pay per impression. See Figure 13.5.

5. **Get Creative with Your Content**—Driving engagement is one of the keys to success on Facebook, especially since Facebook ranks businesses differently than personal pages. Getting likes, shares, and comments has never been so important to your organic reach. But in order to effectively do this, you need to continually share compelling content that piques and demands the interest of your audience. Here are some ideas:

Find us on Facebook

HubSpot ✓
🇫 Like

HubSpot
8 hrs

How can marketing get a "seat at the table"? How can marketing leadership stand on equal footing with the rest of an organization's executive team?

It's all about the data. Know which metrics matter to your company at a particular moment in time. Be consistent in your reporting, and then emphasize the results of your efforts. Own your screw-ups and always relate everything back to sales. Now, you may take your seat.

Marketing Leaders: How to Get "A Seat at the Table"
Learn how you can get your executive team to trust and respect you.

663,800 people like HubSpot.

🇫 Facebook social plugin

FIGURE 13.4 Use Widgets to Build Audience

RIA Compliance Support
riainabox.com

We offer a variety of compliance consulting packages beginning at $99 per month. Come See!

FIGURE 13.5 Facebook Ad Example

- **Post Blogs**—So you just posted a blog post, *10 Interesting Facts about Long-Term Care*. Post this content to your Facebook wall with an engaging question: "What surprises you most about long-term care?"
- **Share Articles by Others**—Think of yourself as the Content DJ filtering through the barrage of content available online and sharing only the best and most relevant articles for your audience.
- **Ask Questions**—This goes back to Dale Carnegie's advice to "become genuinely interested in the other person." Asking questions drives engagement and shows that you're interested. They can be related to your industry or more generalized. Here are some examples:
  - What is your greatest financial concern?
  - What are you doing for Labor Day?
  - Where do you want to retire?
- **Create Events**—Do you have an upcoming seminar, client appreciation event, or speaking engagement? Facebook is the perfect place to create events and promote them to your networks. Consider posting info about the event before, during, and after it's complete. Take pictures and videos, post them after the event, and direct attendees to your Facebook page. People love seeing pictures of themselves, so this is a great way to drive traffic and foster engagement on your page. See Figure 13.6.
- **Create Themes**—Create reoccurring weekly themes like "Trivia Tuesday" or "Throwback Thursday." For example, SEI Advisors uses "Whiteboard Wednesdays" to position their employees as subject matter experts while providing valuable information to their audience. See Figure 13.7.
- **Videos**—We'll delve a little deeper into video in the YouTube chapter, but it's a great idea to post relevant, timely, and interesting videos on your page. Remember the four umbrella goals of empowering, educating, entertaining, and engaging.
- **Polls**—Is there a hot topic that your audience is buzzing about? Create a poll to get their feedback.
- **Quotes**—People love quotes. Create a library of interesting quotes to sprinkle into your posting schedule.
- **Comments**—Ask fans to comment. Instead of simply posting an article, post the article and say, "Do you agree? Comment below and let us know what you think."
- **Use Fill-in-the-Blank Posts**—Fill-in-the-blank posts are great ways to drive engagement. Provide part of a sentence that your audience would be interested in and watch the comments and interaction come in.
  - Example: "For the holiday weekend I'd like to _____."

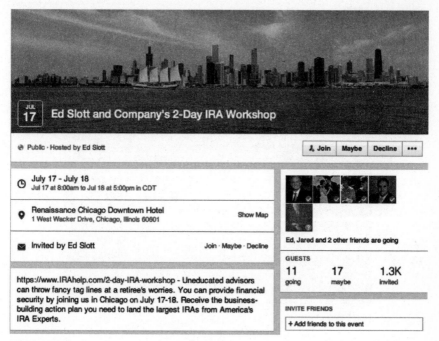

FIGURE 13.6 Facebook Event Page

- ■ **Encourage Check-Ins at Your Location**—When people check-in at your business, all of their friends see it. This is another great way to drive engagement and increase brand visibility.

6. **Stay Active**—You don't want your page to turn into a ghost town. Think of what a ghost town is: vacant buildings, weeds, broken windows, and abandoned sheds. Not only are they creepy, but they're extremely unattractive. I'm willing to bet that you've never sought to re-visit any ghost town you've ever been to, right? Idle Facebook pages are just as unattractive as ghost towns. To be perfectly honest, they scream, "I don't care!" Is that the message you want to send to thousands of people?

   If you invested in a billboard, you wouldn't want it to be outdated or blank. The same rules apply here. Be diligent and consistent with posting and engaging. And remember: It's better to have no Facebook page at all than an abandoned, unused Facebook page with outdated or incomplete information.

7. **Be Patient**—The Facebook world won't stop in its tracks once your business page is up and running. There are millions of businesses

SEI Advisor Network
June 4

Today I helped an advisor...

Like · Comment · Share

Amy Sitnick, Ryan Shanks and 11 others like this.

Richard Walker Butler Adviser/Advisor - Goals-Based Investing: managing
behavioral biases.
June 4 at 12:09pm · Like · 1

Andrew Jameson nicely done, Welz.
June 5 at 1:41pm · Like · 1

FIGURE 13.7   Recurring Weekly Themes on Facebook

competing for your audience's attention, and you need to differentiate
yourself from the crowd. There are several steps you must take to be
successful: set goals, organize and plan, and then define success and
establish key performance indicators. Keep in mind that it takes about six
months to start seeing results, so strive to remain persistent and
optimistic.

As you can see, Facebook is the social network you *must* be on. It's the
network where everyone in the world has a presence, in both their personal
and professional lives. Start developing your page and use these tactics to
increase brand awareness, foster deeper connections with your clients and
community, and ultimately build a greater presence across all of your social
networks.

CHAPTER 14

How Can We Use Twitter?

Twitter is, in many ways, the center of the social media revolution. Simple in nature and forceful in impact, this platform has revitalized the way we, as a culture, communicate. Twitter breaks down barriers of time, space, and media proprietorship to connect real people and real stories in real time. It is freedom of speech and equality at its finest. To merely say it has made an impact wouldn't be enough, for it has shaken the communicative foundations of people, businesses, and establishments all across the globe.

The most important aspect of Twitter is that it's always in the present moment. Other platforms like Facebook and LinkedIn move at a slower pace—conversations and posts can linger for days, whereas on Twitter, tweets will sometimes only last for seconds. Users pump out information in real-time, 24 hours a day and 7 days a week, because the platform is, by its very nature, in the moment. As of January 2014, Twitter had more than 645 million active users, 135,000 people signing up each day, and guess what . . . 9,100 tweets are produced *every* second. That's a *lot* of interaction!

TWITTER IN FINANCIAL SERVICES

Why should financial professionals use Twitter? Many advisors, investors, and agents still cast off Twitter as useless. In this chapter, you'll see why that mindset is incorrect, and that Twitter is actually incredibly useful and beneficial from both a business and reputation perspective. If used correctly and strategically, Twitter is a business gem. Here's why:

- **Your audience is on Twitter**—With more than 645 million active users, it isn't a question that your audience, in some form or another, is on Twitter. By having a presence, you build credibility for your brand and open the doors to millions who may be interested in what you offer.

■ **You have access to the media** —This is huge. Accessing local news stations and publications can be a daunting endeavor—especially for busy financial professionals. With Twitter, you have *instant* access to people and publications that will earn you the exposure your brand needs.

■ **Stay up to date on trends**—On Twitter, you're given moment-by-moment updates on what's going on in your local community and industry. This is key for staying on the cutting edge of trends, news, and ideas.

■ **You don't have to accept people**—On LinkedIn and Facebook, you have to request and approve people in order to connect. With Twitter, those barriers don't exist. You can follow whomever you want. Reciprocally, anybody can follow you. Twitter also doesn't contain heavily private or personal information about you. Simply put, your profile has your picture, a 10-character bio, and a background. Its simple nature makes privacy a non-issue.

■ **Reach the wealthy and the masses** —Because there are no connection barriers on Twitter, you can reach and connect with influencers and high-net-worth individuals. As cited in the *New York Times*, "According to recent research conducted by Scorpio Partnership, a consulting firm, more than 40 percent of high-net-worth individuals younger than 50 viewed social media as an important channel for communicating with their banks."[1] If nothing else, this is a brilliant way to get your brand in front of them.

■ **Keep yourself in front of prospects**—Jude the Certified Financial Planner is a great example of how advisors can use Twitter. He merely engages in conversation, and keeps on the lookout for people who *just might be looking for a financial planner*. Perhaps more importantly, he serves as an educational resource. Who doesn't have questions about finances and retirement?

■ **Improve customer service and damage control**—Whether you have a presence or not, people are talking about you on Twitter—and it's time to join the conversation. Nowadays people are turning to social media for customer support, and by responding to questions and complaints you'll be able to minimize risk and maximize opportunity. Later, we'll talk about client servicing using Twitter. See Figure 14.1.

HOW TO GET STARTED WITH TWITTER

Now that you have a basic understanding of what Twitter is, let's get the ball rolling. You won't be able to connect and grow your business without getting

---

[1]Sonia Kolesnikov-Jessop, "Banks Slow to Embrace Social Media," *New York Times*, March 26, 2012.

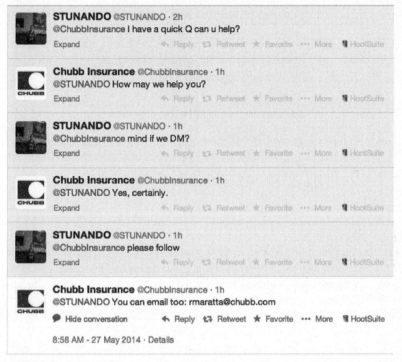

FIGURE 14.1 Twitter Improves Customer Service

started and learning the ins and outs of this platform. Once you decide to create a Twitter page, here are a few steps to follow:

- **Setup/Optimize Your Twitter Profile**—So before you begin to tackle in-depth Twitter marketing campaigns and budgeting ad dollars to promote tweets, make sure you have your basics covered. Below is a checklist of five areas to optimize that will make your individual or firm Twitter profile stand out:
  1. **Profile Picture**—Your profile picture/avatar is going to be the first thing that someone sees. Use a company logo, or if you want, be creative and use a picture of a person or character. Just make sure that whatever image it is, it represents the company as a whole. Also note that you should consider using color instead of a white background, as this will help your brand stand out in someone's feed.
  2. **Twitter Handle**—Your Twitter handle is also your Twitter URL, so it should be an obvious choice that reinforces your brand identity. Keep in mind that your Twitter handle can contain up to 15 characters. If your

FIGURE 14.2 Twitter Bio

company name is already taken or is too long, get creative with abbreviations. We recommend staying away from underscores, however.
3. **Company Bio**—This is your chance to introduce yourself. The challenge: only use 160 characters. Write a clear, concise bio that describes your brand, products, or services. If you have an opportunity to throw in a few keywords, go for it. Twitter also gives you the ability to include live links in your bio so you can drive traffic to a specific product page, another social profile, or any required disclosures. See Figure 14.2.
4. **Location and Web Site**—Be sure to include your physical location, as this dramatically increases your searchability and will also help you connect with your local community. Include a web URL where people can go to learn more about your brand.
5. **Cover Photo**—Last, but definitely not least, is your cover photo. This is prime real estate to portray your brand both for both desktop and mobile viewing. Try incorporating an intriguing graphic, some contact information, or a call to action. It doesn't necessarily need to be a single image. A collage, for instance, can represent brand identity in a more layered fashion, but don't get too exotic. There is already a lot going on in your feed, and you won't want to distract from the most important element—your content. See Figure 14.3.

Also, keep in mind that if you don't have a lot of photography or design services available to you, there are several hundred web sites that provide great, creative backgrounds. Even though this won't be a custom graphic, it is 100 percent better than just leaving the cloud background that Twitter generates automatically.

FIGURE 14.3 Twitter's Cover Photo

- **Start Following People**—Once you have your handle set up, you will be prompted to follow people. Before you start randomly following, think about the goals you have in mind for the specific demographic you'd like to reach. Start by following people you know, and build your feed by following people that you want to know. It's important to be selective when looking at these people. I'm sure you've seen a lot of profile descriptions that say "will follow back," but these are not the individuals you should be looking to add to your social networks.

  The purpose of Twitter (and many other social networking sites) is to build a solid networking foundation of prospective clients, current clients, industry leaders, and partnering businesses. Simply following someone to build your numbers will not only clog your network, but it will damper your social media marketing commitment by blurring the intent, investment, and return strategy.

  Here are some additional ideas of people to consider connecting with:
  - Local media stations (great precursor for getting PR exposure)
  - Local newspapers
  - People you *want* to know
  - Financial publications
  - Other businesses similar to yours
  - Local chambers of commerce
  - Industry leaders
  - Social media thought leaders
  - Better Business Bureaus
  - Athletes
  - Regulatory organizations like FINRA and the SEC
  - Authors
  - Editors of publications

Once you're following users, an extremely beneficial way to strate-
gize and keep your followers organized is to categorize them into lists.
This will save you a *ton* of time while engaging on Twitter. Some
examples of lists you'd create are: industry leaders, financial publications, local media, local businesses, prospects, and so on. When you
separate groups of people into lists, it makes it easy to interact with or
"retweet" a certain demographic of users. Just think: if you log on to
Twitter with the goal of gaining exposure for a recent article you
published, you can go straight to local media and financial publications
lists to promote your content. Lists are key for helping you target the
right people at the right time.

- **Learn the Twitter Lingo**—Twitter lingo can feel like learning a foreign
  language. With the barrage of jargon and symbols, it isn't any wonder
  why you might be skeptical and confused at first. Let's break it down into
  smaller pieces:

  - **Tweets**—So, what *is* a *tweet*? Tweets are the hallmark of Twitter, and
    are basically small bursts of information. Each tweet (a.k.a., post) can
    only be 140 characters long, which challenges users to offer concise
    and rich information.

  - **A Retweet or RT**—When someone shares a tweet by another person
    with their own followers. It shows that they value my content
    enough to share it with *their* network. Let's be honest, getting re-
    tweeted feels like a million bucks. If you want to position yourself in
    front of bigwigs and/or influencers, retweet their content. It's a
    great way to get noticed and stay top of mind. (Remember: If
    someone RTs your content, don't forget to thank them. It's proper
    etiquette.)

  - **@replies or @mentions**—When someone tweets you directly or about
    you. It's similar to tagging someone on Facebook and when you
    @mention someone it is public for anyone to see. By adding the
    @ symbol in front of a user's name it turns their name into a hyperlink
    and connects back to the person's profile when clicked on. Use this
    feature to capture someone's attention or link to another user's profile.
    For example: "Tune into @9News at 8am to see my interview live with
    @ryansheckron!" or "@WSJ Great article on Tax Laws. Check out my
    recent blog post on the topic and reach out if you need a resource."

  - **Direct message**—Like most other platforms, you can send direct
    messages to people, which show up in their private inbox. In order
    to direct message a user, they need to be following you back. Direct
    messaging on Twitter is like the communication frontage road. It's
    much more effective than trying to squeak your way through people's
    jam-packed e-mail inboxes. Remember: only 140 characters.

- **URL shortener**—Because the character limit in Twitter is only 140 characters, it is good to shorten URLs. While Twitter has a built in URL shortener, you may consider alternative shorteners like Bit.ly or TinyURL that also allow you to track the number of clicks each URL receives. This is great for learning what your audience is most receptive to.
- **Favoriting**—A great way of keeping a record of any tweets that you want to refer back to, whether that's someone recommending you, testimonials, or interesting news. You can find all your "favorite'd" tweets in one convenient place on your profile.
- **Hashtags (#)**—The # symbol was created organically by Twitter users as a way to categorize conversations. #finserv is a public conversation on Twitter for people who—you guessed it—are interested in financial services. Using hashtags can lead to increased exposure, more followers, higher engagement and interaction levels, strategic connections, and much more.

Now that you know the basics, it's time to dive in and start building a following. With social media, you literally *become* the media. If you've ever run an ad in a newspaper or on the radio, you are essentially renting someone else's audience. With social media, you have the opportunity to build and own your audience and, on Twitter, that equates to followers.

Ever wonder how some companies amass so many followers? Well, it goes back to the basics of good ol' networking: create valuable content and participate in the conversation. Social media is a dialogue, so start by listening to what others have to say and work to create interesting, valuable content that will add to the conversation while positioning you and your brand as experts in the field.

WHAT TO TWEET

The great and maybe somewhat hard thing about Twitter is the large amount of content you should be putting out daily. Twitter is like a radio station: different users are listening in at different times, which means that, in order to keep your followers happy, you should be putting out quality content on a consistent basis. When it comes to posting, tweet a balanced mix of information. In addition to your company blog posts, third-party articles, landing pages, and replies to conversations and retweets, other tweet suggestions include:

- **Like a Facebook page**—"@MorningstarInc, thanks for the follow. Check out our Facebook page too! [link to Facebook page]"

- **Promote your e-mail newsletter**—"Curious about how to use Twitter? Check out our newsletter for tips on how #advisors can use #Twitter [link to newsletter signup]"
- **Share a video**—"New video about how investors are using social media. You'll be surprised! [link to video]"
- **Share an e-book or white paper**—"New white paper containing latest stats on long-term care. Check it out! [link to landing page]"
- **Share a tool**—"Need a budget? My free software & easy workbook is here, endorsed by Dr. Phil [link to tool's download page]."
- **Promote and conduct a webinar**—During the webinar include a unique hashtag so that users can share appropriate nuggets of information with their followers.
- **Tweet about upcoming events**—"Client appreciation event tomorrow night! Don't forget to RSVP [link to registration page]"
- **Tweet a photo**—"New renovations in the office! What do you think?"
- **Tweet a poll**—"What CRM do you use? Let us know [link to survey]"
- **Ask for volunteers**—Beta test a product or service.

WHAT NOT TO TWEET

On social media, we all risk putting our foot in our mouth at some point or another . . . and on a very public stage. By now, you probably have an idea of how to build a network and rapport on Twitter, but are you aware of the conversational mines you should avoid? Here are 10 ways to lose respect on Twitter:

1. **Talking Trash**—Making negative comments about your competition/ peers puts you on the fast track to losing respect. Avoid it at all costs. And don't engage with other tweeters who do that.
2. **Intense Political and Religious Sentiment**—There is a time and place for having politically and religiously charged conversations. And it's okay to share your opinions on Twitter from time to time. But don't oversaturate your feed with politically and religiously charged tweets. It may be turning away prospects and influencers without you even knowing it.
3. **Narcissism**—When you are networking at an event, you tend to remember those with interesting stories and the people who listened to you. No one wants to follow up with the guy who spent the whole night talking about how great he was. Don't be that person on Twitter.
4. **A Lack of Purpose**—If your tweet falls outside of a purpose or strategy, reconsider posting it. Like your blogs, it's important to keep your tweets purposeful, relevant, timely, and concise.

5. **Not Giving Props**—If someone walked up and congratulated you on an awesome presentation, would you look at them and then walk away? I hope not. When people give you a shout out or RT your content, say thanks. It's simple, but powerful.

6. **Vacancy**—Haven't tweeted in a few weeks or months? This basically spells out "I don't care" to your followers. If you don't have time to post, outsource your social media, create RSS feeds, or delete your account until you can engage on a regular basis.

7. **Not Separating Personal from Ultra-Personal**—People don't mind knowing about the birth of your precious new grandson, but they don't want to hear or see the play-by-play of the messy delivery. Know how to separate the personal from the ultra-personal.

8. **Getting into Tweet Fights**—As a well-respected and well-known professional, it's highly likely you'll face criticism and/or opposing viewpoints from time to time. Let's just say that many people are *vocal* on social media—and it may not always be in your favor. Don't get into a tweet fight. Instead, express gratitude for their honesty and/or address their concerns. If their behavior gets out of control, flag their account.

9. **Complaining**—Don't make your followers call the wahmbulance. Sure, there may be a time when you want to convey a sincere opinion that lacks positivity—that's what social media is all about! But aim to be slow to complain and quick to be positive.

10. **Being a Billboard**—Twitter wasn't created for companies to post ads about their business. In fact, it was created so people—of all statuses and from all walks of life—could have real-time conversations about anything and everything. Don't be a virtual billboard. Be conversational and create a personality.

Remember, Twitter is qualitatively different from the other key social media sites. Its users value brief and timely content in real time, and the back-and-forth banter that's the hallmark of a good electronic cocktail party. Develop the skills to use it well, and Twitter will provide you with engaged clients, online credibility, and a few good stories to tell at more conventional cocktail parties.

CHAPTER 15

How Can We Use YouTube?

Before the birth of the Internet and social media, there was an elusive barrier between those who were on television and radio, and those who were not. In fact, the barrier was so profound that it elevated those on television and radio to a certain stardom. Without such access to the media, it was unlikely that you'd generate a robust and committed following.

With the development of social media, however, there is no longer a barrier between the bleachers and the playing field. With a mere video recorder, camera, or even cellphone, you can upload videos to your very own YouTube channel in a matter of seconds. This simple ability has transformed the way that we, as a global community, communicate. It's quite remarkable, for it has increased democratization and established a unique space for people, businesses, and organizations to spread their messages.

YouTube is a platform for original content creators and people all across the globe to connect, inform, and inspire others via short videos.

I'm sure you're wondering—So what? As a financial professional, how can I use this platform for my business? What type of videos would I upload? How can I stay compliant?

Why should you be on YouTube?

- More than 1 billion unique users log onto YouTube each month.
- More than 6 billion hours of YouTube videos are watched every month.
- More content is uploaded to YouTube in a 60-day period than the three major U.S. television networks created in 60 years.
- Sixty percent of boomers and 40 percent of seniors say watching online video on sites like YouTube has become an important part of their day.
- Seventy-five percent of boomers and 68 percent of seniors report taking some sort of action after viewing a video.
- Forty-one percent of seniors were encouraged by an online video to share a link of the video with someone.

Does the Financial Industry Regulatory Authority (FINRA) and the Securities and Exchange Commission (SEC) allow financial companies to use YouTube for marketing?

Yes, of course. But just like other social media platforms, such as Facebook and LinkedIn, there are guidelines. It all comes back to the static versus dynamic content conversation. Static content includes your advisor website and social media profiles (not the feed). Videos can also be considered static content since they are a singular event that is unchanging. Static content needs to be approved by your compliance department before publishing it.

Most social media activity is considered dynamic content, as it is unscripted and usually involves some type of real-time interaction. Any communication that can be commented on is usually considered dynamic also. This type of content does not require pre-approval, but it does need to be archived. As you can see, YouTube is in somewhat of a gray area because it's both a video and part of a social media platform.

SIX TIPS FOR STAYING COMPLIANT ON YOUTUBE

The rules for playing within the regulatory boundaries of YouTube are much the same as those related to other forms of social media:

1. Before you dive in, double-check with your own compliance department to find out what is and isn't allowed.
2. Treat YouTube videos as static content. Submit a script for pre-approval to your compliance team and turn off the comments and thumbs-up/thumbs-down functions.
3. Archive.
4. Add a disclaimer.
5. Include YouTube use in your company's social media policy. Let investors know that YouTube (and your other social networks) will be used for company announcements. In April 2013, the SEC announced that companies can use social media for company announcements, as long as investors have been informed of what types of social media will be used for this communication.
6. The golden rule of social media: Don't do anything on social media that you wouldn't do off social media. This includes language that you wouldn't use on your website or in an educational seminar for your clients.

The bottom line is that millions of businesses are using YouTube, including financial professionals. For many in the financial industry, this is to establish credibility and increase exposure. Similar to your blog, you want to position yourself as the expert in your videos. By producing interesting, useful, and timely content, you send the message that you know what you're talking about. This is key to retaining client relationships, attracting new clients, and building your reputation.

EIGHT WAYS FINANCIAL PROFESSIONALS ARE USING VIDEO

Similar to the other social media platforms, the key here is putting yourself in the shoes of your customer. If you were a potential client, what would you want to watch? Here are eight ideas of what I consider the most popular types of videos.

1. **Welcome videos**—Create a welcome video for your website. Video allows you to connect with people in a way that is virtually impossible to do on paper. It allows you to make an impact and make an impression. When a new client walks into your office, they will feel like they already have a relationship with you. Include a brief story about your background, hobbies, favorite sports team, family, or business, and you'll be surprised how many people will ask you about it.

2. **Educational Video**—When it comes to the financial industry, there is so much to learn. There is also a lot of misinformation out there. Why not create educational videos that address topics that are important to your audience? As long as you don't offer specific, one-size-fits-all financial advice, this can be an incredibly powerful resource for your prospects and clients. As seen in Figure 15.1, companies like BlackRock are using YouTube to educate their audience.

FIGURE 15.1 BlackRock's Educational Video on YouTube

3. **Guest interviews**—Not sure what to say or do for your video? Why not invite a guest speaker to come and do a live interview? Brittney Castro, CFP®, is a true pioneer of this strategy. On her YouTube channel, Financially Wise Women, she brings in a wide range of professionals to interview—from yogis to law professionals—to discuss their professional and financial lives. The question that ties all of the interviews together is, "What does it mean to you to be a financially wise woman?" This strategy has earned more than 13,000 views on her channel.

4. **Financial news**—Broadcast pertinent and relevant financial news. Several advisors host a weekly financial news recap to inform their audience about the most important discussions taking place and how it will affect them.

5. **Themed shows**—Piggy-backing on the financial news idea, you can also develop themed shows where you talk about financial-related topics such as law, tax planning, and real estate. Perhaps you have guest speakers or interviews. The goal here is to keep your audience interested and engaged.

6. **Video responses**—This is very popular in the YouTube world. Is there a television show, blog, article, current event, debate, or story that you want to comment on? YouTube is the perfect place to do it. Create a short video of yourself responding to an important issue. If you season it with slight controversy, it is likely to pique the interest of your audience.

7. **Human interest**—Your videos don't just have to be finance related. You can create videos about a whole plethora of topics: travel, golf, culinary, wine and spirits, the Olympics, you name it. As long as it aligns with your audience's interests, it's okay to weave in some human interest. Bryan Weiss of Marian Financial Partners created a YouTube video called, "You Won't Believe What I Saw on the Golf Course . . .".[1] In this video, he talks about an abnormal situation he ran into on the golf course and then related it back to investing. This is a creative way to pique interest and offer insight.

8. **Video for landing pages**—When it comes to website landing pages, the purpose—whether you're a business, association, or individual—is often to capture your visitor's attention and encourage them to want to learn more. This can be done by entering contact information, signing up for an event, making a purchase, or simply driving them to a different part of your website. With video being the hot commodity in marketing, it's no surprise that more and more organizations are choosing to optimize their landing pages with video. Moreover, adding

---

[1]Marian Financial Partners, "You Won't Believe What I Saw on the Golf Course . . ." YouTube, June 4, 2012. https://www.youtube.com/watch?v=Tfrgqd8o0kE.

video to your landing pages will improve opt-ins (visitors who grant permission to e-mail or contact them in the future) and click-throughs by up to 70 percent.

When you are creating your landing page, it's important to experiment with your registration fields and video topics. Typically, the more information required to complete a registration form, the fewer who will actually complete it and take the next step. This is also typical when video length increases. The trick? Keep everything short, simple and to the point. Don't stray from the purpose of the video and the landing page—to turn visitors into new relationships.

By creating powerful content, you build a following—fans, so to speak. Just think, if you were to run a news or radio ad, you would essentially be renting their audience for a brief period of time. But if you have a well-rounded, established YouTube channel, you can build your own audience—an audience that is loyal and interested in you. The larger and more engaged the audience, the more power and influence you'll have.

SIX STEPS TO GETTING STARTED WITH VIDEO

There are a lot of moving parts to a video project, so plan ahead. These tips show you how.

1. **Content Planning**—As discussed earlier, there are several types of videos you can create. But where to start? If you've ever written, created, recorded, and edited a video, you know how difficult and tedious it can actually be. First, writing a compelling and engaging script that will entice your audience to continue watching is a complex and creative task. Fortunately, there are several things you can keep in mind to ease the stress.
   - Keep it short: you have approximately 7 to 15 seconds to explain to your listener what your video is about. Think about it like the topic sentence of an article or story. Consider opening with a question.
   - Explain the benefits of staying engaged and how it will be of value to them.
   - Have a clear call to action: Tell them what to do.
   - Be yourself! The last thing a listener wants to hear is some monotonous voice trying to sell them something. Be charismatic and engaging.
   - Give thanks: Always end your video by giving the listener appreciation for their time and attention.

2. **Planning the Set**—When it comes to recording the video, it's important to realize that the imagery of your video matters as much as the message. The background, your clothing, and even your hair need to match the point that you're making.
    - Don't make the background distracting. Your background should match your message, so if you're trying to promote your business, don't record your video in your bedroom or a random setting.
    - Dress professionally. Err on the side of dressing too nice versus not nicely enough.
    - Wear powder. Depending on the lighting, you may find yourself with a shiny nose or forehead, and powder can prevent this.
3. **Recording Your Video**—It is important to remember that you don't have to have a cast and crew on a Hollywood stage and a big production company to make a successful video. Those days are nearly gone. A webcam and microphone will serve just as well. People will watch your videos because you are an expert in your field with information relevant to them.
    - Purchase a quality microphone. High-quality audio is essential to maintaining your listener's attention. A good quality microphone can be purchased on Amazon for $100 to $200 and will be well worth your investment.
    - Speak clearly and look directly into the camera. It should feel like the person on the camera is talking directly to the listener.
4. **Editing and Effects**—Editing your video is key to enhancing and making your video even more creative. While this may seem like a difficult task, with the advancement of technology and do-it-yourself applications like iMovie and Camtasia, you may be surprised at how easy it can be. Don't have the time? There are several inexpensive options available. Below are some key elements to keep in mind when editing your video.
    - Add background music or additional animations that match your message.
    - Add your logo and company information at the beginning and the end of your video.
5. **Publishing to YouTube**—Now that you've created a video, it's time to share it with the world. Upload your video to YouTube and be sure to optimize it for Search Engine Optimization (SEO).
    - Create a powerful title by using keywords in the first few words. Additionally, you can add a colon after your initial keywords and rephrase your title for maximum effect. For example, your video on saving money for college might be called "College Savings Plans: The 529 Plan and Your Child."

- When it comes to the description, start by listing your full URL. Next, create a keyword-rich description. This will help you be found more easily by people searching YouTube for your type of content.

6. **Distributing Your Video**—The final elements of optimizing your usage of the video are uploading your video to YouTube; embedding it on your landing page, site, or profiles; and sharing links to your video on your social networks. In the next section we'll go into more depth on key distribution tactics, but here are a few of the highlights.

   - Keep your most important content above the fold. Your conversion rates will increase if visitors don't have to scroll down to view a video or complete a form.
   - Limit your visitors' options: exclude additional links or other items that will distract visitors from the purpose of the video.
   - Appeal to skimmers: many of your visitors may be individuals who aren't searching out a specific product or service. It's for this reason that you need to make use of headers, sub-headers, bold text, bullets, white space, and graphics such as arrows or buttons to draw a reader's eye toward your call to action.

If you want to stay on the cutting edge of online marketing, it is essential to build a branded YouTube account and use it as much as possible. With the rapid growth of videos and YouTube's presence now on TV sets, it won't be a surprise if its use grows exponentially in the next few years. Now is the time to jump on the bandwagon.

CASE STUDY: MATSON MONEY

Matson Money Inc. first became aware of social media through a marketing conference in early 2008. Eric Matson writes here about what happened next, and how video came to play a part in the firm's strategy.

Until 2008, networks like Facebook and YouTube seemed more like entertainment for teenagers than a tool we would use to help our investment business. When we started to see more and more marketers using social networks to spread their messages, we decided to see what we could do with it too.

Our first video was shot and posted in late summer of 2008—it had fewer than 50 views. In comparison to the many viral videos on the Internet that might seem like a failure, but we realized that we could build on that number and actively engage our existing advisors and clients to participate and communicate with us in a new way. We didn't need a video to go viral in order to reach the audience that we wanted to reach.

We realized that we needed to master the process of quickly shooting video, editing, uploading, posting, and communicating about each video. For the following six months, we focused on building the infrastructure to support regular videos and e-mail communication to promote them. We had to purchase cameras, build blog sites that would become the hub for the videos, write compliance policies, and create a system and process for communicating with each new post.

Four years later, we post three to five new videos each week, with more than 50,000 views on videos and nearly 2 million minutes of viewing time of our videos and live web broadcasts.

CHAPTER 16

How Can We Use Google+?

It may be one of the newer social media platforms out there, but Google+ is quickly catching up to other platforms like Facebook, LinkedIn, Twitter, Instagram, and Pinterest. With such a dizzying array or platforms available to reach investors, advisors, or clients, it may be easier to think of Google+ as just another social media platform to devote your time and energy to; however, doing so would be a mistake.

In fact, Google+ can help you:

- Strengthen and advance your brand
- Reach new audiences
- Build your online connections
- Stay engaged with and satisfy your existing clientele
- Drive more website traffic
- Position yourself and/or your company as an authority on certain subjects
- Improve search engine optimization (SEO)

With benefits such as these, many of them unique to Google, Google+ is certainly here to stay. To capitalize on this new medium, start with these simple tips to get the most out your Google+ social media efforts.

- **Establish a Strong Google+ Page Presence and Profile**—As with most social media platforms, you can customize your Google+ page to reflect your expertise and brand. Yet before you can create a Google+ page, you must first complete a Google profile, as this profile effectively serves as your Google+ About page. Visitors to your Google+ page can click on this About tab to learn more about you and your firm, so this is the ideal location to include:
  - A professional photo
  - Your biography

FIGURE 16.1   A Strong Google+ Page Presence and Profile Example

- Company's address, hours of operation, and contact info
- A few brief items highlighting your expertise
- Links to other company departments or to articles that have cited you

  Make sure your content and calls to action are clear, and emphasize the benefits and solutions you can provide rather than the features of a certain product or services. See Figure 16.1.

- **Set Controls**—Google+ makes it easy to customize the About page with different levels of privacy that determine who among your list of followers or connections may see certain aspects of your profile. For example, if an individual advisor prefers to receive e-mails instead of phone calls from prospects, they can establish this e-mail-only privacy setting quickly simply by making the phone number unavailable. Or let's say an asset management firm has a new product they'd like to promote only to investors with greater than $1 million in assets; they, too, can configure their settings to ensure only qualifying individuals can see that particular content.

- **Build Broader Engagement and Brand Awareness**—Although Facebook, Twitter, and LinkedIn are still going strong, Google+ is only getting stronger. According to a recent study of 3 million user interactions with 2,500 or more brand-oriented posts from 7 different social media networks, Google+ branding posts are actually more powerful in generating engagement. In fact, posts generated by Google+ get nearly the same engagement level per follower as Facebook produces, and it garners almost twice as much engagement per follower as Twitter posts do.

As for bolstering brand recognition and credibility, simply adding a Google+ sharing badge and the +1 button to all the Web-based content you generate will jumpstart your campaign credibility and visibility. What's more, you can use Google+ to search for comments or mentions about yourself or your company. Not only will this give you a glimpse into how the public perceives your brand so you can make adjustments as necessary, but it also helps to keep you top of mind for advisors and managers at the top of their social media game. Of course, to really impart your authority on the topics you see via comments on your thread or company responses to mentions, be sure to respond to every thread, mention, or comment, and consider re-sharing posts to support your brand. It only takes 10 seconds to type a quick response of appreciation or to +1 a comment, and it can elevate both your authority and brand likeability. (If you want to adopt this strategy, as an advisor, you will need to adjust your compliance policies and procedures to take this activity into account. While we discuss this more later, you will want to shape your responses, and your recordkeeping of those responses, to comply with applicable requirements.)

- **Get Involved with Google+ Communities**—In my last book, *The Millionaire Zone* (Hyperion, 2007), research found that the wealthy made better use of their social networks, ultimately helping them achieve greater wealth than those who did not. The Google+ platform takes this concept to another level. One of the most appealing new aspects of Google+ is its Community feature, a tool that helps groups of users develop around certain shared interests. Users can either join an existing community and contribute to the conversation there, or they can create a community around a different topic of interest. Either way, getting active in the Google+ Community significantly extends your reach and allows you to cultivate relationships and interact with centers of influence, prospective investors, and advisors. Additionally, Google+ affords you the opportunity to participate in communities using your brand name—something that, as of this printing, is unavailable with Facebook. See Figure 16.2.

It's also worth mentioning that if your business or organization establishes a community, you get a couple of extra benefits. In addition to

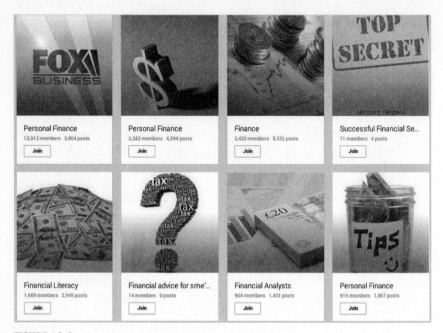

FIGURE 16.2   Google+ Community Feature

having your community featured on your About tab, which makes it even easier for site visitors to connect with you by joining your group and/or following your page, your company will appear at the top of the community page's right column, helping to reinforce your brand expertise in the eyes of your members.

- **Develop Google+ Circles to Reach New Audiences and Qualified Prospects**—Whether you're looking to convert qualified leads to clients or advisors or to make contact with new audiences, you should segment your posts to ensure the right content is seen by the right groups of followers. Google+ simplifies this task with its circles. In Google+ lingo, circles are essentially groups of followers you'd like to connect with and/ or engage, and your Google+ account site already features three such circles—one for friends, one for family, and one for acquaintances. Furthermore, advisors and managers are also encouraged to create their own circles to connect with even more targeted niches.

  Asset managers, for example, may choose to create one circle for their elite advisors as well as one for their more average advisors, while advisors might consider building circles for their A, B, and C clients, centers of influence, or industry groups. It's also possible for the same follower to be part of several circles (e.g., one of your aunts is also a B-level client, leading you to create a new Family B Clients circle), which provides even more opportunities to broaden and maintain your client base. And just as with your Google+ profile, you can decide which of your circles will be able to see certain content.

- **Huddle Up with Prospective Investors and Advisors as Well as Existing Clientele**—In yet another way to connect with your different groups of followers wherever they may be, Google+ has developed a tool you can now use to reach out to fans and followers via mobile phone—text or SMS huddles. After ensuring desired participants have the Google+ mobile application on their smartphones, you can issue a text message to every member of certain groups simultaneously. Then, each time a huddle participant replies with a question or comment, it can be seen by everyone in the huddle. Often affectionately referred to as a text message party chat, huddles tend to work best with smaller groups, for obvious reasons.

- **Stay Engaged with Current Clients, Advisors, and Circles of Influence**—We've already established that Google+ is a useful component of any prospecting strategy, but your Google+ page is also key to staying engaged with your existing clients, advisor list, and circles of influence. To ensure your current fans don't feel left out in the cold, add helpful new content to your Google+ page regularly, respond to any comments or questions immediately, stay in touch with your circles of followers, join and participate in any Google+ communities your members may belong to, or try hosting a special huddle devoted to a new solution your followers may be interested in exploring. In short, don't lose track of the people who currently support you in a blind effort to acquire leads.

While incorporating another social media platform into your overall marketing campaign may seem daunting, most experts agree that by devoting just 15 minutes a day to cultivating your Google+ presence and following, you'll soon see the fruits of your labor take root in the form of new investors and happy clients. The same principle also applies to managers, firms, and brokers as they seek to hire and retain strong advisors. So familiarize yourself with all the benefits that Google+ provides and then get to work on creating a keyword-heavy and thoughtful Google+ page.

CHAPTER 17

What Other Social Media Platforms Can Professionals Use?

Now that we've gone over the big five networks you should definitely be on—LinkedIn, Facebook, Twitter, Google+, and YouTube—you should have a better understanding of a proper social media presence on the Internet. Hopefully, you've set up a profile on at least one of the major networks, have a better understanding of what they do and why you should be on them, and you've optimized your profiles so you can grow your brand, gain new clients, and deepen your relationships with your current community.

But what about all those other networks out there? I understand, it seems like there's a new one popping up every day. So how do you decide where to spend your time and energy? Besides the main five we've already discussed, investment professionals are experimenting with a number of other social media platforms. In this chapter, I'll provide a quick overview of what these platforms are.

INSTAGRAM

With more than 200 million users logging in each month and more than 60 million photos uploaded every single day, Instagram is a social force to be reckoned with. Instagram is a photo-sharing social platform where each user has a profile and can upload photos (plain or stylized) for followers to view, enjoy, like, and comment. It may seem like a simple photo-sharing site, but many businesses and advisors are using Instagram to their benefit.

One of the main keys to Instagram's marketing potential for businesses is the fact that it is, first and foremost, a mobile application. If you've kept up with any of the social media trends around the Web, you know mobile is important. Some 91 percent of American adults own a cell phone, and 50 percent of these owners download apps like Instagram. All Instagram actions occur on users' mobile devices as they go about their day.

Instagram allows users to share photos not only with their direct Instagram network, but also through their Twitter and Facebook feeds. Cross-pollinating these different networks helps simultaneously build and strengthen a following. If your Instagram network is new or small, it's okay because you can just share your photos to Facebook or Twitter if you want more eyes on a picture you've created. The same hashtag, @mentions, liking, and commenting practices that occur on Facebook, Twitter, and LinkedIn also apply to Instagram. Because it is becoming more integrated with the traditional social platforms, it will be harder and harder to ignore Instagram in the future.

How Can I Use Instagram in Financial Services?

So, how does all of this apply to companies in the financial services industry? By giving your followers a behind the scenes look at your work environment, promoting your office and events in pictures, and showing the personality and people of your company through images, you give a human element to your brand and become easier to connect with.

There are a few ways you can use Instagram in your social media efforts, without having to build a full-blown Instagram presence:

- *Test the waters with a personal account*—Download Instagram for your own personal use. Pay attention to how comfortable you are using it and who and what you stumble across in your actions. By following other financial services companies, you can see how competitors are using this platform and if it may be applicable to your business as well.
- *Take advantage of Instagram's photo-enhancing tools*—If you are already posting photos on your social feeds, you can add filters from the Instagram app to enhance your photos, adding an aura of cool and making them more engaging. People love looking at filtered photos, especially since they add an artistic touch to life and offer a different experience than the other networks.
- *Get the most out of a hashtag*—Whether you're hosting an event or attending one, there's likely a hashtag associated with it. Don't just add the event hashtag when you use Twitter; Instagram loves hashtags too! Take a picture of the turnout for your client appreciation event, or the panel you're sitting in on at a conference. Filter it, hashtag it, share it, and you'll get a lot of mileage out of your Instagram account!

FIGURE 17.1   Financial Times and Learnvest on Instagram

Think of Instagram as an extension of the work and best practices you're already doing on social media, and it might just become your next favorite social hangout too. While this is rather uncharted territory for financial services, both *Financial Times* and Learnvest use their Instagram accounts to share photos from company and industry events, and provide helpful financial tips and information about upcoming events. See Figure 17.1.

PINTEREST

Pinterest is a popular, fast-growing network on the Internet right now. The website offers a way to organize and share content-related images from all over the Web in one spot. Picture Pinterest like an online corkboard or refrigerator with people showing off their interests. You share your favorite images from around the Internet or from your computer called pins and organize them by themes or categories on a board. If someone likes what you've pinned, they will re-pin it themselves, but it will always be attached to your company's profile as it gets passed along (which helps create brand awareness).

Reaching a predominantly female demographic, Pinterest in 2013 was actually the fastest growing content-sharing platform on the Internet. Comprised of these virtual pinboards, Pinterest allows users to keep track of their favorite things—such as recipes, sports gear, blog posts, financial resources, fashion, and more. While at first glance it may seem like this platform is solely for crafty soccer moms in mini-vans, it should not stray far from your radar. It offers the opportunity not only to promote your brand in a creative way, but to also reach out to the female demographic.

I know what you're wondering: "A scrapbooking site for financial services? Why do I need that?" Well, while Pinterest is generally known to cater to woman looking to scout out recipes and crafts, this is actually a good thing! It's estimated that by 2019, women will make up two-thirds of America's wealthy population. Pinterest presents an excellent opportunity to collaborate with these potential clients on a very personal and sometimes viral level. At the time of this writing, Pinterest is the third most-used social network in the United States and is valued at $4 billion. Not bad for a newcomer to the social media scene.

Some other things worth knowing:

- As of late 2013, Pinterest had more than 70 million users and more than 30 *billion* pins.
- Eighty percent of Pinterest users are women, while 50 percent of all Pinterest users have children. Pinterest gives advisors access to this untapped market and their families.
- Twenty-eight percent of Pinterest users have an annual household income of $100,000. These users have assets to invest and manage.
- More than 20 percent of Facebook-connected users—more than 2 million members—are on Pinterest every day. These users are connected, engaged in all social media platforms, and they have made it a part of their lifestyle.
- Pinterest hit 10 million U.S. monthly unique visitors faster than any independent site in history.
- Twenty-five percent of Fortune Global 100 companies reported having Pinterest accounts in 2012.[1] BNP Paribas had an extensive collection of pins, with more than 600 followers.

---

[1]Brian Honigman, "100 Fascinating Social Media Statistics and Figures From 2012," *Huffington Post*, November 29, 2012, updated January 29, 2013, www.huffingtonpost .com/brian-honigman/100-fascinating-social-me_b_2185281.html.

How Can I Use Pinterest For Financial Services?

So, now that you know about the basics of Pinterest, here are some ways you can utilize the site for your financial business:

- *Get visual*—Infographics are a great way to share financial information that is also engaging to look at. Create an infographic about savings or general financial tips, like the example in Figure 17.2, or simply take one of the best pictures from an event or meeting and post it on your board.

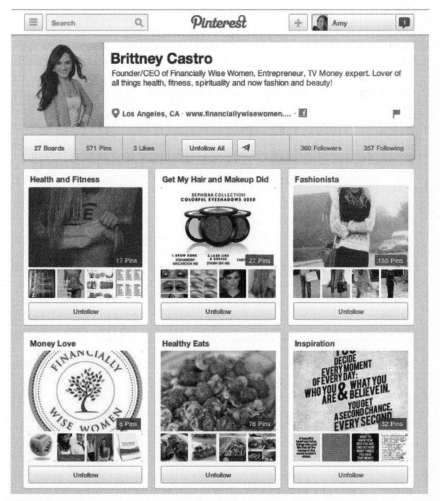

FIGURE 17.2   Brittney Castro, owner of Financially Wise Women on Pinterest

- *Share your interests*—Pinterest allows users to connect to one another on a deeper level of shared hobbies, aspirations, and values. Consider pinning popular images that you also like. Did you find a quote that you find inspiring? Pin it and I'm sure others will agree. Brittney Castro, owner of Financially Wise Women, uses Pinterest to connect with her female audience by posting boards on topics such as health and fitness, fashion, and money. See Figure 17.2.
- *Show the ideal life (or retirement)*—Users pin pictures of the ideal lifestyle that they want to have. Imagine you're writing a story for your customers and using images from Pinterest and around the Web to illustrate what their stories looks like.
- *Show your personality*—Share the inner workings of your office. Did someone bring in cookies for the staff? Share it. Does your business have a charity cause? Have a board dedicated to literacy, animal rescue, or whatever it is that your business supports.
- *Measure results*—Just like Facebook, a business account allows you to track pins and usage with analytics.
- *Share repurposed content*—Create boards to share your blogs, YouTube videos, or media appearances. Wintergreen Advisers LLC uses Pinterest to share educational video content on subjects such as "What is dollar-cost averaging?" and "What characteristics should a value investor have?" See Figure 17.3.

The more you start exploring and pinning, the more ideas and connections you will generate. Pinterest will help you continue to grow your online presence and establish your brand—and you might even find something delicious to make for dinner along the way!

SLIDESHARE

When the National Investment Company Service Association (NICSA), the association for operations professionals in the investment industry, wanted to extend its reach and leverage its efforts, CEO Theresa Hamacher turned to social media. Among the platforms she uses is SlideShare and with great success. She posts presentations there "because it's a public forum like YouTube, so others can access it." And, the presentation format of NICSA's content allows her to "convey technical information in an easy-to-digest format." As an example of the power of SlideShare, NICSA posted a presentation on the new hedge fund rules in Europe, which has received a whopping 12,000 views. See Figure 17.4.

FIGURE 17.3   Wintergreen Advisers on Pinterest

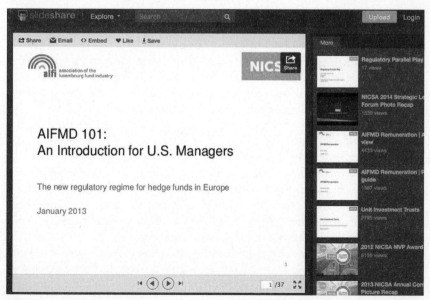

FIGURE 17.4   NICSA's SlideShare Post Garners 12,000 Views

SlideShare is more of a tool than a social network and it's something you should absolutely be using with your company. SlideShare is a website that allows you to share and view presentations in the form of slideshows, PDFs, or video, making it incredibly easy to spread content. It's becoming one of the go-to methods for sharing presentations and distributing information between businesses and customers.

SlideShare gets 130 million page views and 60 million visitors each month. Companies are finding they can increase leads, distribute content, and position themselves as experts in their field by uploading high-quality presentations to SlideShare and sharing among their networks.

Why Would I Use SlideShare for Financial Services?

SlideShare has many applications for the financial services industry. Here are just a few.

- *Great for SEO*—SlideShare is excellent for search engine optimization, helping your website to pop up in searches and to link and direct people back to your page. With SlideShare, you can generate referral traffic from links on your other networks, your business channel, and natural Google searches, and use it to cross-pollinate your social platforms.
- *Position Yourself as an Expert*—Having a presentation on SlideShare helps to position you or your organization as an expert in whatever topic or industry you post in. SlideShare presentations are viewed as high-quality business materials where people can learn valuable information and spread information easily. See Figure 17.5.
- *Low Cost, Easy To Use*—You can always test the waters with Slide-Share's Basic Free membership, which lets you peruse the website, watch presentations, and share with your network. If you want to get more involved and load videos/presentations, consider the Silver Pro Plan at $19/month. This gets you their analytics program, private uploads, 10 video uploads, and basic branding control. The $50/month Gold Plan gets even more features.
- *Repurposing Content*—Imagine all the ways you could utilize SlideShare to your advantage. If you wanted to set up a webinar for your customers, you can post it to SlideShare and develop an even larger audience, or if you have an excellent PowerPoint presentation, you now have an easy platform to distribute it among your followers.
- *Use Analytics to your Advantage*—Analytics are provided on your SlideShare dashboard, so you can log in and find out how you are doing, see how many people have viewed your presentation, and even find out the path people took to arrive to your page with the traffic and geography

FIGURE 17.5   Use SlideShare to Position Yourself as an Expert

sources. As with analytics on any network, these stats are very valuable for assessing how you are doing, how customers and clients are interacting with your brand, and how you can see what practices work best so you can continue forward in the most powerful way.

- *Client Development*—When you upgrade your subscription to Silver or Pro, SlideShare offers a feature that allows you to create and name a campaign to add to any of your slides, files, or presentations that you wish. In a part of your presentation, whether beginning, middle, or end, you can create a custom message and ask for a name, e-mail address, or phone number from the viewer. You can offer a newsletter or free download and, if the viewer is enjoying your presentation, he or she can opt to receive your company's newsletter or special offer.

If you are a financial professional, business, or advisor who wants to position yourself or organization as an expert, and you have presentations and information to share, SlideShare is the place to be.

SKYPE

Most people know Skype as an international Internet communication service that is simple to use and extremely low cost. But, most people don't know how advantageous Skype is for business communication. Skype can be used to send large file transfers in a matter of minutes, conduct video conferences, and easily communicate with fellow employees.

Founded in 2003, Skype reported 300 million regular users in late 2013—meaning they use the service at least once every month. As more peer-to-peer networking services emerge using social media, it is no surprise that Skype's system model has been such a success. The original founders of Skype sold the service to eBay in October 2005 for $2.6 billion. Six years later, in May 2011, Microsoft announced that it had agreed to acquire Skype for $8.5 billion (32 times Skype's operating profits), a 300 percent increase in value. It's obvious that Skype is growing, and its popularity in the professional sector is making an impact.

How Can I Use Skype for Financial Services?

Due to the wide range of features that Skype offers for personal and business communications, I've broken down the most beneficial features that can provide value and worth to your organization's operations.

- *Build Relationships*—We all know the importance of face-to-face interaction in the business and not-for-profit world. This type of interaction helps create and nurture lasting relationships between consumers and employees alike. Skype allows you to conduct video calls and conferencing anywhere in the world. The application allows you to put a human face to your recommendations and better gauge client reactions.
- *Cut Costs*—As I pointed out earlier, calls to other users within the Skype service are free, and so are one-to-one video calls, instant messaging, and screen sharing. International calls can be conducted at a fraction of traditional phone costs. Skype also offers low rates with services such as pay as you go, subscriptions, and premium memberships.
- *Increase Your Productivity*—Services such as screen sharing, file transfers, video conference calling, call forwarding, customer service tools, and more can allow your firm to stay connected—internally and externally—from its own computer network. You can hold a meeting online and share a proposal, show files and designs to employees, and work with other service providers such as web developers.

Of course, Skype comes with some caveats. Since its operations are conducted on a busy Internet highway, the system can get clogged and calls can get broken up or even lost from time to time. Additionally, security and privacy can be an issue. However, the benefits of Skype tend to outweigh its possible negative impact. The social media giant Facebook has even jumped on board—you can now see your friends' latest Facebook news through Skype.

VINE

Vine is a mobile app that allows users to create six-second looping video snippets with their mobile device. Think of it like Twitter, but for short video clips instead of text. These videos can then be shared on your Twitter and Facebook personal profiles. (Note: Business pages are exempt from sharing.) Vine videos are easy to create and don't require you to be a professional videographer or editor. All you have to do is simply tap the camera icon to start recording and then tap the video to stop and restart the recording. To search Vine videos on Twitter for a specific topic, enter, "vine.co" and then your keyword. (For example, "vine.co investing.") When viewing Vine videos in your Twitter feed, simply click on the video to get it to stop the loop.

How Can I Use Vine for Financial Services?

Vine is the video equivalent to adding an image to your tweets. It's a customized way to visually engage a viewer with your message. Much like other forms of social media, financial firms are creatively using Vine to highlight new products and services, tell a story about their brand, offer behind-the-scenes office insight and personality, and connect with consumers. Here are some examples of how businesses are using Vine to their advantage:

- *Illustrate a Message*—American Family Insurance (@AmFam) is constantly using the app to visually share simple messages and promote their content. By creating helpful how-to videos, AmFam generates high engagement and shares while keeping their brand top-of-mind.
- *Show Your Work*—A portfolio manager from Chicago (@bbolan1) uses Vine videos on Twitter to show customers he's hard at work managing his buy and hold recommendation service, Home Run Investor.
- *Promote an event*—My personal favorite is Morningstar Advisor's Vine campaign launched in June 2013 to "celebrate 25 years of sharing investing ideas and insight at the Morningstar Investment Conference." They invited conference attendees to tweet Vine videos finishing the sentence, "Investing is . . .". The videos flew in attached to the conference's hashtag, #MIC25. This is a great example of how to have your audience create content for you using this app. Check out Bill Winterberg's (@BillWinterberg) creative response to the campaign challenge in Figure 17.6.

Because Vine is linked to Twitter, if you're comfortable tweeting away and attaching images to your tweets, it's easy to consider this tool as a next step for a social media savvy professional. Those who enjoy the creative

Bill Winterberg CFP®
@BillWinterberg

☑ Follow

Investing is... #mic25 @mstaradvisor **Morningstar**
Advisor #StopMotion vine.co/v/blunPdVToW7

11:19 AM - 10 Jun 2013

Ⓥ Vine @vineapp

6 RETWEETS 3 FAVORITES

FIGURE 17.6   Bill Winterberg on Vine

process of social media may enjoy the new opportunity for artistic inspiration that Vine provides. On the other hand, if you're just starting up in the social media scene and still finding your feet, Vine isn't something you should be concerned about learning. Focus on the basics of growing your network and engaging on LinkedIn, Facebook, and Twitter. It's critical you walk before you run with your social media. Once you get comfortable using these platforms, then you can start exploring different social media applications.

As you can see, there is a plethora of social networks to be involved in. They all have their unique advantages, audiences, limitations, and beneficial aspects of business and social interaction. I advise you to research them all, but don't forget to consider the most relevant networks among the basics (Facebook, YouTube, LinkedIn, Twitter, and Google+) and then move on.

PART Four

Marketing and Business Development

CHAPTER 18

How Do We Decide Which Social Media Platforms to Use?

You have to use the networks as a listening device.
—Blane Warrene, co-founder, Arkovi

With new social media platforms popping up every year, it's hard to know where to start when building a social media strategy. There are the obvious ones, but there are a host of others. Who would have thought Pinterest or Vine would now be something advisors or asset managers might use?

In other chapters in this book, we guide you in ways to manage specific social media networks. Here, we want to talk about how you might go about choosing particular platforms, how to use platforms simultaneously, and how your goals and audience fit in. As always, be sure to read on; while you may think you know what to do by the headlines, some valuable nuggets of help are within our discussion.

THREE QUESTIONS TO ASK . . . AND IT ALL STARTS WITH COMPLIANCE

For financial professionals, choosing the right platform(s) might first be dictated by your compliance policy. Oftentimes, as we address later, firms will develop a specific social media policy to guide their activities.

But in choosing the best platform, one needs to answer these three questions (see Figure 18.1):

Platform	Primary Audience	Best Practices	Total Users 14
Linked in	Professionals, Recruiters	Engage in professional networking, demonstrate leadership, find target audiences/employees	300,000,000
facebook	Friends, Family	Create a personal network to share with friends and family: updates, videos, and images	1,310,000,000
twitter	Influencers	Engage with key influencers and listen to the voices of clients and prospects	645,750,000
slideshare	General	Publish & share educated content (e.g., research, speech) in powerpoint, PDF, or infographic formats	60MM visitors/mo
You Tube	Skews Younger (ages 18-34)	Create & share videos (i.e., How-to videos) that reach the masses	1,000,000,000
Google+	General	Explore network and increase a brand's SEO and visibility	1,150,000,000*
Pinterest	Women	Organize and share content-related images (i.e., retirement planning) to increase brand exposure	70,000,000

FIGURE 18.1   Social Networking Platforms at a Glance

1. What do we want to accomplish?
2. Where are our clients, prospects, or influencers? What social networks do they frequent?
3. Can I remain compliant using those platforms?

A CASE: CHOOSING THE RIGHT PLATFORMS

Fans of the National Investment Company Service Association (NICSA) can follow the organization all over social media, via LinkedIn, Twitter, You-Tube, and even on Pinterest, where it posts pictures of past conferences.

It wasn't always so. NICSA, which promotes best practices within the investment industry, sensed a need for new approaches a few years ago, says President Theresa Hamacher.

At the time, the group was encountering resistance to e-mail outreach. Social media offered a new way to draw in people. Hamacher says a younger NICSA staff member also encouraged more blogging on the group's site as shorter-form content became more popular online.

Hamacher, a former CIO at Pioneer Investments who became NICSA's president in 2008, says she was convinced of the power of social media about two years ago, when 1,000 people started following NICSA's new LinkedIn group.

- **Know Your Audience**—Most social media blogs in the financial space are business-to-consumer enterprises aimed at large-scale education. That approach doesn't work so well with a B2B audience with more sophisticated needs, Hamacher says. "What we've learned is you really have to think about what it is you're trying to achieve with your social media, and set some goals for yourself," she says.
- **Know What You Represent**—Having many followers on Twitter is not a compelling need for NICSA, and the group doesn't believe that following all of its followers is consistent with its professional image. Instead, it focuses on professionals who are corporate members of the organization. "It's thinking about the individuals rather than the numbers, which I think is a message that resonates with financial advisors," Hamacher says.
- **Plan for Patience**—Working on a successful Twitter strategy alone took about 18 months. "If you expect to have great success with this overnight, you're not going to," Hamacher says. "But we've found as our reputation develops, more and more of our members are following us back."

Dealing with multiple platforms, however, is a challenge. "We have a different login for every social media channel," Hamacher says. "Just managing that can be a nightmare for small business. There haven't been a lot of great solutions." See Figure 18.2.

Part of the reason Hamacher became involved with Finect, a social media site for financial advisors, is its ability to share content compliantly on

FIGURE 18.2 NICSA Posts Event Presentations on Pinterest

multiple platforms easily. Says Hamacher, "I like that it's a very integrated presence."

THREE STEPS TO CHOOSING THE RIGHT SOCIAL MEDIA PLATFORMS

While Hamacher's story may make it sound easy, it isn't always, whether you're a small firm doing it all yourself or working within a large company where things might move slowly or approvals are time consuming. Here are three steps to get you going:

1. **Conduct Some Discovery**—By "discovery," I mean going on a fact-finding mission. You can accomplish this even without a defined compliance policy. Consider Blane Warrene's advice at the start of this chapter. Begin a listening program across Twitter, LinkedIn, Google+, Facebook, YouTube, or any other platform you're considering. Are your customers there? Do you see an audience that is important to you or your firm? Are your influencers, who help you shape the voice and visibility of your organization, also present there? See Figure 18.3.

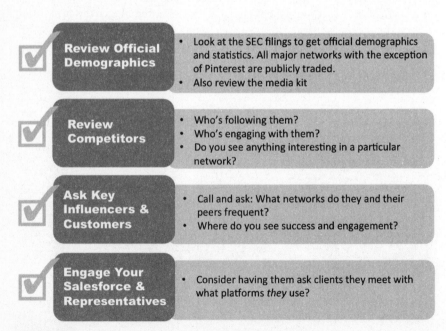

FIGURE 18.3   Checklist for Social Media Platform Selection

Here are some additional tips when conducting discovery of networks:

- **Avoid Familiar Faces**—One big mistake: going where your friends are. "Obviously, what's most important is to figure out where your clients or ideal audience is," Warrene says. "But often we're drawn to go to where our own influencers and friends are first because it's comfortable."
- **Check Accessible Data, Insights**—As part of the discovery process, look for data such as the number of users, profile insights, and trends. For example, people rave about LinkedIn because it offers information such as the job seniority of its members. Such data is accessible on LinkedIn, but it's more limited on Facebook, Twitter, and YouTube. On Facebook, says Warrene, a user might be able to see and access friends, but he or she may not be able to see their profiles—something you often can do at LinkedIn.
- **Beta Test Advertising**—One way that institutions and enterprises can get access to data is by conducting an advertising campaign. If you execute beta advertising or other test on Facebook, for example, you will almost definitely get significant demographic information, and that's a good way to see if your audience is there.
- **Start Small**—As a consultant, Warrene recommends that a small business spend $500 to $1,000 over one to three months to see what kind of results they get, even by taking an existing campaign and moving it into social media. Of course, the bigger the firm, often the more leverage you have: "If Vanguard says to Facebook that we want to test $25,000 on the network, they'll open their kimono," Warrene says.
- **View Competitors**—Also be sure to look at your competitors: What kind of traction, if any, do they have? Consider your direct competitors and those firms you bump up against the most; you'll get some insight into where your customers may be based.

2. **Go Back to the Policy**—You now know enough to say, "This is where we need to be, not only from a compliance but a governance perspective." That's where the policy comes into play: Define the networks you want to use. It almost bleeds into the third step: *Can* we stay compliant using this network? Your organization may decide that its hub is its web site. You may find yourself asking, "If we distribute information on YouTube and on Twitter because we see engagement, can we archive it and supervise it?" If so, wrap that up into the policy.

3. **Connecting the Dots**—The final step is ensuring that the platform is flexible enough that you can connect the dots between compliance, marketing, and human capital.

You have a team that's going to be active on that social media platform. But there might be some questions you need to address to activate the team (or yourself):

- **Connecting to the Social World: Firewall?**—Can employees even go to the social network identified or is it prevented? Will they see "your access has been blocked" after investing time in training and content development?
- **Connecting to Marketing: Connectivity?**—Is there connectivity from the firm's marketing into the network? In other words, will the advisor or firm be able to talk to this network properly to publish content— whether we use Salesforce, Eloqua (a marketing automation software, like MailChimp for the enterprise), or other marketing and communication tools? If not, it may mean you opt for another initiative or undertake this as a new project. However, most marketing automation tools are indeed connected to the various social networks, including Mailchimp, ConstantContact, Salesforce, and Eloqua. As an example, if the firm selects YouTube, can you actually upload them by accessing YouTube directly or any other marketing tool or platform you might be using? Any firm or professional can do much of this themselves without outsourcing, but you'll need to consider the technical issues. Of course, if you choose YouTube, that's a platform generally contained to video. But other platforms such as Pinterest and Facebook support a variety of mediums: video, auditory, images, and so on.
- **Connecting to Your People: Compliance?**—Clearly, you won't move forward on any platform you choose without the compliance education and then the protocol training on the selected network(s). That should include everyone from the most senior to the most junior. Generally, this group should include people ranging from those who will supervise social media to those on the road actually doing the publishing, engaging, and/or responding. Your organization's social media users need to have a clear vision for compliance as well as the etiquette and protocol. "Each network has its own science that one has to learn," Warrene points out. One final reminder: Don't overlook your compliance leaders when it comes to training. Too often, they are ignored and end up lacking the ability to understand what they're looking at.

In short, choosing the right platform isn't as daunting as it sounds: It all starts with your audience. Many firms begin with a single effort on a single platform; that's a great way to get the ball rolling and learn. But, if you have the time or resources to conduct some discovery on the various networks, you can gather invaluable information for your longer-term planning and resource allocation.

CHAPTER 19

How Do We Integrate Social Media with Overall Marketing?

We are at a point where we think of social [media] in a box. But social media will soon be part of all media.
—Mark McKenna, chief marketing officer, Putnam Investments

Talk to any marketing leader, and many will tell you they can't help but think about social media. In fact, they might even have their CEO breathing down their necks over the subject.

That's what happened at Putnam Investments, manager of $153 billion, when CEO Bob Reynolds woke up one day and said: I want to be on Twitter.

"Bob has a passion for technology and communications, so we put together a task force and explored the options," CMO Mark McKenna says. But that wasn't enough. McKenna recalled that his boss turned to him and said, "Let me be clear. I want to tweet *tomorrow*."

You can be sure McKenna wouldn't have been able to meet his boss's demand if he didn't have a larger vision for how marketing needed to work at Putnam.

This larger marketing vision can play on the consumer side as well. I'm reminded of the time when I developed a national campaign to give away one million copies of a free budget kit to help Americans save. The campaign led to over 60,000 orders in a matter of a few days, due to a combination of traditional PR (the *Washington Post*), an appearance on *Dr. Phil*, and social media or the word-of-mouth effect. Today, the free tools continue to be accessed by thousands each year with minimal effort, thanks largely to social media.

As David Edwards, a financial advisor at Heron Financial Group, puts it, "If you don't have a marketing plan, none of these social media efforts will help." That's because you have to know who you are (and what you offer)—and whom you want to reach.

THE CHALLENGES OF UNIFYING SOCIAL MEDIA WITH OVERALL MARKETING

First, let's step back. Is it difficult to unify a firm's social media efforts with their overall marketing plans and goals?

Yes and no.

Lindsay Tiles, managing director of corporate public relations at Charles Schwab and a leader of social media efforts there, says, "It's not challenging; it's just that there are more levers to pull."

She's right. Social media is simply another channel to get your message out—but in a far deeper way. Social media isn't just about pushing content out; it can be about *engaging* your audience.

Say you have a white paper on impact investing and you want to reach family offices. You could just distribute that content in the social media world, but take it a step further. You might invite readers to engage, perhaps by commenting on the content, encouraging them to share it, or inviting them to an event (online or offline) to learn more. That engagement could require new people or processes on your end.

Another challenge across firms, says Citi social media director Frank Eliason, is that "social media efforts need to match the culture of the company—and that's not always the case." Companies need to consider:

- What are we striving to do?
- What are the social components to marketing efforts?

It helps when the message comes from the top. Using Putnam as an example of culture, McKenna says he would sit down with Reynolds to discuss strategic moves—moves that McKenna would execute that very afternoon.

Another challenge: measuring social media. One case in point is Citi's Private Pass, which offers early access to concert tickets for their credit card customers. Citi has turned that service into a social media activity, empowering cardholders heading off to see, say, Billy Joel in concert, to then start talking about the experience—and build the Citi brand and reach in the process. See Figure 19.1.

The resulting conversation is analyzed and its metrics flow across the overall organization, it's not retained just within the marketing unit itself.

FIGURE 19.1   Citi's Private Pass Encourages Cardholders to Share Through Social
Media

Another essential step in incorporating social media into marketing plans
includes recruiting employees skilled in social media. This leads many firms to
hire from places like digital agencies, colleges, or the blogosphere, or to invest
in their employees' social media education—something many top schools
from Columbia University to the University of Texas at Dallas now offer.[1]

But once you get into the groove and make social outreach a daily or
weekly habit, it simply becomes a core part of one's overall marketing efforts.
In the end, it can make the challenge of building relationships more efficient
and more impactful.

TWO APPROACHES TO INCORPORATING SOCIAL MEDIA INTO MARKETING

If you're looking to leverage social media, remember that it should not stand
alone. Social media can (and should) be a way to extend your other marketing
efforts.

---

[1]Eric Dybala, "Top 20 Social Media Universities," *Social Media Delivered*, March 2,
2012, www.socialmediadelivered.com/2012/03/02/top-20-social-media-universities-
by-socialmediadel.

There are two primary approaches to incorporating social media, depending on how you're structured and what you're trying to accomplish:

1. **New Media to Traditional Media**—This approach involves creating a digital or social media strategy first. That strategy might involve specific campaigns and ongoing content shared on Facebook, Twitter, and/or LinkedIn. Then, you review other marketing efforts and look for synergies and duplication.
2. **Traditional Media to New Media**—A traditional marketing or PR initiative might add social media components or work with its social media manager to give legs to the effort.

THE NEW MODEL: GETTING YOUR FIRM BEHIND A SOCIAL MEDIA PROGRAM

However a firm chooses to go about marketing with social media, one thing is clear: It's all about change—and bringing together key stakeholders.

Sunayna Tuteja, director of social business at TD Ameritrade, explains that the adoption of social media first began with start-up firms, where change is the mantra, and ideas could be quickly implemented.

Today, however, the fundamentals of social media are more broadly grasped. "Everyone knows what Twitter is and how it's used," she says. That's changed the model of how one transforms a firm into a social one, able not only to operate in the outside social world but internally as well, often in large and complex organizations.

"The early model," she continues, "was a command and control model—someone had to take the bull by the horns, whether it was in employee training or best practices, and then roll it out. But that's not sustainable from a long perspective."

The new model? Enablement and empowerment. As you manage change when moving your practice into the social world, consider these implications:

- **Reactive versus Proactive**—Whether it's managing their brand, customer service, or client engagement, firms have to ask if they want to react to what's said about them on social media or move proactively to shape their reputation.
- **The Risk of Delay**—Anything a consumer posts is public, and remains in its place there forever. Regulators will naturally ask: "What did you do with this post on this date and how was it resolved?" Clearly, developing policies and identifying or building the right platforms doesn't happen

overnight. If a company needs resources, there is a significant mountain of risk of not doing it.

- **Governance Structure**—The decision to enter a social property has an impact on everyone and only underscores the importance of clarity around roles and decision making. Firms need to have either a leader who can make unilateral decisions (generally reporting to either technology or marketing) or a governance structure involving key stakeholders.

THREE SOCIAL MEDIA ELEMENTS OF MARKETING

In the financial industry, larger companies typically develop marketing plans mid-year, seeking budget approval during the summer for the following year. Whether you work with a formal or informal process, you may still want to consider these key elements:

1. **Goals**—Financial advisor David Edwards underscores the importance of having a marketing plan and specific goals; without it, your social media efforts are dead. If you're a small firm, determine what you're striving to accomplish and then the efforts needed to get you there. Edwards set a goal of doubling assets every two years. Advisors might consider other goals such as:
   - New accounts or assets over a specific time period or from a specific campaign
   - Increases in engagement—Are more people viewing your content or sharing it with their peers? How does that compare to last year or last month?
   - A growth in your online community
2. **Budget**—While social media can cost less than other forms of marketing and outreach, it may still require a budget. If you're just getting started, take the test-and-learn approach. Test with a small amount, even as little as a few hundred dollars a month or just your time. Schwab's Tiles points out that many firms even reduce budgets for marketing and put more toward digital content. Today, most agree that the key is having good content. Small firms should realize their best content might come from their most passionate people, and such content may cost almost nothing if done properly.
3. **Reporting**—If you report on marketing activities, don't forget social media. Consider including metrics and even comments from the social world in reports on a monthly or even daily basis. It's smart to provide executives with a summary of how social media supported an initiative or met a business objective in a simple but compelling PowerPoint

presentation. At Citi, metrics "used to be fans and followers," says Eliason. Today, firms are monitoring metrics such as the following, which could be assembled either internally or by an outside agency:

- **Site visits and new customers**—Whether you're focused on content or a campaign, you can track their metrics through Google Analytics (www.google.com/analytics)
- **Engagement**—Through the number of views, comments, and shares of your content
- **Share of voice**[2]—Are you driving the conversation? How much of the conversation in the social media world are you driving compared to competitors? Tools like SalesForce (www.salesforcemarketingcloud .com; formerly Radian6) and Sprinklr (www.sprinklr.com) are used by Citi to understand. But share of voice, a common measure with traditional offline marketing, is changing, as Putnam underscores.

Indeed, many firms have shifted how they measure their success as technology and social media has evolved. "It used to be, whether you were a phone or computer company, how many ads were you running at Lotus Software or Microsoft," says McKenna, who formerly worked at an ad agency. "You'd say to the client: your share of voice is 11 percent and your top three competitors outspent you. Now, you need to up your spending."

Today, the focus has shifted *away* from share of voice as firms run fewer product-centric ads and instead concentrate more on creating compelling content that educates and informs (a strategy I've long embraced because it's more authentic and effective and less costly).

Let's take a closer look at Putnam and how its outreach and marketing has shifted with the boom in social media usage.

PUTNAM RETAIL: ASSET MANAGER MOVING FROM TRADITIONAL TO DIGITAL MEDIA

In the wake of the financial crisis, many investors and advisors were scratching their heads: What happened to our portfolios? Did we do something wrong with asset allocation? Do the old models still hold true?

Those questions led Putnam to create a suite of four absolute return funds and then turn the conversation to hedging risk. To accomplish that, they used digital marketing coupled with traditional marketing to drive their message.

---

[2]Peter Meinertzhagen, "How to Calculate Share of Voice for Organic Search," *The YouMoz Blog*, November 29, 2013, http://moz.com/ugc/how-to-calculate-share-of-voice-for-organic-search.

One key to their strategy? "We try to look at the intersection of what's topical in the market and what we can share that's relevant to that topic," says McKenna.

As Putnam sought to spotlight the issues getting attention in the industry and their solutions, they took some key steps:

- **Invested in both paid and unpaid media**—Putnam conducted paid search and paid advertising. They bought keywords on Google around the terms "absolute return funds," created a blog (www.absolutereturnblog.com), produced videos and white papers, ran broad-based advertising in *The Wall Street Journal* and *The New York Times*, and shared this all through social media, including Twitter.
- **Developed visually compelling content**—Putnam relies on an in-house team and production capabilities that turn videos around quickly.
- **Hired a journalist to identify trending topics**—Identifying topics is a daily task. That effort helps the team shape the content and thought leadership they then produce and share in the social media world.
- **Leveraged CEO Bob Reynolds**—Reynolds' participation in social media helps bolster the team's efforts and create a culture of rapid response. For example, his focus on the retirement crisis through Twitter has led to more than 6,000 followers and a culture of quick turnaround. See Figure 19.2.

FIGURE 19.2 Putnam's Bob Reynolds Brings Business and Personal to Twitter

- **Captured analytics**—By monitoring analytics, from keywords to content with the most engagement, "we can determine where to spend the next dollar," says McKenna. Those analytics also help inform the sales group about whom to meet when they make in-person visits. "Better to meet someone who's already engaged with us online and expressed interest, than to meet someone who hasn't," he notes.
- **Moved away from return on investment (ROI)**—As discussed above, Putnam is focused less on the traditional "share of voice" measurement than they are on things like engagement, site visits, time on site, time on specific content, and registrations to their online tool, FundVisualizer.

Putnam's experience warrants the attention of others in the financial industry. To manage their marketing, businesses will need new tools for measuring emerging methods of engagement.

A SMALL ADVISOR AND HIS BIG-TIME MARKETING PLAN

Financial advisor Edwards is focused—*keenly* focused—on what his business is and whom he wants to reach. That focus, combined with the power of social media, is enabling him to compete with the goliaths.

Today, he manages $140 million through 90 families, up from $60 million in 2010. His goal is to grow to $250 million next year, doubling every two years.

Edwards offers this advice for smaller firms trying to reach their audience effectively:

- **Define your ideal prospects**—"On the one side of the client spectrum are individual accounts, and on the other side, institutional accounts. We can't compete there." So Edwards targets clients with between $1 million and $10 million in assets—professionals who are busy, aren't working with an advisor, and may have faced a life event recently. How did he get to this client definition? Many in the industry know that answer: "Because it takes as much energy on a $200,000 portfolio as a $1 million portfolio."
- **Reflect your marketing in all materials**—Be sure all materials online and in paper reflect your audience. Be visual, clear, and concise—yet personable. Be sure every employee in your firm understands the marketing strategy.

- **Let your audience drive your marketing**—Edwards points to a friend who focuses his advisory practice on medical professionals. "There's a huge hospital system nearby; they can focus just on that and do well hosting quarterly dinners where they ask a client to bring a friend. That won't work for me." Edwards' clients are throughout Europe and the United States, and they're pressed for time.

He recalls the time he tried assembling a dinner with four couples in Connecticut. "Half couldn't come because their kids had lacrosse practice. So, I have a problem accessing clients through traditional means." What does work for Edwards is meeting over wine or beer and leveraging social media. Before he meets a client, he'll review their LinkedIn profile, check for friends in common and their education, and access Fidelity's Referral-EDGE, which provides him free access to additional information on millions of individuals, foundations, and other potential clients. He's also made sure he can easily be found online—a topic discussed in detail in Chapter 22 on search engine optimization (SEO).

Given his growth goals over the next five years, it's no surprise that Edwards sees the need to manage his marketing needs in new ways. His clients have more complex lives and their investment needs are more sophisticated. His marketing, coupled with social media, needs to respond in kind.

FIVE WAYS TO GIVE SOCIAL MEDIA LEGS TO YOUR MARKETING EFFORTS

Sometimes a business doesn't know how good they've got it. One mistake the financial industry in general has consistently made is not fully leveraging the efforts already taking place internally, largely because of silos and layers of bureaucracy.

Too often, firms have events and content already being produced that could simply be given more legs through the social media channel. Stop and think about your own firm or organization. What are you doing now that could be shared elsewhere?

Since economies are the name of the game today, you'll want to consider these other ways of expanding your social media efforts.

- **Appearances and Live Events**—If you or someone in your firm spoke at an event, chances are there's no reason you wouldn't want many more to hear the message. So:

- Record it for YouTube and then share it.
- Take photos and tweet it out and write an article with a visual.
- Post the PowerPoint presentation on SlideShare.
- Consider a "Tweetup," bringing a group of Twitter followers to your event. (Learn more with "How Tweetups Work.[3])

- **Online Events**—Are you thinking of hosting a webinar? Consider partnering to expand your audience, maybe with your local newspaper. Share the invitation link through the various social platforms (profiles, groups, and an article). Then follow some of the same suggestions as above.

- **E-mail**—If you have an e-mail program, perhaps a weekly newsletter, be sure to add the various share buttons, available by almost all e-mailing tools such as Constant Contact, VerticalResponse, MyEmma, and ExactTarget.

- **Research**—Engage in an online survey to get valuable feedback while generating content that could spread your message and generate attention by reporters and bloggers. As one example, Finect conducted an "Investor Social Media Behavior Survey" with individual investors that led to more than 200 responses, valuable insights, and repeated sharing by news organizations, marketing firms, and investors. It's a powerful example of spending very little but getting very broad reach. But don't forget that good content is essential to engaging others—the media, industry associations, and more—in adopting or sharing that content themselves. See Figure 19.3.

- **PR**—Maybe you or your CEO conducted a radio or TV interview. Surely some preparation notes were developed, or maybe even a script. Did you ever think about turning that into a short article that highlights the appearance—perhaps with a photo using your iPhone? As an example, take a recent appearance on Fox to discuss financial literacy among millennials. One could easily just make the appearance and call it a day. But since I often do my own prep with Q&A, it's quite easy to turn my notes into an article and then share it through social media (with the video link) as well as to customers in a weekly newsletter. If you have something newsworthy to announce, tease the appearance beforehand through social media. Keep in mind those keywords and hashtags so others can find you and your content. See Figure 19.4.

---

[3]Amy Hunter, "How Tweetups Work." HowStuffWorks.com, http://computer
.howstuffworks.com/internet/social-networking/information/tweetup.htm.

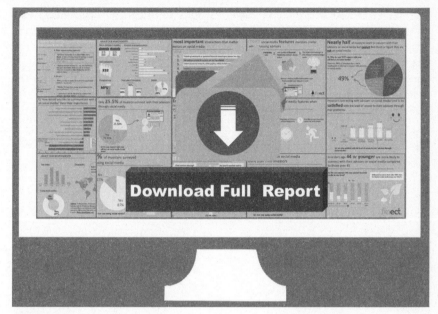

FIGURE 19.3   Consider a Call to Action to Access Valuable Research

FIGURE 19.4   Leveraging a TV Appearance through Social Media

We've talked about some powerful ways to integrate social media into your regular marketing efforts. From large companies like Putnam to small registered investment advisors (RIAs), they're doing it, and not always with big budgets. In fact, enjoying the benefits of social media can often mean just looking at what's right in front of you—the research you're producing or the event you're about to hold—and taking it one step further.

CHAPTER 20

How Do We Measure Social Media ROI?

O ne of the biggest questions on the subject of social media is: How do you measure your return on investment (ROI)? How do you find out where your time and dollars are going on these various networks?

When you're dealing with investments and direct marketing campaigns, it's easier to measure the results of your spending, but this can be more difficult with social networks. The social media ROI concept is still in its infancy, but there are many tools and tactics on how to measure the return, or at least how to analyze how effective your social media presence is.

DEFINING SUCCESS WITH ROI AND KPI

There is no doubt that figuring out your ROI is an important factor in determining where to put marketing dollars. If you're not getting tangible, direct results immediately, why spend the money on it, right? Well, not really. As marketers struggle to wrap their heads around how and where social media plays a role in marketing efforts and budgets, there is a shift to start analyzing what really matters for long-term success: the value of the relationships acquired and maintained through social media.

Instead of trying to calculate the exact dollar amount acquired from each new client that you gained solely from social media compared to the dollar amount spent on social media assets (technology, staff, time), try changing the metrics. When it comes to social media and digital marketing, the measurement needs to encompass factors that are significantly broader than this.

Think back to the last time you attended a trade conference, a chamber networking event, or an impromptu coffee meeting with a prospective client. During these occasions, I'm guessing you engaged in conversation, exchanged pleasantries, passed out business cards, and gave brilliant elevator speeches.

In other words, you spread the seeds of your business or mission with hopes that some would grow into lasting relationships.

Many seeds withered and faded, but others probably developed into fruitful returns on your investment of time and energy.

Similar to real-life relationship-building meetings and events, social media offers the platforms to spread the seeds of your business or cause to the world. Think about it: The Internet is just an extension of real life, and in some cases people are actually spending more time conversing and interacting online than in person.

Measuring the growth of these seeds can be a challenging concept to grasp, but it begins by shifting the definition of your return on investment (ROI) and developing a solid list of key performance indicators (KPI). Below are three indispensable strategies to consider when it comes to measuring social media ROI.

THREE STRATEGIES TO MEASURING YOUR SOCIAL MEDIA ROI

When it comes to measuring your social media ROI, here are three strategies to keep in mind.

1. **Change Your Perspective**—Back in the day (let's say the 1990s), it was easy to launch a marketing campaign and measure the success via bottom-line growth. With social media marketing, it's a little different. Many advisors (understandably) struggle with grasping the benefits and potential returns of social media. With a little shift in perspective, however, the benefits and/or returns are hard to ignore.
   - **Cost savings**—Let me state the obvious: social media is cheap and in many cases free. By having stellar social media processes and operations, you will save your company or yourself a boatload of money that otherwise would be spent on costly marketing campaigns. Don't ignore this when examining benefits and returns.

     For example, are you spending thousands of dollars each month with a public relations firm? I've had people say to me, "Gosh, we spend $10,000 per month on a part-time PR firm. How can social media *not* be a part of this? And for less!" With social media, you'll be able to cut back on costs by reaching out and contacting editors and reporters directly through Twitter and other social channels.
   - **Search engine rankings**—Google is the number-one search engine in the world and is an integral part of many people's day-to-day lives.

Think of social media as the vehicle to increased search engine rankings and, ultimately, worldwide exposure.

- **Cost avoidance**—Whether you've accepted it or not, people are talking about your organization on social media. It's the new marketplace, the new bar where everyone goes to chat and spread the news. Whether or not you choose to participate in this conversation is up to you. I don't know about you, but if I knew people were talking about me in real life, I'd want to be there to save face. On social media, you have the power to not only listen in, but also monitor the conversations that are buzzing about your business. Just think— putting an end to one negative conversation may result in one new client that may have never looked twice before. See Figure 20.1.
- **Sales and revenue**—Just because the bottom line is no longer the only measure of success doesn't mean it should be ignored. Continue to measure the relationship between your business' bottom line and your social media efforts.

Still shaking your head? According to *WSJ Online*, New Hampshire-based advisor Mark Scribner landed a $2.6 million 401(k) rollover account and a large insurance policy from a client's

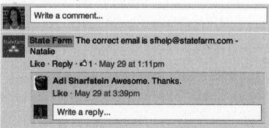

Adi Sharfstein
I tried emailing becky@sfhelp.com about your companies continued stonewalling on my diminished value claim and your servers are rejecting my email. Have I been blocked? Why is it so it so difficult to contact you people or to get a phone call back? Is this how you prevent paying out to people (that aren't your shareholders or customers)? You just drag it along as far and for as long as you can in the hopes that we just give up? Well, I have news for you, I'm not giving up. You have my email, my phone number, my insurance companies phone number, and my home address. Why is this so difficult?

Like · Comment · May 29 at 12:45pm

Write a comment...

State Farm The correct email is sfhelp@statefarm.com - Natalie
Like · Reply · 🖒1 · May 29 at 1:11pm

Adi Sharfstein Awesome. Thanks.
Like · May 29 at 3:39pm

Write a reply...

FIGURE 20.1 Sharing on Social Media May Keep Clients Happy

boss by re-connecting on LinkedIn with an acquaintance he hadn't spoken to in 15 years.

- **Social capital**—Social capital refers to the collective or economic benefits of knowing people. In other words, the more people you know, the more likely you are to gain referrals and prospects, get preferential treatment, and develop your celebrity, so to speak. When you take the time to let your audience know you care by listening and responding to what they say and providing thoughtful content, the relationships you are building begin to become invaluable. Show authenticity toward your current and prospective clients and get to know them, and they will no longer be just fans and followers, but brand evangelists. Over time, you will see these relationships benefit your bottom line.

2. **Keep Track of the Seeds That Grow With KPI**—Key performance indicators are the mediums through which your business assesses success. I cannot emphasize enough the importance of measuring your performance. You'll waste years of time and energy if you fail to do so. Here's how you can get started:

   - **Create categories**—Choose metrics that you can translate into business categories, such as sales, leads, customer satisfaction, customer interaction, and so on. Determine these categories based on the goals of your firm. For example, if you're seeking to increase referrals, use referrals as a unit of measurement.
   - **Stop fixating on your likes**—Define more than just attention metrics (number of followers, etc.). For financial professionals, it takes time to develop a large following. And, while it's great to have as many followers as possible, it's essential to expand your attention to other areas such as higher search engine rankings, follower engagement (likes, comments, shares), and weekly total reach.
   - **KPIs for each social network**—Each network is different. On Facebook you may measure your weekly total reach, whereas on YouTube you may measure the number of video views. Regardless, make sure you tailor KPIs to the specific network.

3. **Check Out these Monitoring Gems**—Listed below are links to some excellent free tools to help you gauge the performance of your social media marketing and outreach. The information and insights you obtain from these sources will be useful in all realms of your business.

   - **Facebook Insights:** Facebook Insights is a great tool to measure the impact of your posts, how many people are talking about your page, demographics, and your weekly total reach outside of your fanbase. You can access insights by logging into your business page and clicking on the admin panel.

- **Google Analytics** (www.google.com/analytics): With Google Analytics, you can insert a line of code into your website and keep track of how people get to your site, how they navigate through it, and how long they stay.
- **YouTube channel stats** (www.youtube.com/analytics): With YouTube's analytics, you can keep track of video views, demographics, playback locations, traffic sources, audience retention, subscribers, views and more.
- **Going Up!** (www.goingup.com): This is another free web analytics package that helps you monitor traffic trends, SEO, keywords, and user profile data.
- **LinkedIn** (www.linkedin.com): LinkedIn is not necessarily a monitoring tool, but it can provide good information about your connections. Use it to keep track of your competitors, industry trends, and hot discussions.

To sum it up, there really is no one universal understanding of success in the social media world. Rather, success depends on how you define it. Regardless of your goals, you must define success on a large scale (ROI), and then acquire small-scale key performance indicators. These indicators will help you analyze and evaluate how your social media presence and actions are doing, how you can improve, and most importantly, how your relationships are developing and growing.

CHAPTER 21

What Types of Content Work Best?

When it comes to doing business in today's wired society, social and digital media are absolute musts. There's simply no point to avoiding it, as social media has fast gone from nice to have to must have. Content is at the heart of all social media activity. It's what your audience craves, and everything you post is considered content. But the Web is saturated with content, both good and bad, from the factually informative to the practically irrelevant. So how can your voice be heard over all this noise? What kind of content works best? The key is to provide your audience only with effective, targeted content that speaks directly to their needs or desires.

THE BENEFITS OF CONTENT MARKETING

Creating great content is certainly worth the effort. When delivered to the right people, outstanding content can:

- **Enhance your social media presence**—Each time you post knowledgeable content, particularly if you do it consistently, you establish yourself as an influencer in a relatively short span of time.
- **Elevate and solidify your brand**—This goes hand-in-hand with building up a strong social and digital media presence. People are simply more likely to purchase a product or use the services of a brand they've come to recognize.
- **Position yourself as the go-to authority on a particular issue**—Stellar content, especially if it's laser-targeted, can go a tremendous way toward culturing a perception of yourself or your firm as *the* authority and resource for a particular need. For example, an advisor who specializes in annuities and creates plenty of annuity-centric content will appeal to

FIGURE 21.1   PIMCO's Plain Talk Gets Noticed

any potential investor currently researching annuity products. Likewise, asset managers who position themselves as the best firm for advisors in the business of working with high-net-worth investors by continually posting solid and leading content will earn extra credibility as the right firm to join.

- **Spark discussions that improve engagement**—It's not enough to rely on the sales pitches, jingles, and billboards that were so effective a decade ago. You must provide your audience with real value. If you do this regularly via blogs or other posts, you can create a dialogue with your prospects, and this is the type of engagement that produces results. As an example, PIMCO isn't shy about taking positions and communicating them on social media. In 2012, PIMCO's former "Bond King" Bill Gross came out swinging against the most recent easing plans from the Federal Reserve and European Central Banks. The comment came just days after the Fed unveiled its plan for a third round of quantitative easing—or QE3—and generated lots of engagement. See Figure 21.1.
- **Boost your credibility**—Again, the more content you produce on a specific subject, the stronger your credibility becomes, especially since your content proves—rather than just implies—that you're an expert.
- **Increase your exposure and reach**—Great content is almost always picked up and re-circulated, opening the doors to several opportunities to further your reach. For example, bloggers may ask you to contribute a guest blog post, while other media outlets will be eager to publish your content. Not only does this increase the number of links back to your own website (which improves search engine rankings), but it also puts you in front of all-new yet qualified audiences.
- **Drive more traffic to your website and improve your search engine ranking**—It's a simple equation: Search engine optimization (SEO) Keywords + Content + Frequency = better search engine rankings, and as a result, more traffic to your site. If you hope to land on the first page of a

consumer's search results, be sure to weave plenty of SEO keywords into your every post.

- **Grow your list of followers and fans**—Whether prospects find your content via search engine or through word of mouth, being known as a great resource will naturally lead to an uptick in your followers.
- **Generate qualified, warm, and interested leads**—The people reading your burgeoning content cache (which indicates they have an interest in what you have to say or offer) can easily be engaged and converted to new relationships.
- **Be repurposed and reused for a multitude of reasons**—Even the biggest asset management firms have caught on to one of the best benefits of economies of scale, and that is that original content can be reshaped, repurposed, and reused to appeal to different audiences or to meet different goals.
- **Help recruit great talent**—Good content speaks to the future employee. It tells them not only about your firm and investing philosophy, for example, but how much you get it—how current you are. Indeed, many young people I've spoken to are making decisions about firms they want to join based on the firms' openness to utilizing social media.

To realize all of the amazing benefits strong and savvy social and digital media can deliver, we'll touch on the key components to crafting a winning social media presence with impactful content that works.

SIX STEPS TO SUCCESSFUL CONTENT MARKETING

Here are six steps I have found that work to build successful content marketing.

1. **Develop an Editorial Calendar to Ensure Consistency and Frequency**—First things first. If you really want to knock your social media out of the park and ensure your messaging is always on target, develop a consistent content and posting schedule. In magazine and publishing parlance, this kind of schedule is known as an editorial calendar. It outlines which topics you want to address and when, how each topic will be delivered (i.e., via blog or article, video, e-mail, etc.), and the audience for which it's meant.

   In the world of social media content, however, it's not uncommon to use multiple editorial calendars, one for each platform you use. If, for example, you use Facebook to connect with and engage potential investors, Twitter to advance your industry brand recognition, and

LinkedIn to foster relationships with other professionals, you'll want an editorial calendar for each. Then determine how many touches each channel should receive on a daily/weekly/monthly/yearly basis, and build a timeline around those engagement goals. Finally, think of the type of content that will appeal to your various audiences, and tie every touch to a particular subject about which you're passionate. Your editorial calendar will also make it easy to identify chances to craft seasonal promotions or other seasonably salient content, and these are great opportunities to try to connect more personally with your prospects and clients.

When you're just beginning your editorial calendar, it's easy to feel overwhelmed by the task, so start by assigning your content touches for the next month. As you gauge the effectiveness of your content and gather comments or discussions from your audience, deciding what to cover in the upcoming weeks and months will only get easier, as will ensuring your content has a consistent tone.

2. **Develop Content that Builds Your (or Your Firm's) Authority and Credibility**—Would you rather put your assets in the hands of a fly-by-night planner or those of a respectable advisor authority? Think about when it comes to making a living. Most advisors would rather work with an authoritative and reputable asset manager than with a relatively unknown firm. The fact is, regardless of whether they're conscious of it, advisors work toward being perceived as *the authority* on certain specialties, be it retirement or college planning, even if only locally. It's the same for asset managers. They're aiming to become *the authority* on a certain type of fund, employee culture, product, or retirement planning tool.

Now consider this brief etymological (the study of word origins) treatment: What would you call someone who writes and distributes words, sentences, and paragraphs, or the stuff that we collectively know as content? Most of us would call that person an author. Ever wondered from whence that word author came? Yep, the word *author* shares the same root as the word *authority*. Therefore, an *author* is someone who serves as *the authority* on a certain subject. So the more authoring you do, even if you don't use a byline, the more you feed your audience's collective need for authoritative resources with whom they can trust and work.

3. **Original Content Is Always Best**—The simple fact of the matter is the most effective and long-lived content comes straight from your keyboard, and the more frequently the better. A regular blog is ideal, but you can also create whitepapers or compile interesting research, produce brief but

entertaining and informative videos, record podcasts, or design clever branding and engaging social media posts. But where can you look for inspiration? This is possibly the most difficult aspect of writing, since without a great idea to build your content around, you could find yourself going in circles.

Bill Winterberg, a certified financial planner who writes about tech issues in the financial advisory space, knows a great deal about creating stellar original content. A longtime industry insider who knows the landscape from both sides of the fence, he founded FPPad in 1998, a blog dedicated to serving as a leading source of news, thought leadership, and insight on financial planning technology. From its roots as a blog, FPPad has now developed into a premier consulting and media source for financial planners and wealth advisors.

According to Winterberg, your own book of business is a treasure trove of potential content ideas. "You know your clients and the problems they're dealing with best, and they're answering questions and creating solutions every day," he says. "Just go through your client plans, portfolios, and concerns, and all the solutions you've identified. This is perfect material for online content."

But no matter where you get your inspiration, how can advisors and asset managers be sure they're creating good content? Generally speaking, the best content is:

- **Unique or groundbreaking**—On top of grabbing your readers' attention right out of the gate, anything different, groundbreaking, or new you create will likely shoot to the top of search engine pages and correspondingly, to the top of your followers' minds and news threads.
- **Informative and beneficial to the reader**—Face it, if your content is neither, why on earth would anybody waste their time reading it? Don't bury the information or benefits you want your readers to take away. Bring it right to the fore and make it the centerpiece.
- **Thought provoking**—Any time you can get your readers to think, you've scored a hit. Ideally, your content will have them thinking of how the subject matter could affect them, which naturally segues into them reaching out to you.
- **Actionable and engaging**—If you provide your readers with plenty of content, whether via your website or other social media outlets, that compels them to take action and engage in discussions with you. You'll see exponential growth in your social media network as well as in actual leads to new relationships.

That said, don't forget the importance of regularly checking your analytics to ensure your idea of great content aligns with what your audience finds to be worthy. "The user ultimately decides what's good content," says Frank Gosch, who serves as media giant Hearst's SEO and analytics director. "If you create content and then through your analytics you see people didn't engage with your content, then either the content isn't as good as you think it is or it doesn't meet what people are looking for."

If you think you've posted something truly special but your analytics reveal low engagement rates, it's time to reassess your content.

4. **Use Purposeful, Goal-Driven Content that Brands, Engages, and Sells—** The next step in taking your content in the right direction entails determining what your goals are and what you want each communication to achieve. Social media experts tend to agree that virtually all of your content should speak to at least a couple if not all of these three end goals: branding, engagement, or selling.

"At a high level, every piece of content you make should have all three of these elements," says Winterberg. Here are tips for working these goals into your content, to keep in mind when crafting purposeful content.

Branding

Branding is the work you do to get your ideal prospects, whether investors or new advisors, to recognize you or your company as an industry leader. To solidify your brand, use a measure of consistency in everything you produce: Always use the same types of font and format; use your logo and graphic components in a consistent manner; employ the same signature music that plays on your website, podcast, or video.

One firm that's found tremendous success with social media is Transamerica. They've become quite adept at creating content that marries their brand to certain life insurance products. The image in Figure 21.2 was featured on Transamerica's Facebook page one year, where it garnered almost 90,000 likes. It's easy to see why this branding effort was such a success: There's nothing cuter than a baby, and their clever headline ties the imagery to real-life events that might naturally lead people to think about a need for life insurance without dwelling on the unpleasantness of mortality. Content featuring a brief but compelling lead like this, coupled with a powerful and memorable image and strategic logo positioning, is an outstanding way to advance your brand in the minds of your target audience.

Engagement

One of the primary aims of any digital or social media campaign is to engage your audience. How do you know if your audience is

FIGURE 21.2 Transamerica's Facebook Page

engaged? Prospective investors, clients, and potential recruits become engaged every time they participate in your social media efforts—via their use of comments on blog posts or use of likes, for example. Smart advisors and asset management firms engage their audiences in a variety of ways, but one of the best ways to leverage your engaging content is to build prospect lists or generate leads.

An easy way for advisors to capitalize on engagement-driven content and its lead-generating potential is to offer their readers and visitors what's known as opt-in engagement opportunities. These opt-ins can be attached to almost any type of content on a multitude of platforms; by incorporating some sort of reward for users who leave you their contact information or review an educational guide, for example, you'll see engagement rates climb.

"When someone stumbles on to your site, what's there that's going to compel them to engage with you?" asks Winterberg. "In some cases, they might provide an e-mail address because they thought you were funny, but not everyone will be so liberal. That's where the incentive carries some real weight; someone gets rewards by offering you their e-mail." He suggests using incentives such as:

- Your information-packed newsletter
- Interesting research
- Free or trial site membership
- Proprietary content that could benefit them
- Free gym or club memberships
- Gift cards for services such as Starbucks or iTunes

While asset management firms can also use the same kinds of opt-in engagement strategies, their ultimate goal is usually to recruit new advisors. LPL Financial, for example, uses two different avenues to generate their leads. First, they rely on paid Twitter promotional tweets. According to their senior vice president of brand marketing and delivery, Melissa Socci, "We use this medium to say we want more followers and that we want advisors to know who we are, so we've been sharing some great videos about some of our other advisors." They also use LinkedIn to drive new store sales or advisor acquisition.

Selling

This word can be interpreted in a couple of different ways, so Bill Winterberg offers this advice: "Remember, selling doesn't necessarily mean, 'If you act now, you'll save 10 percent off your financial plan.' But make no mistake: every financial planning piece I do is about selling myself as a tech expert. I publish it so they can get 10 [video blog] episodes that get them thinking about me and how I could help their business."

Content that's geared toward selling doesn't necessarily result in a financial transaction, although it well could. Financial products and services aren't as commoditized as other industries are, *so what you're really selling is yourself or your firm.*

By posting content that proves your expertise in a certain niche, you're laying the groundwork for acquiring new clients and relationships—from partners to thought leaders. When the time comes and your readers decide to get an advisor, that advisor will be you. The same logic applies to asset managers selling their companies. Not only can their selling content assure consumers that, for example, their 529 plans are ideal for their needs and ultimately result in a sale, but they can also create similar content aimed at boosting their credibility and likeability among the advisor community. This can result in advisors signing on to work with them.

5. **Incorporate Video into Your Social Media Activities**—You've probably noticed that many of the people interviewed for this chapter mention the use of videos. And for good reason: Adding videos to your social media efforts is the latest and most effective means of distinguishing yourself or your firm from the competition. Why?

   According to Gosch, "Video is underutilized. Content needs to be geared to what the customer wants, which has become visual aspects like video, and video is helpful in earning trust." And while the Web is overrun by text content, the realm of video is largely untapped and consumers genuinely enjoy video content. You already know how the imagery, graphics, and other visualizations in your web and PR content elevate it from other more static content, so it's not a huge leap in logic to take visualization to the next natural level: video. What's more, videos meet all three characteristics of good content:

- They're wonderful branding vehicles, as the use of consistent background imagery, charts, and other visual elements allows viewers to recognize your brand. What other channel allows you to keep your logo on display for longer than 10 seconds?
- Videos provide limitless opportunities to engage with your audience, the least of which is the fact customers can now put a face to your name or company. In addition to imparting essential information, you can use this medium to address your audience's questions or respond to comments they've made elsewhere, and they're perfect for pitching opt-in incentives, like a free transcript of the video.
- Yep, videos can also sell. If you speak well, use appropriate gestures, and deliver content of benefit, they can help you market yourself or your company. What better way is there to illustrate a new tool, product, or technological innovation?

Once you start posting video content, it's important not to lose sight of the importance of that boring old print content. For now at least, that's still social media's bread and butter. So heed the advice of April Rudin, founder of Rudin Marketing.

"We're in a transformational time, so you need to do both," Rudin says, "because some prefer video and others print. One mistake firms and advisors make is to commit to one platform or one way of communication when best practices are to be available in both places. In fact, they each (print and video content) need to reside in different places on the Internet."

The time to act and get into the video game is now, so do some research or talk to other advisors and firms about how best to start producing video content. Then start posting videos to your own site, YouTube, and Facebook.

6. **Reuse and Repurpose Your Best Content**—One of the best things about a robust stable of social media content is that it allows you to go back and repurpose certain posts to meet different goals or to address a different audience. And why shouldn't you? Plenty of big-name asset managers and social media-savvy advisors do it all the time, and some even mandate that all content be created with the aim of being repurposed. Your greatest content asset is your blog, and you can definitely mine it for additional posting opportunities.

10 Ways to Repurpose Content

Here are just a few (okay, 10) ways to repurpose your blog content to meet a variety of goals on several social media platforms.

1. Take three to five key points or insights from your blog and post them on Facebook.
2. Using the same three to five insights, organize them into a paragraph, and share them in a LinkedIn group announcement.
3. Schedule anywhere from 5 to 15 tweets featuring key phrases or points from your blog.
4. Based on your analytics, run a "Best of XXX Blog 2015" blog series featuring your five or six most popular blogs.
5. If your blog is recent and contains useful industry trends, turn it into a press release as soon as you can.
6. Create a written or video Q&A spot based on questions you've gotten or seen in comments or posts.
7. Use information you've discussed in blogs or data from your research and convert it into charts to capitalize on the visual appeal.
8. Condense your blog content into an informative podcast.
9. Turn an interview you conducted into a blog post.
10. Post a series of photo montages from the photos you've used in blogs and other postings over the years.

Now that you know which kind of content works best and how to apply it to different audiences, get out there and create a social media storm!

CHAPTER 22

How Do We Use SEO to Reach Key Audiences?

*Financial services companies have content galore, but they're not
good at making that content available, and so they're losing
opportunities when people search—free opportunities.*
     —Frank Eliason, director of global social media, Citi

Y ou've used them when you shop for flowers to send to Mom's home across
the country or when you're looking for your favorite restaurant while
travelling on business.

Search engines, that is. Not just Google, but Yahoo! and a host of others.

You know the Internet is crucial, but how can you use it to ensure that
potential clients, consumers, or partners find you, your firm, or your content?
How can you make sure that your precious time and resources are used
effectively?

Are you an asset manager who wants end investors or financial advisors
to find your content online? Are you an advisor who wants someone
searching for his next financial planner to discover your name? The better
the visibility you have on the search results page, the more visits or clicks you
will get for your content, website, or group.

In short, search engine optimization (SEO) leads consumers to you.

THREE WAYS SEO IS CHANGING RIGHT NOW

SEO has been around for years, but one thing remains constant: the mystery
surrounding it. Still, there are lots of key things to know—from the latest best
practices to the biggest mistakes.

Despite its age, SEO has progressed. In short, it matters more than ever. And the experience is more visual than ever. Have you noticed fewer words and more pictures?

Let's look at three factors driving SEO today:

- **Content Is King**—Search engines appreciate good content, and they will rank it at or toward the top of a search results page. And the race is on for good content. It allows a small firm to compete with a big firm if the smaller one produces effective blogs or articles online, a practice that is increasingly easy to do.
- **Black Hat Strategies**—These refer to attempts to jimmy the SEO system. It's the spam and junk strategies one might put into place to show a boost in traffic—and perhaps to justify their cost. The good news, according to Frank Gosch, senior director of search and analytics at Hearst, is that search engines in the past three years have become better at detecting these strategies, and penalizing and removing sites that apply them from SEO results.
- **Social Visibility**—Just five years ago, content found by search engines typically featured only articles; today it's taken a giant leap forward to include broader social visibility. "Search engines now leverage the information they get from social media about brand sites and include them into the consideration when they do rankings," Gosch explains. Think about your LinkedIn or Facebook profile that now appears in search engines. (Okay, maybe you haven't checked yours, but surely you've searched for those of others and found them.)

A CASE STUDY: HERON FINANCIAL GROUP

David Edwards of Heron Financial Group, a wealth management practice in New York City, says, "If you don't have a rock-solid marketing plan, all the SEO and social media in the world won't help you. But if you have a marketing plan, then social media and SEO is a force multiplier."

Edwards felt SEO was important—"I have to assume my clients are also Googling me, just as I'm Googling them." His goal was to appear among the top three firms when someone performs a search with his name or for a New York wealth management firm. That isn't easy, because "there's a bunch of David Edwards out there."

As a result of his SEO efforts, Heron Financial appears among the top three firms in searches. What's his return on investment (ROI) for his efforts? "Who cares! If we're adding one family every week and doubling assets every two years, it's clear by the hard work we've done defining our ideal client and executing with search and an Internet presence," Edwards said.

Moreover, as Edwards points out: "We can go head-to-head with the big guys who spend thousands: They have 100 times our assets and 100 times our marketing budget, but we're on a level playing field."

What did Edwards do so right?

- **Defined His Ideal Client**
  - $500,000 minimum investable assets. Ideally $1 million to $10 million in AUM
  - Time-stressed executive
  - Is *not* already managing his own money successfully or working with a good advisor
  - Has had a triggering life event causing him to re-think his financial life, such as:
    - Change in marital status: marriage or divorce
    - Birth of a child or grandchild
    - Promotion, job change, or pending retirement
    - Windfall such as restricted stock, stock options, sale of a business, or inheritance
- **Leveraged Tags**—Tags matter. Edwards has a description tag that appears in the search results and lives on the home page of his site. He's also thinking about how people might search for him: "New York" and "wealth manager," for example, so he knows it's critical these words appear on his site. See Figure 22.1.
- **Shared Content to Drive Inbound Links**—As a result of Edwards' content, appearances, commentaries, and more, Heron has generated multiple links from other worthwhile sites (those that don't traffic in spam) back to his site. "Every time David Edwards or Heron is mentioned elsewhere or posted—in a blog, a tweet, or a retweet—it adds to the thousands of links. This is an important lesson: You might start your social media and SEO efforts and see very little over the next few months. You're thinking, 'Oh my gosh, I'm wasting my time,'" says Edwards. "But it takes time for those high-quality links to propagate in the online world."
- **Hired Help**—With a fairly small shop to run, and wanting to make even greater progress, Edwards hired help. His SEO expert can't tell him what tags to use if he doesn't know who he's trying to reach as part of his marketing plan, but once armed with that information, the expert provided tools and techniques to help establish the keywords to use.

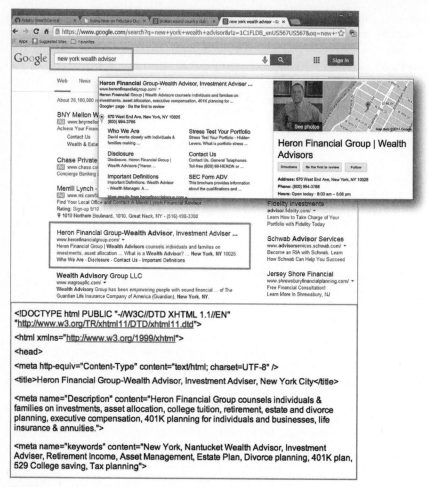

FIGURE 22.1   Heron's Title and Description in a Search Result and Tags Behind the Scene

TOP MISTAKES THE FINANCIAL INDUSTRY MAKES

With this evolution of SEO and the industry's own turtle-like speed of innovation and adoption, it's easy to see that financial firms might be more prone to errors. Let's take a look at some of the biggest missteps and why they occur.

- **Do Once, Then Done**—Experts often say people who tiptoe into SEO think of it as something they do once, rather than as an ongoing strategy.

SEO and related content are fundamental to any online presence. Everyone who's contributing to the publishing process online—whether it's editorial or marketing—needs to be mindful of SEO, says Hearst's Gosch.

- **Focus on Paid Search**—Citi's Frank Eliason says that many times firms focus on paid search. The problem, he points out, is that search terms then get bid up a great deal. For example, take the term *credit cards*. Say a consumer—you—conducts a search for the best credit cards. Naturally, you want good, relevant content coming to the top so you can move on to find that card. But, Eliason says, too often the industry has been focused on paid search in which firms pay to buy a word or phrase—credit cards—so that when you perform that search, their firm's offer will appear first. This focus on paid ads, says Eliason, isn't helping the customer: "We're not good at thinking like a customer; we think more like a company." Better ways to think about search would be to consider why the customer is looking for a credit card in the first place: "I have a bill coming up," or, "I'm frustrated with an existing provider." By failing to think about the customer and focusing instead on paid search, firms will (a) spend more money and (b) fail to address specific consumer needs which could be addressed through free and/or educational content. See Figure 22.2.

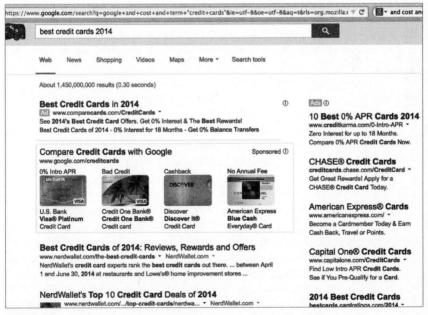

FIGURE 22.2 A Search for Credit Cards Reveals Many Paid Ads

■ **Low-Hanging Fruit**—Bill Winterberg, certified financial planner and
founder of financial tech news source FPPad, says another common
mistake is simply not addressing the low-hanging fruit. Examples of
simple mistakes that could be addressed quickly include:

  ■ Leveraging and sharing existing content, as discussed earlier.
  ■ Failing to take existing content and make it searchable. One example:
    failing to put text around images, which by their nature, cannot be
    found in search engines.
  ■ Having titles that don't get to the heart of the content or consumer's
    questions.

Now that we've talked about some of the mistakes when it comes to
being SEO-friendly, let's move on to how to make your content a friend of
search engines.

FIVE KEYS TO BUILDING SEO-FRIENDLY CONTENT

It's clear you don't need to be a rocket scientist—or a Googler—to know how
to make SEO-friendly content. But there are a few things you should know.
Some of it may be a bit technical, but we'll try to keep it to the main points.
Here are five keys to building SEO-friendly content:

1. **Improved Crawlability**—We know we don't want to crawl in today's
   fast-paced tech world, so we need to give our content some help.
   Crawlability refers to the ease with which a search engine can crawl
   and access your content. While search crawlers are always crawling for
   content, the goal is to make your site and content even more accessible.
       "You can have great content, but some technologies that power
   websites can impact crawlability," Gosch points out.
       Adding text around images and ensuring content is readable in the
   HTML code are a couple ways to build crawlability. "The crawler is the
   VIP, so get the red carpet out for him," says Gosch.
2. **On-Page Optimization**—Optimizing your site involves two elements:
   a. **Technical**—This is about ensuring you have the right tags in the
      source code of your web pages so that your relevant content can be
      discovered by consumers using search engines. This includes the title
      tag and various meta-tags as well as descriptive tags for images and
      content. Gosch says the title tag is the most important tag for rankings
      since it can be influenced by a publisher (website owner) directly. The
      words you use there do indeed matter as they can, in turn, lead those
      travelling the Web to find you online. See Figure 22.3.

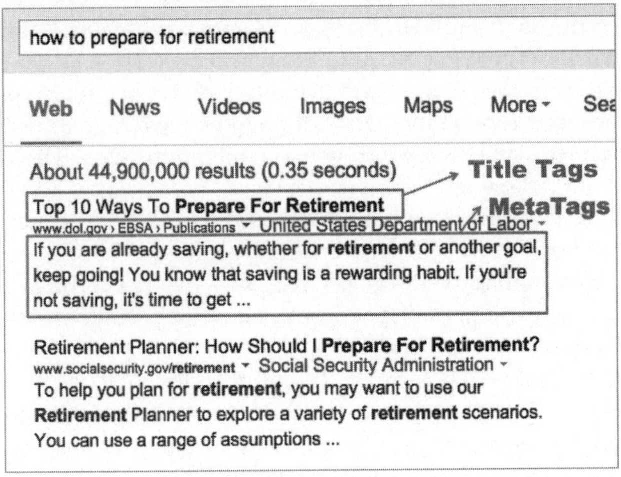


```
<head>
<title>Top 10 Ways To Prepare For Retirement</title>
<meta name="description" content="Description Here">
<meta http-equiv="content-type" content="text/html;charset=UTF-8">
</head>
```

FIGURE 22.3 How Title Tags and Meta-Tags Display on Search Engine and the Example of Meta Tags Code

b. **Editorial Content**—Once your pages (and the source code behind them) have the relevant tags available, you need to fill them with relevant editorial content. You may have heard about optimizing your site. On-page editorial is about optimizing your page content. Make sure your content is both visually and informationally appealing to your audience. The search engines appreciate this. Your site should be built for users and not search engines. Use videos and photos for an improved user experience, but make sure they are compliant with search engine requirements so that they, too, can be found.

3. **Content Strategy**—This is the heart of what we're talking about: creating and sharing content that people will consume—matching those *searching* for something with those who *have something* relevant to offer. Content can include not just old-fashioned text articles or blogs, but videos, audio, and even short content bursts shared in the social media world.
4. **Organic Link-Building**—Engaging with consumers or other target audiences isn't just about creating good content; it's about providing ways for them to find you. There are ways that you can build linkage across the

webosphere that will help bring you a greater potential audience and increase your presence in SEO results. Think about organic links—separate from those you might actually pay for—as recommendations; the more relevant quality links that point to your pages, the more likely your content will be shown to users searching for such. These strategies include the following:

- **RSS feeds**—Just about any content management system has the capability for an RSS feed enabling people to access your content regularly and automatically. Other sites might publish your feed on their pages and provide you links as a result. The RSS feed automatically adds a link to your blog.

- **Internal Links**—These are links within your content to other relevant writing you've created on your blog or website. Say you post a piece, "Top Dividend-Paying Stocks," but earlier you also produced a related article, "Stocks That Have Increased their Dividend;" feel free to reference the latter within the former.

- **Partner Links**—If a professional association, for example, asks for an article from you on a particular topic, ask for a link back to your site to be included when they publish it.

- **Other strategies**—These include the use of local directories, online public relations, and related online community activities such as guest blogging or posting.

(For more, you might read "Link Building Tactics," by Jon Cooper of PointBlank SEO.[1])

Gosch offers this warning about link-building: "If you do it wrong, the result will be the opposite of what you intended. If you have good content, you don't have to worry much, because the nature of the Web and the social nature will lead people to naturally find you." And that leads to our final point.

5. **Social Media**—Perhaps one of the best ways to help others find you and your content is to build and leverage your relationships through social media. In this case, it's about share-ability—can your friends, colleagues, customers, and others easily share and interact with your content? Follow not only some of the strategies and examples discussed in this book, but also remember *the power of nice*. Little things like reaching out to someone and commenting on their article or blog; offering help to someone you meet on LinkedIn or at an event; calling a customer or prospect who sent in some feedback—all of these random acts of kindness may well lead to more relationships and more references (links) to you or your firm.

---

[1]Jon Cooper, "Link Building Tactics—The Complete List," *PointBlankSEO*, April 1, 2012, http://pointblankseo.com/link-building-strategies.

MULTIPLE OFFICES? HOW A FIRM OR ADVISOR CAN REACH LOCALLY VIA SEO

Most would agree that not only do relationships matter in the online world, they matter locally—right at home where your clients or prospects live. So how can you reach them?

Sure, you can have a presence on Yelp or any number of directories, but let's take it a step further. See Figure 22.4.

Let's say you have offices in Denver, Seattle, and Chicago. You want people in those areas to find you if they search online. This is called geo-targeting, and it's why you need to get your business or organization into Google, says Gosch. There are a few ways to accomplish this:

- **Set up your site as a local business**—Include the local address with a map. If you have multiple offices, Gosch suggest creating separate sites for each office or subsites so you would individually optimize for each of them.

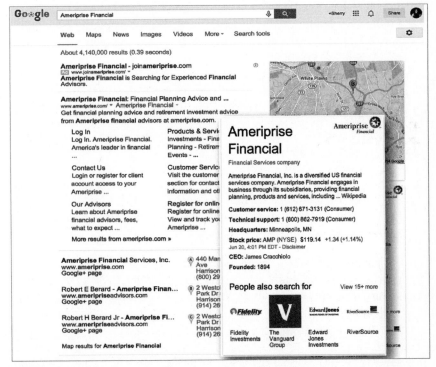

FIGURE 22.4 Create a Google+ Page to Increase SEO Results of Your Local Business

- **Create a Google+ page**—It's free and will help your firm appear in search, maps, mobile, and more. See Chapter 16 on Google+.
- **Get your site into directories**—The Yellow Pages is perhaps the most known. You'll want to be careful of the reputation of directories and be sure it is a good source. You might use MozLocal[2] to make sure you have listings in some of the highest quality sites, suggests Scott Landon of SEO firm HigherVisibility.
- **Become active in the local community**—Engage with your local audience and reflect your efforts in your content on your site.

WHEN TO HIRE HELP

So if all of this has you wondering if you can do it yourself, let us offer some guidance.

- **Small Firms, or Just Getting Started**—If you're a smaller firm operating a smaller site, most of this you can do yourself. The blogging platform WordPress has plug-ins that help you deploy the most important tags, for example. A small site would also be one that serves primarily as an online brochure about your firm with a way to contact you and perhaps schedule a call or appointment.
- **Large Firms, Large Sites**—For larger sites or sites that have been around for a long time or changed publishing systems, you probably need someone to review and understand your legacy systems and content. The larger a site becomes and the more people contributing to the content living on the site, the greater the need you have to build an effective SEO strategy.

  Remember, there's always work to be done because SEO is always changing. If you do want to get help, you can hire someone for as little as a few hundred dollars a month. Advisor David Edwards spent just $1,000 with an SEO expert who teaches at a college and found it made a big difference in his site's searchability.

Citi's Eliason already sees the next direction for SEO. In the recent past, best practices involved adding the right tags to content, tags that could help the content turn up more easily in Web searches. But increasingly, Eliason

---

[2]MozLocal (www.moz.com) creates and maintains business listings on the sites, apps, and directories that factor most into local search engine results.

says, it'll be more important to know what sort of content particular individuals are using in order to rank blog posts, articles, and other material for Web searches. As content becomes more sharable and accessible, consumers will be able to see what peer groups are reading, accessing, and even finding relevant.

Right now, that sort of SEO is not so easy in the financial world. "The focus in our industry has been on words, rather than on social media and people," says Eliason.

CHAPTER 23

How Can We Leverage Paid Social Media Promotions?

By now, it's clear that a social media presence is imperative to success in this bold new digitally competitive industry. And for good reason: In addition to establishing a respected brand and managing public perception of the company, social media creates bridges that lead you to audiences you've never touched before. And arguably one of the most appealing aspects of social media marketing is that it can all be done at surprisingly modest expense.

That said, once an advisor or firm has established a strong social media presence and taken full advantage of its myriad of free marketing methods, there is still plenty of juice to be squeezed from this enticing and potent fruit. Incorporating some paid social media promotions and advertisements into your social media campaigns is a great way to increase your impact and speed up your success.

WHY PAID PROMOTIONS MAY BE BENEFICIAL

The fact is, paid social media has leveled the playing field a bit. It allows advisors and asset managers alike to reach fresh audiences previously considered beyond their reach, whether it was due to prohibitive advertising costs or ineffective, uncertain distribution methodologies. That means paid social media is every bit as effective for the smallest of businesses as it is for the biggest names on the Fortune 500 list.

When using paid social advertisements, not only will your name and brand gain even greater recognition and credibility, but you'll also be exposed to new, qualified audiences you've never before reached. Other significant benefits include increased website traffic, a broadened social media network, a longer list of ideal followers, and countless opportunities for spreading online word-of-mouth referrals.

What's more, when compared to traditional—and more costly—advertising routes such as newspaper ads and TV or radio spots that use something of a shotgun approach (essentially shooting your message out to a massive audience, hoping it hits at least some of your target prospects), paid social media offers advisors and firms two powerful points of leverage:

- Pinpoint access to your precisely targeted audience
- Affordable options to fit almost any organization's budget

How is this possible? No matter which platform you choose—Facebook, LinkedIn, or Twitter—they all capture valuable information about each user. The data includes not only demographic information such as age, gender, location, and businesses to which investors and industry pros are connected, but also pyschographic data like relationship status, hobbies and interests, family life, job titles, professions, and so on. In addition to all of this helpful prospecting info, Twitter has gone one step beyond the competition by introducing keyword filters, which allow you to drill down even deeper by filtering site subscribers for those who often use specific keywords and targeting your ad directly at them. So if you try filtering by "#invest" or "#retirement," you'll uncover prospects who already have your topics of expertise on the brain. This is clearly an extremely powerful and effective way to ensure your message is delivered only to people who match your specified criteria.

As for the paid aspect of this strategy, your expenses are minimal because each of these sites offers pay-per-click advertising and posts. This gives you the option to pay only if your ad is clicked on, or, if you're using Twitter, you only pay if your ad is replied to, retweeted, or favorited. Additionally, each platform allows you to control how much you spend on paid ads and promotions by using what's known as the bid system. By setting your daily budget for each platform you use, the bid system ensures you'll never pay anything beyond what you're comfortable spending. Once you've maxed out your daily budget, your ad simply stops running.

STEPS TOWARD STARTING YOUR PAID SOCIAL MEDIA CAMPAIGN

Paid promotions will expand your reach and ultimately generate prospects for you when done strategically. Here are a few things to consider when diving in to the paid social media space.

- **Determine which platform will give you the biggest bang for your buck**—Before you begin, set your marketing goals to determine which social media network you want to use. As with any marketing campaign, the tools you use to employ paid social media will be determined by your overall goals. Once you've identified these goals, you can select the best social media platform or platforms to ensure your campaign succeeds. Looking to attract more local followers? Then Facebook and/or Twitter might be good tools for reaching this goal. Trying to promote an event to a specific level of business professional? Perhaps LinkedIn would be best for such an endeavor. Just because you are active on all three, doesn't mean you need to advertise on all three. That being said, if your campaign will benefit from exposure on each of these platforms, then tailor your message for each site and promote across all networks.
- **Develop informative, intriguing content**—Because it is free and accessible to pretty much everyone, the social media marketplace is saturated with information, ads, comments, and more. Rather than adding to that clutter, you must elevate and distinguish yourself from the general online jumble, and smart paid social media promotions and advertisements can do just that—but only if you have the right content. Nobody will click on or share an ad or post just because they happen upon it, but they will click on ads and posts that speak directly to their interests or needs. To ensure you get the best results from your paid social media marketing, make sure your promotions include attention-grabbing headlines, enticing images, and above all, powerful calls to action.
- **Plot out your cross-promotion strategy**—Paid ads and promotions can be incredibly beneficial to your organization, serving as a full complement to all your other marketing endeavors. Determine how you can incorporate your social media ads and promos in other marketing venues such as e-mails, wherein you can include links to these ads and posts. Your web site is another great place to cross-promote with your paid social media marketing efforts, as you can easily add your most successful posts and ads to your site and encourage people to share them.

NETWORK-SPECIFIC ADVICE

As we mentioned earlier, each platform has its own capabilities and targeting methods when it comes to paid promotions and advertisements. Make sure

that you understand your options beforehand, so you are not inefficiently spending marketing funds. Below are a few network specific tips:

- **Use Facebook and LinkedIn ads to attract a bigger following and expand brand awareness**—Arguably the most popular of all the social media platforms, Facebook sells advertisements (which appear in prospects' newsfeeds and on the top right side of their screens) that can be very effective in generating both brand awareness and ideal prospects, and those prospects are based on quality over quantity. The same precision targeting can also be achieved with LinkedIn, where you're also able to choose your audience based on broad categories like Parents or Baby Boomers, as well as any hashtagged interests. This is an unparalleled way for advisors to reach people in certain age groups and locales, as well as for asset managers to locate professionals with a specific industry expertise.

  So, if you've written an informative and actionable article on college financial planning strategies, your Facebook and LinkedIn ads can be configured so they appear only on the pages of both men and women in your city or region with children between the ages of 4 and 18.

- **Complement Facebook and LinkedIn ads with promoted posts**—A promoted Facebook or LinkedIn post ensures other consumers will see your post, in addition to your existing Facebook fans or LinkedIn connections, making it a powerful tool in its own right. It can become an even stronger tool when paired with your other ads. Promoted posts on Facebook and LinkedIn will appear directly in your target prospects' newsfeeds, which expands your reach tremendously, as anyone who goes to a prospect's page will also see your promoted posts.

  With Facebook, you have two options to promote posts:

  1. You can elect to promote your post to a very finely-tuned target audience just as with their ads.
  2. You can promote your post to friends of individuals who already like your page.

  Again, anytime another user sees a post from a company one of their friends likes, it only serves to reinforce your credibility and generate what's known as social word-of-mouth marketing.

- **Twitter ads can benefit your bottom line and deliver word-of-mouth future clients**—In Twitter's platform, the most common ad is called a promoted tweet. Promoted tweets are essentially regular tweets that appear in the newsfeeds of users well beyond your current network of followers. Additionally, even though these users may not be following you directly, they can still re-tweet your post, reply to it, or favorite it. This is a way to grow your social community of followers very quickly, all while leaving impressions on new investors you couldn't access previously.

The goal of these advertisements and promotions is to increase your social media footprint in the most efficient and effective way possible. To make sure you are doing so, it is important to track and measure the success rates of all paid campaigns, just as you would with any direct mail, e-mail, or radio campaign. Each major platform has its own set of analytics tools for you to gauge how well each ad or post has performed. This is a wonderful way to duplicate your most successful pieces—simply use older and proven-effective content, ads, or posts as templates for creating similar but new content to promote. These analytics tools will also reveal what time or day of the week you get the most traction for posting, so you can ensure you sync your paid social media efforts with your target audience's online activity.

There no question that a well-planned paid social media marketing campaign offers a variety of new benefits, but if you have some trepidation about taking the plunge, Facebook, Twitter, and LinkedIn all offer detailed tutorials and guides to using their paid social media tools. These advertisement methods are constantly changing and evolving, so specific platform guides can help you stay on top of your options. You can also turn to a professional social media company to help craft and outline a winning paid social media strategy on your behalf.

CHAPTER 24

How Do We Avoid Copyright Problems?

One of the key social media strategies we've outlined in this book is the creation of blogs, articles, and other content that allows financial professionals to engage with many people at one time. Such writing helps establish your brand as a thought leader, which can deepen relationships with existing clients and help attract outside investors to your business. Financial bloggers, for example, frequently comment on things they see elsewhere on the Internet: an interesting article in a magazine or newspaper website, even a post on another blog.

If you are writing your own content, however, you need to take care. The extent to which you use material from outside sources may cross a line. Replicating other people's material in your own blog requires attention to detail, proportion, and a sense of fairness.

Remember, the content that you read elsewhere on the Internet often is protected by copyright laws. Wholesale duplication of someone else's material without attribution—and sometime even with attribution—is plagiarism.

You can't just cut and paste something from another site, for example, and post it on your own blog. And it's an easy mistake to make if you're not conscious of it while you're writing.

MASTERING THE RULES OF FAIR USE

What if you attribute the source of the material and cite where it came from? After all, a key point of blogging is to generate a conversation among like-minded people where ideas are shared, explored, and often criticized, with an eye toward clarifying issues and sometimes reaching consensus. Every day you can find bloggers commenting on developments around the world. What's the harm?

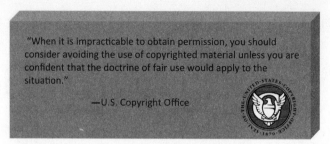

FIGURE 24.1   A Quote from U.S. Copyright Office

A public interest certainly exists in these kinds of interactions. Nevertheless, limits still exist on how other people's writing may be used toward that end. It's called the concept of fair use, and its aim is to strike a middle ground between free speech and the rights of writers to protect their work from infringement.

The University of Minnesota provides a good breakdown of fair use concepts[1] on one of its websites. Keep in mind that experts say that no one factor can be decisive; all criteria has to be considered. (By the way, the university provides an online tool[2] to help writers evaluate whether using material in a certain fashion violates fair use.)

Here are three key points to keep in mind at the moment you sit down in front of your computer and start crafting your piece based on material that you've read elsewhere. Remember that these are guidelines, and circumstances and context govern whether you've crossed a line (see Figure 24.1):

- **In what way are you using the material?** Commercial and for-profit uses are viewed unfavorably; while not-for-profit purposes, education, scholarship, research, news reporting, criticism, and commentary are generally more acceptable.
- **How much material are you using?** One of the standards for measuring whether fair use crosses into infringement is the amount and percentage of the written work that makes its way into your blog. Generally speaking, the less material you use, the less likely you're crossing a line. (But the proportion of what you're using matters, too; it's harder to argue fair use if you're reproducing just a few hundred words of a work that's not much more than that in its complete length.)

---

[1]"Understanding Fair Use," University of Minnesota, Copyright Information and Resources, https://www.lib.umn.edu/copyright/fairuse.
[2]"Thinking Through Fair Use," University of Minnesota, Copyright Information and Resources, https://www.lib.umn.edu/copyright/fairthoughts.

■ **What kind of material are you using?** Another important fair use concept is how substantial the borrowed material is in relation to the complete written work. Reproducing from the heart of the work, the University of Minnesota says, is more of a problem than reproducing something that's more peripheral within the work.

STANDARDS FOR USING PHOTOS AND GRAPHICS

The rules governing the borrowing of written content also apply to photos and graphics. Financial advisors who face budget challenges and are tempted to copy a stock photo off Google Images or elsewhere on the Internet for use on their own website or in marketing materials should be warned: You can easily face a $1,000 fine as a result of a copyright violation. Photos typically are the biggest source of offense.

The culture of the Web and the nature of sharing thoughts, pictures, and other material on social sites have contributed to some of the misunderstanding over how much borrowing can be done. When everyone shares, there's sometimes a belief at some level that the material belongs to everyone. Make no mistake: There is only one true owner, and it's the individual who created the material in the first place. You can no more appropriate another person's creative work wholesale than you can drive off with the person's automobile when they've left the keys in the car.

The good news is there are simple rules that financial professionals can keep in mind to avoid legal entanglements with images:[3]

■ **Know what's protected.** From the moment of its creation, any original graphic image, photograph, or design automatically enjoys copyright protection.
■ **Someone else's license isn't yours.** Someone on the Internet may be sharing an image to which they have rights, but the mere act of sharing doesn't transfer those rights to you or anyone else.
■ **Seek permission.** When you've come across exactly the right image for your next marketing campaign, take the next step and obtain the owner's approval to use it. You want to ensure you have whatever licenses are necessary, and remember to credit the photographer or designer in your own work.
■ **Linking doesn't cut it.** It's a common misconception: You can use the photo as long as you link to its source. It's not so; attaching a link as a

---

[3]Helpful information about image copyright rules and how to license stock photos can be found at www.stockphotorights.com.

citation for the source is totally different from having the right to reproduce the photo.

- **Consider free or low-cost images.** Good news: there are many online firms that offer such photos and graphics, and you will be pleasantly surprised at the quality of the material. Here are a few sites:
  - Shutterstock.com. A subscription service that's good if you have continuous need for stock images.
  - morgueFile (free)
  - Microsoft Images (free)
  - freeimages (free)
  - RGB Stock (free)
  - iStock. Purchase credits on this site to download images.

Good-quality images always improve the overall excellence of marketing content, which leads to greater engagement with you target audience. But just as advisors are obliged to comply with federal and state regulations in the course of their business, they also need to know how to use text and images in the course of their marketing efforts.

The good news is you easily can achieve your goals in this part of your business without running afoul of copyright.

CHAPTER **25**

How Do We Track and Defend Our Reputation on Social Media?

I talked at the beginning of the book about a Boston-based firm. We were meeting with the head of the advisor network, the chief marketing officer, and others, talking about the opportunities with social media.

Then, the head of customer service piped up and asked, "Why would we want to be on social media when people can say things that hurt your brand?"

The CMO instantly chimed in, "It's happening anyway. This is a way to manage our brand."

I thought to myself, "Wow, she really gets it. I can understand his fear, but isn't it more worrisome to have hundreds or thousands of customers out there, saying things about you or your products, and you're not aware of it? Does turning your eyes away help? Or does it actually create more risk, leaving you vulnerable to the day when something big will happen, and you'll be totally unprepared for how to address it?"

Failure to use social media in some way poses a greater risk—a risk that your reputation will be shaped by the conversations happening out there, conversations that are led by others, not by you. The new online world presents an opportunity to know what's being said, and to manage it. How you respond says a great deal about your firm and its leaders.

The old adage—In business, your reputation is your livelihood—is perhaps more accurate today than at any other time in history. No business or profession—including advisors and planners—can expect to thrive and remain relevant in today's fast-paced and tech-savvy world without maintaining a strong web presence. In fact, the Internet has become such an integral component of daily life that consumers rely on it for just about everything, and that includes researching advisors and planners like you. So, developing and keeping a dynamic online strategy is absolutely crucial to creating a reputable brand. This means that in addition to keeping an active and engaging website, you must also take advantage of other web-based referral and marketing sources like blogs, LinkedIn, Twitter, Facebook, and other online media.

Yet despite the obvious benefits of a well-rounded online and social media strategy, some advisors remain hesitant to use these online tools due to one simple but frightening possibility: You can't control what's being said about you in cyberspace, and that could potentially threaten the reputation you worked so hard to build. This makes the Internet something of a double-edged sword—not only does it allow you to promote your brand easily, but it also affords your clients, prospects, and even competitors the ability to express their thoughts about you or your organization just as easily.

KEY METHODS TO MANAGE AND ENHANCE YOUR WEB PRESENCE

Managing an online strategy and reputation can become even more of a challenge for financial industry professionals and leaders, as there are barriers preventing advisors from interacting on the Web in ways professionals in other industries can, with great ease and virtually no restrictions. In fact, this is a common excuse advisors often pull out to avoid getting engaged in social media and digital marketing, but conversations are already happening and judgments are being formed regardless of whether you are online to manage them, so why not err on the side of caution? After all, even the smallest stain on your record is fair game, from a poor comment on a review site to a negative newspaper editorial, and it can appear anywhere on the Web, threatening your business's online reputation. So what, if anything, can you do about it?

Here are some steps to take:

- **Set an Alert for Yourself**—In order to handle occurrences immediately, you need to know what is being said about you and your firm so you can take action as swiftly as possible to offset the negativity. In addition to regularly running a search on your name and your company's name through Google to see what shows up on the all-important first page, try setting up Google Alerts for yourself and your company (see Figure 25.1). These alerts will help keep you regularly apprised of any new information posted about you. Alerts will also give you a head-start in crafting your response to a particular posting. It's also worth checking out Mention .com, another great site for finding more in-depth social media posts and conversations that Google Alerts may miss. When it comes to your reputation, you don't want to leave anything to chance.

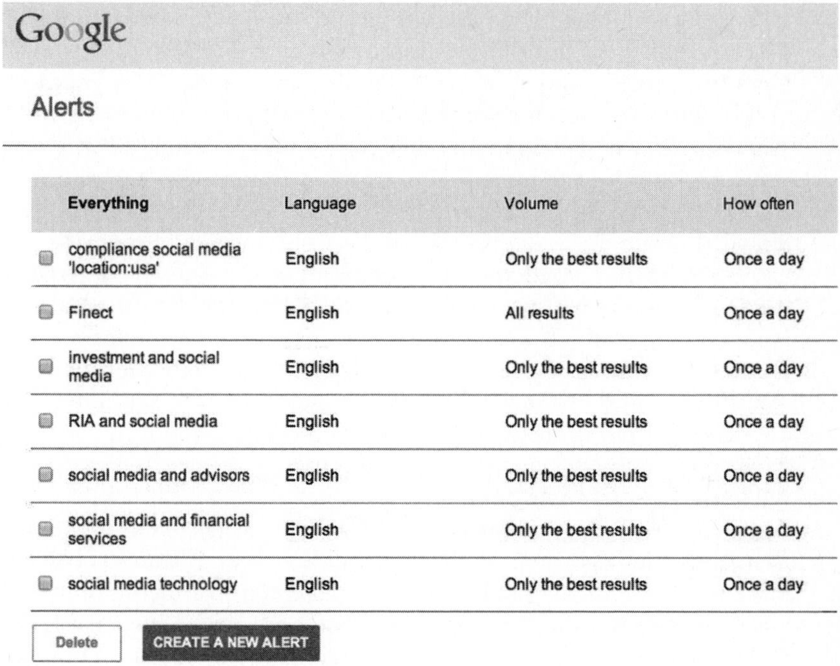

Google

Alerts

Everything	Language	Volume	How often
compliance social media 'location:usa'	English	Only the best results	Once a day
Finect	English	All results	Once a day
investment and social media	English	Only the best results	Once a day
RIA and social media	English	Only the best results	Once a day
social media and advisors	English	Only the best results	Once a day
social media and financial services	English	Only the best results	Once a day
social media technology	English	Only the best results	Once a day

Delete   CREATE A NEW ALERT

FIGURE 25.1   Set Up Google Alerts

- **Put a Powerful Social Media System in Place**—If you want to keep criticism at bay, one of the best ways is by managing your reputation in a way that puts your best social media foot forward. In addition to maintaining a dynamic website, be sure to keep a comprehensive company profile alive on as many relevant social media platforms as you can, and create and stick to a content deployment schedule. These practices, along with your website and blog, will together weave a portrait of who you and your company are because they allow you to exhibit the positive persona you want your online reputation to embody. And the more active you are, the more likely you are to appear among the top listings on popular search engines. It's really quite simple: Having more social profiles and by-lined content appear on the first page of a Google search simply leaves less room for the odd nugget of negativity to overwhelm what's otherwise a stellar reputation.
- **Blog and Blog Again**—Your website should feature an advisor blog that you rely on to share helpful information and keep your business top of mind, but you can also use that blog to generate positive stories and buzz

about your firm. Not only is the blog on your website a great resource for developing content that only you control, but it also provides outstanding search engine optimization. Make certain you capitalize on these opportunities to craft original content that speaks to who you are, what you do, and why you do it, and that you're always putting out original content that is a genuine reflection of the trustworthy expert you are. Again, the more content you share on the Web, the stronger your intended image on search results will be.

If you're ever faced with a reputation crisis, redouble your social media efforts. Try writing two blogs posts a week instead of just one and see if you can contribute to your partners' sites or online industry trade journals as a guest. Remember to include lots of links back to your website and use those long-tail keywords to get your blog and website to appear at the top of the search results. As a rule, the more content you have online, the better chance you have at pushing negative reflections off the initial search results page.

- **Always Know What Profiles You Have Set Up**—You should only create as many profiles as you have the time and resources to manage, but the more you have, the more likely you will get wind of criticism on social media. Sometimes there are pages on the Internet with your name on them, and you might not even be aware that they exist. Take for example, Google+. When you set up a Google+ Local Business Page, it automatically creates a Google Places Profile for you. You need to make sure that these pages are up to date. A good way to do that is by, again, searching for yourself online. Go through the first few pages of results and make sure they are first and foremost pages you are aware of, and secondly, complete with accurate information.
- **Consider Using a Reputation Management Service**—If you'd rather pay someone to keep track of your Internet appearances and online reputation, consider hiring a professional company do it for you. Companies like socialmention.com and reputation.com will monitor the Web for posts about you, and many of them will develop original content for your website or blog by tailoring a strategy that meets both your business and budget needs.
- **Have a Pre-Approved Response Ready to Go**—If there's a chance someone does say something unfavorable online, you may want to be ready to respond quickly, so that you can avoid any further issues. Have a general response pre-scripted and approved by your compliance team, so that if an issue arises, you don't have to wait days to respond. Most upset and irritated comments are better dealt with sooner rather than later.

DUKING IT OUT IN THE SOCIAL WORLD

We've talked about some ways to manage your reputation. Don't forget that building a positive reputation is all about transparency: Companies that have issues to hide may well be more susceptible to the negative reputation impact that operating in the social media world might bring.

But what do you do when something negative actually occurs online between parties? When do you move something offline—perhaps in a live phone conversation—versus engaging in a back-and-forth diatribe online, which can leave a permanent negative footprint?

As one example, marketing manager Sherry created a compelling article and infographic on women and wealth, carefully citing sources of various statistics and obtaining her boss's review before posting and sharing it on social media. Unfortunately, a thought leader with a major international company (with thousands of followers) commented through Twitter that perhaps the infographic was "inadvertently sexist." Specifically, Sherry was told that she was stereotyping women when she suggested they are more interested in topics such as babies and fashion. See Figure 25.2. Now, it's easy for anyone to make even a slightly negative comment since, after all, it's controversy that makes news—and generates followers! Still, no one likes anything negative.

FIGURE 25.2 A Keyword Cloud—Featured in a Graphic—Highlights the Terms Women Search for Online

What did Sherry do in this situation?

- Reply to the primary comment in a personalized and thoughtful way. Sherry replied by thanking her for the comment and explaining that she hadn't seen it that way. Her transparency led the person who left the comment to start following her.
- Sherry also replied directly to all others who commented on the original comment.
- Finally, Sherry avoided trying to act defensive or challenge their views. Instead, she took it as an opportunity to take feedback and build new relationships.

However, depending on the issue, it may make sense to obtain the contact information of someone and have a direct phone conversation rather than hashing something out in the social media world. Then, once the parties come to an understanding, a proper comment or new post can then be shared online, perhaps even incorporating the original commenter.

To maintain an untarnished reputation as an expert in this constantly evolving profession, you have to jump in to social media with both feet. Granted, it does take work and time, but in an era where news travels faster now than ever before, you must maintain a bold online presence if you hope to stay competitive. And if your reputation does take a hit from a negative comment, take the time to digest it and decide what actions you'll take to remedy the issue, but then move on and leave it in your past. Spend your energy repopulating the Web with content only you control, and you'll be back on top in no time.

CHAPTER 26

How Can We Use Social Media to Promote Our Events?

Consider the bad old days of public relations. If your financial firm had news of an event or an important hire, it would prepare a press release that it would e-mail or snail-mail to area newspaper editors and other local media. You would cross your fingers and hope the editors would publish it and provide you with the attention you craved from their audiences.

Some firms are still doing publicity that way, but the world is changing rapidly. The good news is that social media is providing alternatives to old-school PR practices in ways that help drive brand awareness and amplify your core message—as well as introduce you to new investor clients. You don't have to rely on gatekeepers to promote your message about your next event or a new service offering at your practice.

CREATE A SHAREABLE STORY

The first step in the process is crafting your story. What you say about your news, and the way you say it, will bear heavily on the success you have in trying to share it. It must be written in a way that makes people want to read it.

So consider the Four Cs as you sit down to write your story:

1. **Clarity.** Every story has a point. Every good story makes the point clear and doesn't force the readers to scratch their heads to understand what you're getting at.
2. **Compelling.** Why should people care about this? Give them a reason to take an interest in what you're saying. What's in it for them? How would they benefit from knowing your message?
3. **Concise.** Readers are busy and getting busier. The professionals who understand this will respect their audience's time, and craft their message in the most trenchant manner possible.

4. **Consistency.** This is easy to get wrong. When you're promoting an event or other similar PR activity across multiple media, your message has to maintain similar visuals, titles, and reasons someone should attend, regardless of whom you're conveying it to. Are you saying the same thing on your website that you are in your press release? Are you sending different messages to different media? You don't want to blur your brand.

HOW TO FIND INFLUENCERS

Now that you have a story or event to share, you need to find someone to share it with who will help you get the word out. Welcome to the world of *influencers*—people who have a following in social media and can influence the way issues are discussed. These include the usual suspects such as editors in local media, but they also include local thought leaders such as fellow professionals or investors with a point of view. Building an online relationship with them can help your chances that they will share news of your activities with their own followers.

A key first step is to review the articles and other materials your influencers have published online. You want to share your own point of view about what they're saying on their platform. You can even ask if they would be willing to provide a point of view that you can use in your own story (which, of course, you would source back to them).

There are several methods for finding leaders and influencers via social media, depending on which platform they use. The three key channels—LinkedIn, Twitter, and Facebook—all have their own playbooks for obtaining the best results. Let's look at each one in turn.

For LinkedIn

LinkedIn Groups consist of members of the platform who share common interests. They typically are built around themes or sponsors, and are a great way to locate influencers in a particular industry. In financial services some good ones are:

- *Financial Advisor* Magazine[1]
- Financial Advisor Network[2]
- Compliance & Audit Professionals in Banking and Financial Services[3]

---

[1]https://www.linkedin.com/groups/Financial-Advisor-Magazine-2220033.
[2]https://www.linkedin.com/groups/Financial-Advisor-Network-FAN-54278.
[3]https://www.linkedin.com/groups/Compliance-Audit-Professionals-in-Banking-4021725.

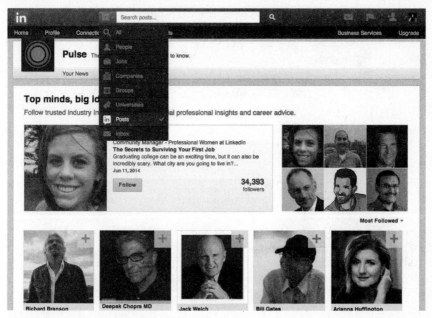

FIGURE 26.1   LinkedIn Influencers

LinkedIn Influencers allows thought leaders to share content directly with users. Articles can be searched by keyword that will take you to another page that will show you the authors of pieces using those keywords. See Figure 26.1.

For Twitter

- Use the Search function to query keywords and industry publications, such as @ThinkAdvisor (for *ThinkAdvisor* magazine) and @NEWSfromIN (for *Investment News*). Once you find the industry publications, navigate to their lists and you will likely find their journalists and editors. See Figure 26.2.
- Follow hashtags for events and people related to your media goals.
- External apps such as Simply Measured (http://simplymeasured.com), Followerwonk (http://followerwonk.com), and InkyBee (www.inkybee .com) use Twitter Analytics to help you gather information on thought leaders.

FIGURE 26.2 Twitter Influencers

For Facebook

Now that you've found these influencers and media resources on LinkedIn and Twitter, use Facebook search to seek out these same industry leaders. Being connected on multiple networks will expand your reach.

While you're at it, research and join industry-relevant Facebook groups. In the search window type: "Groups named [keyword]."

INFLUENCERS: A NEW MINDSET

Creating your lists of influencers and joining related groups is just the beginning. The biggest change from old-school PR to the more modern age is a shift in your mindset—instead of constantly pitching story ideas and releases to local editors, you build connections with influencers. You do this by being truly engaged in what they are posting on their sites:

- **Repost their content.** If you Tweet about someone's content and mention them, for example, they can retweet you. This expands your post to their (larger) group of followers.
- **Leave comments.** You can leave comments on their posts or send non-spam messages directly to them via their social sites. Start conversations and develop a rapport.
- **Share their events with your own followers.**
- **Set up a Google Alert for key influencers.** This will help you stay on top of what's happening with them.

Finally, if you do ever use a quote or example from an influencer in your content, make sure you not only give them credit, but tag them and tweet at them when you share it. This will encourage sharing on their part as well, further boosting your reach.

IT'S NOT JUST ABOUT TEXT

Just as public relations has evolved, so too has the way we share news. Make your news stand out by crafting content beyond words. Consider posting your newsworthy content accompanied by graphics, video, images, a podcast, or a pre-recorded webinar.

Remember, consistency is key. Journalists and influencers get tons of pitches every single day; if your pitch is not relevant in that moment, it doesn't mean they are not interested. Developing a rapport can keep you top-of-mind for when that magical media moment can happen.

PROMOTING YOUR EVENTS VIA SOCIAL MEDIA

Putting on a local event—a panel discussion on economic trends, or something social such as a wine and cheese party—is a classic strategy for advisors and managers to broaden their reach among clients and potential investors. In fact, Fisher Investments conducts regular networking events so that clients can network among each other in local areas.

Yet the work can be daunting: setting a topic, a date and location, a budget, lining up potential speakers, and of course, promoting it far and wide. The proper use of social media can really make a difference. Here's how to do it.

Prior to the Event

- Define your marketing budget for the event.
- Consider a partner to join you—a local publication, firm, or nonprofit—to help spread the word.
- Create a video promoting the event that you can post on the landing page of your website and forward via e-mail and social networks.
- Identify a list of current clients who live locally and should be at the top of the invitation list. Reach out to them on social media. A client who is enthusiastic about what you're planning is more likely to want to share the news with his own followers than would a stranger.
- Define a hashtag and take care to employ it over multiple social media platforms:
  - When crafting an ideal hashtag, we recommend RUSS (Relevant, Unique, Short, and Sweet).
  - To generate buzz just before the event, pass your hashtag along to your invited guests and ask them to share it with their followers.
  - Create a Twitter list and keep tables on people using your hashtag. These are the folks you want to stay in conversation with.

    As an example, I partnered with *Financial Advisor* (FA) magazine to execute an idea for a Compliant Social Media Summit for financial professionals. Our efforts led to a surprising 700 registered professionals, far more than expected. As part of the effort, we executed a number of key activities, including the following (see Figure 26.3):
  - Created a unique hashtag: #compliantSM.
  - Asked speakers to tweet out registration info using the hashtag.
  - Promoted the event by highlighting—in a quick, engaging way—very specific issues the speakers would address.

FIGURE 26.3 Hashtag Promotion

- Identified the relevant LinkedIn groups with appropriated audiences.
- Posted the event info with a direct link to sign-up in relevant LinkedIn groups.
- Shared it with our own list of customers and partners.
- Worked with FA magazine to ensure they, too, promoted it.

Promoting the Event

- Start this part of the process one and a half to two months before the event; offer prizes or other incentives for people who sign up earliest.
- Create an event page that outlines all of the key details. This page can appear on your website using a service such as EventBrite, or try Facebook Events (https://www.facebook.com/events/list).
- Give some thought to what sort of data you'd like to obtain (something besides just a name and e-mail address). This is an opportunity to gather valuable demographic info: website, a guest's role in his company, the size of his company, the social media channels he uses—so you can follow back—and how he heard about the event.
- For Facebook events: After the event page is created, make sure to go into Facebook as yourself (not the business), say that you are attending the event, and then invite all of your connections personally.

     Facebook and LinkedIn's hyper-targeted ad platforms offer good promotional opportunities. You can target by zip code, age, gender, likes/interests, and many other factors. Don't forget to use your hashtag here, too. Record your activities in a spreadsheet and adjust as necessary.

     When promoting an event via social media, identify any professional allies that could help the effort. It can be useful to collaborate with a partner in the community who has a similar reach to yours, but not an exact one. Think CPA, estate planning attorney, real estate agent, and so on.

Consider a series of e-mails when reaching out to potential guests in this fashion: a registration e-mail, a confirmation e-mail, a reminder e-mail, a follow-up e-mail, and a lead-nurturing e-mail (about your company, with a call to action).

Provide pre-written tweets using your hashtag in all of your e-mails. Check out ClicktoTweet.com (http://clicktotweet.com), a platform for Twitter promotions, to create links.

Encourage current clients to invite appropriate, interested friends and family to the event. And if there is going to be a theme for the event—Estate Planning, for example—source and share specific blog articles regarding that topic for the month leading up to your event.

During the Event

- In your opening introduction, mention your social networks and encourage people to connect and share during the event.
- Using presentation slides? Include your Twitter handle and hashtag.
- Include social media icons and the event hashtag on any event signage.
- People like to see themselves on social media. Take pictures while the event is going on and pass it along on your social networks.
- Tell your guests to share comments on social media using your hashtag, and stream live updates in a public area.

After the Event

- The work doesn't end once the guests leave the premises (online or offline). Indeed, this could be the most crucial part of the process.
- Using your social media channels or a short e-mail, follow up with people you met and chatted with individually.
- Collecting business cards? Use them to set up LinkedIn connections.
- Use your event to generate future content:
  - Blogs (or long-form LinkedIn posts)—Turn breakout session topics into a series of posts.
  - Images—Take photos and short videos and post them during and after the event.
  - Videos —Turn any videotaped sessions into an on-demand webinar or a promotion for your next event or testimonial.

Events are a great way to engage with new clients and build on existing ones. They are powerful for that one-to-one dialogue and visual connection that can't always happen online. Events may not always make sense, but if they do, be sure to take advantage of the many ways to give them legs. With a little planning, your event can be buzz-worthy and organically shared with lots of new potential attendees using the power of social media.

CHAPTER 27

Do We Need a Social Media Manager?

By now, establishing a social and digital media presence and campaign has transformed from a question of "Should I?" into "How do I?" But as we've learned, implementing one of these plans requires knowledge of not only the variety of social media platforms and how to use them, but also how best to leverage these sites to achieve your desired results. Marketing is crucial to any organization, whether it be a single independent advisor, a large asset management firm, or even an association, and social marketing has become something your consumers (both investors and advisors alike) have come to expect. If you don't have a social or digital media presence, your competitors likely do—and you risk losing market share.

Asset management firms typically have an easier row to hoe, since they often have a much larger marketing budget, but individual advisors must also invest in marketing. At this point, many of you may be asking, "But isn't the beauty of social media marketing based on the logic that it's more or less free?"

While the simple answer is yes—many powerful social media avenues can be capitalized upon for nary a cent—it doesn't take into account all the man-hours required to make it successful. Let's explore some ways you can determine if hiring a social media manager is best, or if you're better off to manage it yourself.

SO WHAT DOES A SOCIAL MEDIA MANAGER DO?

You may be surprised at just how many hats an ace social media manager wears, especially one working in the financial services industry. In addition to monitoring and supervising your everyday social media activities, they're responsible for managing your client relationships and your brand. Sometimes, depending on the nature of your business, these efforts get support from others within the company, such as those working in traditional client servicing. And of course, you can also design this position to fulfill any of your industry- or goal-specific needs.

Primary responsibilities of a social media manager include:

- **Creating content**—Just as with any form of marketing, the quality of content determines its success. But in addition to creating original content, your social media manager must also be able to adapt, vary, and repurpose content for certain networks or platforms, such as taking one posting concept and then applying it to other major social networking platforms, including the ability to take a complex concept and whittle it down to a 140-character tweet. This person should also have the skills to create images to complement posts.
- **Spreading the news**—In this industry, relevant news stories are constantly breaking, so your social media manager must be able to sort through it all to identify the pieces most salient to your audience and then create content around it. In addition to regularly taking the industry pulse and reacting to changes in social networks, your social media manager should also have PR experience so they can introduce you to editors and media outlets looking for experts on certain topics, both of which should ultimately lead to an expanded reach.
- **Analyzing marketing efforts**—A good social media manager will be able to provide you with detailed analytics on your social media endeavors, such as supported customer cases, leads cultivated and generated, and your overall reach. They should also actively test new content or campaign strategies, analyze the data, and then take action based on what they've learned.
- **Facilitating the growth of your community**—Simply having followers or fans does not a community make. Real communities interact with and engage each other, so your social media manager should be able to ask questions and plant discussions to encourage this kind of interaction, as well as monitor the community for spammers. This skill can prove tremendously powerful, as a recent MSI study revealed that increased community engagement can lead to as much as a 25 percent spike in revenue.
- **Performing customer service**—The person who fills your social media manager role will represent your firm to everyone from potential clients, customers, or recruits, to fans and media representatives. Consequently, they'll likely be deluged with questions and comments regarding everything from your company's services and products to its culture and ideals, so they need to be able to deal with a variety of personalities and

communicate well with people in different buying stages, such as researchers, prospects and clients.

- **Managing and funneling leads**—In addition to launching content and campaigns aimed at lead generation, social media managers must also be able to engage with potential clients or recruits directly and identify which require further cultivation to deliver them the appropriate content. They must also be able to articulate the benefits of your services or products with ease.
- **Cognizant about compliance**—It's not enough in the financial space to know the nuts and bolts of social media. A social media manager also needs a deep understanding of the regulatory rules as they apply to the particular sector of their business, be it brokerage, registered investment advisor (RIA), or financial advisor in the retail-banking sector. Regulation has been a constant in the industry for decades, and key agencies have been issuing guidance about social media use in recent years. A social media manager must know these rules cold.

All of these qualities are ideal in a social media manager, considering that more than half of businesses report acquiring a customer from Facebook, 40 percent acquired clients through LinkedIn, and more than 35 percent have gotten clients from Twitter.

HOW CAN ADVISORS AND ASSET MANAGERS FURTHER BENEFIT FROM HIRING A SOCIAL MEDIA MANAGER?

Having a qualified person as your social media manager can benefit an advisor's business or an asset management firm's bottom line in a number of other ways:

- Ensure your social media efforts maintain a unified voice and consistent message.
- Boost your search engine optimization (SEO) by already knowing how to incorporate SEO into content that's attractive to search engines.
- Serve as a liaison with other departments to create, develop, and oversee marketing and promotional campaigns.
- Save time by having one person manage the contribution and scheduling process. Let your social media manager delegate and schedule this, and you can focus on doing *your own job*.
- Ensure you reach every audience with the right content distributed via the best social network.

- Expand your reach with positive PR generated by forming relationships with media outlets, journalists, industry experts, and bloggers who can help grow your business for free.
- Position yourself as both the face and voice of your company. Consumers love being able to put a face to a brand, as it engenders trust and likeability.
- Stay current with changing technology and trends. A good social media expert will be able to identify and adapt to changes in platform tools, networks, or other technological trends.
- Maintain and manage your company's reputation by monitoring listing sites such as Google+ Local and review sites such as Yelp, replying to comments or reviews (both positive and negative), as well as trolling the Web for mentions of an advisor or your company name and responding as necessary.
- Post job opportunities on your website as well as sites such as Facebook and LinkedIn.
- Get on board with the new ways to distinguish yourself or your firm from the masses with video. You can hire a social media manager with experience in videos and using YouTube to build your brand, promote a service or recruiting campaign, and engage with users.
- Get valuable intelligence from industry conversations, reviews, and social media efforts other advisors or asset managers are engaged in.
- Prove that you or your firm really is the authoritative expert by having your social manager craft, maintain, and disseminate blogs, articles, Webcasts, valuable research, or whitepapers. This type of content, in addition to tweets, blogs, Facebook posts, and efforts on other social media channels will bolster loyalty among your target audience.

HOW DO I KNOW IF I *SHOULD* HIRE SOMEONE TO MANAGE MY SOCIAL MEDIA?

Begin by considering and answering the following questions honestly. If you answer *No* to two or more of the first list of questions or *Yes* to one or more of the second list, it's a signal you could use some professional help.

First list of questions:
- Do you fully understand the importance and value of using social media as an integral component of your core business strategy?
- In addition to knowing all of the major social media sites, do you understand their key functions and know how to use the sites' features to add value to your business sustainability and growth?

- Have you developed SMART goals that reflect you mission, vision, values, and strategy?
- Do you have a solid understanding of what kind of content to use in social media, when and on what frequency to post it, and the most appropriate platforms on which it should appear?
- Are you comfortable handling social listening, constant interaction, and relationship building while managing both your brand reputation and your social media community on a 24-hour, seven-days-a-week, and 365-days-a-year basis?
- Do you have the tools, resources, energy, and time to manage your own social media community efficiently and effectively?
- Can you perform all of these social media activities while still managing the daily tasks your business demands?

Second list of questions:

- Is keeping up with social media consuming more than two or three hours of your time at work?
- Has your social and digital marketing been preventing you from performing your other key work responsibilities?
- Has social media become such a distraction that it's currently having an adverse effect on your overall productivity?
- Do you now perceive social media to be one of your least favorite tasks simply because it's no longer fun?

Review your answers to these questions and you'll discover whether hiring a social media manager (or several social media workers) is the right move for you or your firm.

WHAT SHOULD ADVISORS OR ASSET MANAGEMENT FIRMS LOOK FOR IN A GOOD SOCIAL MEDIA MANAGER?

If you decide to fill this position, there are a few key qualities your potential social media manager should possess in addition to being passionate and knowledgeable about the field:

- A complete grasp of the regulatory rules around advisor communication in the financial industry in general, and as it relates to social media in particular
- A good working understanding of you or your firm's culture, products, services, and specialties as they relate to the financial industry as a whole

- Experience in sales, marketing, or customer service
- Strong writing and editing skills (it helps to ask for writing samples, especially anything they've done that's related to financial services social media)
- Excellent critical-thinking skills
- The ability to solve problems independently
- A personality that jibes with you or your company culture, as they'll be representing you or your company brand
- Good listening and analytical skills
- Any industry or other contacts that could help build your brand

If you're comfortable with the idea, a great way to gauge a prospective new hire's functional and industry knowledge as well as their personality and communication skills is to ask them to offer criticism or suggestions on your current social media position. If they can offer any constructive feedback, as well as suggestions for improvement in a tactful, diplomatic way, you may have found a winner.

Additionally, when interviewing outside firms or individuals, one of the key things to look at is their own social networks. Are they active on the networks you plan to participate in? Do they have a large following and engagement? If they can't manage social media for their own brand, don't expect them to be successful in managing yours. Also, see what industries they specialize in. The way you manage social media for a restaurant is completely different from how you would manage social media for a financial service company.

Some advisors and firms choose to use both internal resources in addition to outsourcing certain tasks to get the message out, and others elect just to hire a social media communications firm to do it all, particularly when they're just starting out. Whichever way you go, these same capabilities and skills apply and will help you use your time and resources well.

Client Servicing

CHAPTER **28**

How Can Social Media Be Used to Save Time and Money in Servicing Clients?

It's risky not to do client servicing on social media. For most companies, it's going to happen regardless.
— Lindsay Tiles, managing director, corporate public relations, Charles Schwab

Despite the obvious business necessity of satisfying customers, we in the financial industry are still struggling to do so in the social media world.

A broad range of industries are satisfying wealthy consumers and setting their expectations for service—expectations where, in comparison, the financial sector frequently falls short, PricewaterhouseCoopers (PwC) reports in its white paper *The Connected Advisor: The Rise of Digital and Social Advice in Wealth Management.*[1]

"Indeed, attitudes, behaviors, and preferences of the affluent are increasingly being shaped by experiences in other sectors where content, interactions, and features are richer and deliver a more engaging and rewarding experience," the report says. See Figure 28.1.

Why the discrepancy? "Firms have been slow to bring new technologies to meet the challenge for regulatory, privacy and, more importantly, cultural reasons," PwC says.

---

[1] "The Connected Advisor: The Rise of Digital and Social Advice in Wealth Management," PricewaterhouseCoopers, August 2013, www.pwc.com/us/en/asset-management/ investment-management/publications/wealth-management-digital-social-advice-impact .jhtml.

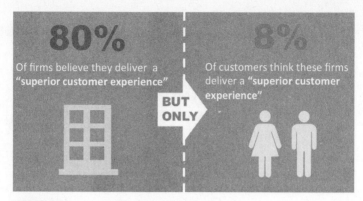

FIGURE 28.1 Identifying the Delivery Gap
Source: James Allen, Frederick F. Reichheld, Barney Hamilton and Rob Markey, "Closing the Delivery Gap," Bain & Company, 2005, http://bain.com/bainweb/pdfs/cms/hotTopics/closingdeliverygap.pdf.

Social care matters because consumers are increasingly counting on it. It matters even more so today because as consumers get more comfortable in using social media, when they do have a bad experience—offline or online—they're more likely to be more vocal.

Given that reality, they are less likely to be tolerant of businesses that fail to measure up when it comes to responding on social platforms to their concerns. The reverse holds true as well—companies that get it right are rewarded.

Evolve24, a Martiz research company specializing in social analytics, conducted a study that found that some 70 percent of customer service complaints made on Twitter go unanswered.[2] Nearly half expected their company to read their tweets. Of the one-third who received a response from the company, 83 percent said they liked or loved hearing from the company.

American Express found similar results in its 2012 Global Customer Service Barometer[3]:

- Only 31 percent of social media users for customer service say they always get an answer or have their complaints resolved. See Figure 28.2.
- Twenty-three percent say they rarely or never get an answer or have their complaint resolved.

---

[2]"Maritz Research and evolve24 Twitter Study," Maritz Research, September 2011, www.maritzresearch.com/~/media/Files/MaritzResearch/e24/ExecutiveSummary TwitterPoll.ashx. Accessed June 8, 2014.
[3]"2012 Global Customer Service Barometer," American Express, May 2, 2012, http://about.americanexpress.com/news/docs/2012x/axp_2012gcsb_us.pdf.

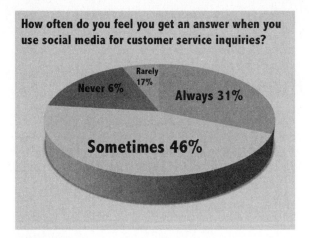

FIGURE 28.2 Social Problem-Solving
Source: American Express 2012 Global Customer Service Barometer

- Still, 60 percent feel companies have generally improved their response times over social media channels. One-third say they have not changed. See Figure 28.3.

What's been surprising is that, even though our use of the Web has evolved, there are still companies that fail to be present in their online

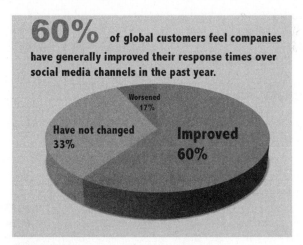

FIGURE 28.3 Improving Response Rates
Source: American Express 2012 Global Customer Service Barometer

customer service even though they promote it, whether it's real-time chat, e-mail, or care through Twitter.

FOUR FACTS TO KNOW

As our use of social media grows, consumer expectations for real-time answers also seem to be growing. It doesn't stop there though. Indeed, the ramifications can run deep and wide, as a Harris Interactive survey found with these four critical client servicing facts:[4]

1. Eighty-nine percent of consumers have stopped doing business with a company after a poor customer service experience.
2. Nearly half (48 percent) of consumers tell someone about their good customer service experiences *all of the time*.[5]
3. Only 27 percent of companies deliver high-quality customer service, according to global customers.[6]
4. Seventy-five percent of global customers have spent more with a company with positive customer experiences—as much as 13 percent more on average, compared to the previous year.

That's right. While many consumers might stop doing business as a result of poor customer service, the flip side is that great social media care can translate into great feelings about the company—and more spending. I'm sure I'm not the only one who's thought, "Yes, I'd pay more just to have someone pick up the phone (or my chat or e-mail request) more quickly so I can move on to the next thing on my list." See Figure 28.4.

OVERCOMING CHALLENGES IN THE FINANCIAL INDUSTRY

What holds the financial industry back from providing great customer care? There are a few hurdles—some obvious, others less so:

---

[4]Harris Interactive, "2011 Customer Experience Impact Report," RightNow, January 10, 2012, www.slideshare.net/RightNow/2011-customer-experience-impact-report.
[5]"2012 Global Customer Service Barometer," American Express.
[6]"2012 Global Consumer Pulse Research," Accenture, November 19, 2012, www.accenture.com/SiteCollectionDocuments/PDF/Accenture-Global-Consumer-Pulse-Research-Study-2012-Key-Findings.pdf.

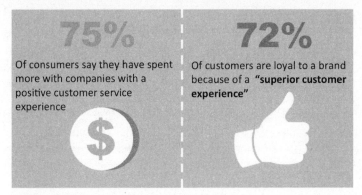

FIGURE 28.4 The Rewards of Great Service
Source: American Express: 2012 Global Customer Service Barometer; Clickfox: 2012 Brand Loyalty Survey, http://web.clickfox.com/2012SurveyResults-BrandLoyalty.html.

- **The Big R (Regulations)**—JPMorgan Chase's Bianca Buckridee, vice president of social media operations, says that while Twitter use is now very common among a lot of people, the regulatory environment adds an overlay. "To a lot of customers, Twitter is very natural," she said at the Wharton Social Media Best Practices Conference.[7] "They might want to send a DM (direct message, which may include personal information). But in the banking industry, your legal and compliance team says, 'Uh-uh. The only thing we can take via direct message is name and zip code.' So we have to route them through other channels."
- **Privacy**—Schwab's Lindsay Tiles echoes these concerns about sharing identifying information over very public channels. The firm will use Twitter's direct message function, and if something requires an exchange of information, will attempt to move the dialogue to the telephone.
- **Not So Quick**—Tiles also notes that immediate answers to customer problems are a big challenge. "Most interactions you have with clients in our industry require some context and some discussion to get the details," she points out.

---

[7]"The Ignored Side of Social Media: Customer Service," *Knowledge@Wharton,* January 2, 2014, https://knowledge.wharton.upenn.edu/article/ignored-side-social-media-customer-service.

SCHWAB: A CLOSER LOOK

Even with some of these hurdles, Schwab is among the firms that have embraced social media care. It recognized that people want to be served in the media they use, and today, that means less old-fashioned face-to-face interaction and more e-care.

Tiles, who drives Schwab's social care, says, "Most customers feel good about the service experience: They use social media as the first dialogue." She goes on to explain, "We engage or follow up with a more personal approach. There's no question we increasingly find investors on social media and wanting their questions answered there."

Schwab views social care as instrumental in three ways:

1. Reaching clients where they are.
2. Increasing loyalty.
3. Supporting the brand and reputation.

"The reputation benefits extend not just to the person you're helping, but to everyone they're connected with," says Tiles. She adds that companies that avoid servicing their clients online face a big risk: "People are saying things about your brand, whether or not you're there to respond."

Most of the time, just acknowledging an issue can lead to its resolution. For example, if someone says, "Why did you send me all this paper?" the company can reply, "We're sorry, but we do it for security reasons." Customers, Tiles says, often are grateful to hear there's a reason for a certain company practice.

Financial professionals can take away a number of lessons from Schwab's customer care program, from staffing the team to dealing with incendiary comments in the social sphere. Let's take a look at how it works:

- **Internal Staffing and Structure**—Schwab's social care team features five to six trained customer service people who take on the social media duty. While watching social traffic, they keep an eye on Twitter and review comments about the brand that call for a response. "There's a group e-mail and whomever's on duty gets back to me—and they're fast," Tiles says.
- **Corporate versus Customer Service Accounts**—One of the social care issues currently under debate in the industry is whether a firm should have separate social media accounts for corporate branding and client servicing. Although the trend seems to be to merge the two, for now Schwab uses separate Twitter accounts that allow them to keep true customer service issues separate from the broader Schwab universe (see Figure 28.5):

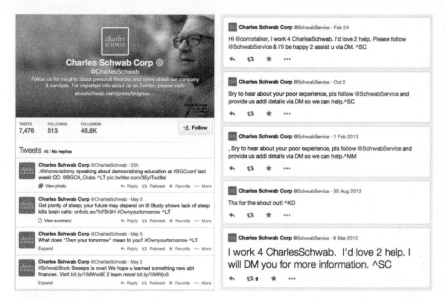

FIGURE 28.5   Schwab's Corporate Twitter Account @charlesschwab and Service Account @schwabservice

- @schwabservice—Used either to thank people for a comment or to reach out to offer further assistance. For example: "I'd like to help you. Please follow me and I'll help you through private channels like DM."
- @charlesschwab.com—Used for corporate-level communications and updates, such as news, events, and educational content.
- **Types of Service Issues**—Depending on the breadth of a firm's business, the issues that emerge on social care can truly run the gamut. For Schwab, they include:
  - **Products and Services**—With the firm's reach into banking, brokerage, and advisory services, questions can be broad—everything from rebates of ATM fees to alternatives for investing cash.
  - **Technical**—These include everything from problems logging in and password resets to customers struggling to make a deposit with their phone.
  - **Brand-Related**—These include comments about the brand, both good and bad, and require that the team set some parameters about what should and should not be addressed online.
- **Addressing Inflammatory and Other Comments**—Responding to inflammatory comments requires an entirely different level of response. In fact, Schwab has identified issues or situations requiring special outreach. In choosing how and whether to respond, the Schwab team asks a few key questions:

- Is there information that needs to be corrected?
- Is it important for our community to see us responding, even if it's an apology for an inconvenience?
- Is it inflammatory? These comments tend to appear on Twitter more than any other channel, and the firm generally opts not to address them: "We try to have reasonable exchanges with reasonable people."

Still, "at the end of the day, it all comes down to good judgment," says Tiles.

CAN SOCIAL CARE HELP YOU SAVE TIME AND MONEY?

So, by now, you may be wondering if servicing clients through social media really saves you any time or money.

Actually, Tiles says, it may *increase* service demands. That's because you're reaching out to people who might not have called or asked for help before. So, a better customer care program may lead people to ask for help when they need it.

Citibank's Frank Eliason, director of global social media and author of @YourService (Wiley), says there are occasions in which social care can help save time and money:

- **Customers Assisting Customers**—This occurs a great deal in online forums within the tech sector—developers help other developers, for instance, through an online forum. This kind of social care can work in financial services, too, Eliason says, until there's a need for greater customer account information.
- **Proactive Communication on Issues**—It's easy for a firm to find itself inundated with calls when an issue or crisis arises—a website gone down, for instance. But firms that are proactive can actually use social care to *reduce* the number of incoming calls and drag on staff from such an event. A simple message displayed to customers online or through social media that says, "We're down but we expect to be back up" can deflect calls and build customer loyalty.

FIVE KEY STEPS TO SETTING UP CLIENT SERVICING ON SOCIAL MEDIA

So by now we know that there's a growing trend to service clients through social media, that clients expect more of their service providers today than ever before, and that the rewards of good social care can extend beyond loyalty to greater spending. Now what?

Let's look at the five key steps to getting a social care program under way:

1. **Choose the Platform(s)**—No surprise: Twitter and Facebook are the top platforms for client serving. But don't feel compelled to use both; you can certainly start with one. Just remember that if you're using your firm's account—say on Twitter—both for corporate communications and customer service purposes, you may be faced with quite a number of issues to address, and rather quickly.

2. **Choose Keywords Carefully**—Think about those key words to describe your social care account or profile. These are key words clients may be using to search for you when they do have a customer service need. For instance, if you wanted to ask your bank a question through Twitter, how would you go about finding their Twitter handle? "Schwab" and "customer service" might be the most logical for that firm. Watch out for common names. If your investment firm is "Smith Investment Advisors," you can be sure you'll get an avalanche of inquiries, and not all for your firm. Tiles suggests using the firm's name with other keywords.

3. **Determine Your Purpose: Reactive or Proactive?**—Determine your social media care philosophy: Will you be reactive only or are you looking to build stronger relationships, perhaps hoping it may lead to even more business? If the latter is the case, consider key words connected with your core product or service areas so you can engage with people on those topics. The audience you reach as a result might not ever mention your brand, but it's still an opportunity to make yourself known.

4. **Promote It**—If you decide to engage in social media care through one of the social networks, be sure to tell the world. Of course, you should share it through your social media accounts, but don't forget the myriad other ways such as company newsletters, e-mails, brochures, and other traditional means. Also remember to tell your employees so they, too, can spread the word.

5. **Staff It Right**—Who's going to manage your social media care efforts? An employee? An outside consultant? You? Determine how you're going to set up the care and feeding of your customers. Be sure people are properly trained and engage in some mock social care to get everyone comfortable before going live.

One final word: If you decide to use social media for client servicing or customer management, commit wholeheartedly. The last thing you want to do is to get a program under way, only to find it taking a back seat to other priorities. You'll only risk losing customers and hurting your brand.

CHAPTER 29

How Can We Use Social Media to Create Client Groups?

As investors and other consumers expand their use of social media to answer their questions about wealth management, financial professionals are following suit, albeit more slowly. A report by FTI Consulting and LinkedIn, Financial Advisors Research 2012, reported that more than 71 percent of financial advisors were using at least one social network for business purposes.[1]

But what does that mean? Financial professionals can be engaged on social media in a variety of ways, from superficial to deeply probing. Advisors can merely follow the tweets of leading wealth managers for news or fresh ideas, or they can develop broad strategies across multiple platforms to attract new clients, strengthen relationships with existing clients, and position their business for future growth. Like everything else in social media, the degree of your involvement is entirely up to you. See Figure 29.1.

But it's important to remember that merely creating profiles or delivering messages on social media won't help you reach your business goals. A number of digital marketing executives in the financial services industry feel that many companies still don't get certain fundamental realities about social media.

THE BIGGEST MARKETING MISUNDERSTANDING ABOUT SOCIAL MEDIA

"Social media is not about a company sending a message, but people interacting with people," says Frank Eliason, the director of global social media at Citi. Engagement is key. Building relationships on social media is no

---

[1] "Financial Advisors Research 2012," FTI Consulting and LinkedIn, http://marketing .linkedin.com/sites/default/files/pdfs/LinkedIn_FinancialAdvisorsResearch_2012.pdf. Accessed June 3, 2014.

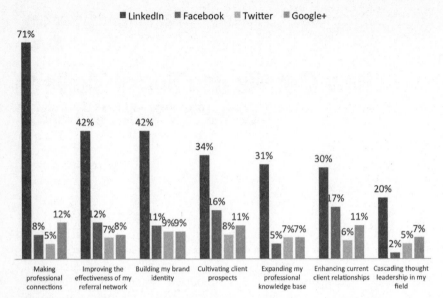

■ LinkedIn   ■ Facebook   ■ Twitter   ■ Google+

FIGURE 29.1   Social Network Use By Business Purpose
Source: FTI Consulting

different in principle than building relationships through networking on the golf course or cocktail parties.

So how can a busy financial professional—someone who's short on time and looking to accomplish things efficiently—best use social media with those ends in mind?

The answer, not to be too flippant, is to throw a cocktail party: an electronic cocktail party. First, stop and think: Who is it you remember at a party? It's the people who share interesting stories or who really listened to you. It's not the people who talked about themselves. The same applies online, whether you're using Twitter or creating a group as a way of bringing like-minded people together.

Now, consider the social events that your financial practice may occasionally sponsor for your investor clientele—a wine and cheese get-together at your office, for example, usually coupled with a short program from an industry expert on a topic such as recent gyrations in the stock market.

There's a social media complement to activities like these. Creating groups on your practice's website is one way to accomplish multiple goals: targeting the right audience, building a following with investors, and also learning about and understanding their own needs.

Your practice is filled with clients with common interests: middle-aged couples looking for ways to build their retirement portfolios or people on the cusp of retiring who need to restructure their wealth. Maybe you work closely with a certain type of client with specialized needs: doctors, teachers, or scientists.

By creating social media groups around these investors' needs, you are inviting people to a party of sorts on your website, where they can learn interesting things about subjects that matter to them, and where they can interact with you and others at the party.

FIVE STEPS TO CREATING SOCIAL MEDIA GROUPS

Here are five things you need to think about as you get ready for that party:

1. **Choose a theme.** Before creating a group, take time to think about your specialization and who your target audience is. For example, if your business is aimed at people who invest in fixed-income securities, you might want to create a group that shares and discusses anything topical to market trends, news, and investment ideas around that subject.

   It will help if you search online to determine whether similar groups already exist—if they do, think about how your group can differentiate itself from the other, preferably in ways that are superior.
2. **Decorate your venue.** The mission of creating a group is to build relationships and to let people know about you. If you're building a special place on your website for your group, one that's open only to them, think about the features that they would find valuable.

   Upload a clear image that is representative of what your group is about. It could be your company's logo or a picture that fits the topic. Structure the site so it features real-time information about topical investment products, and perhaps links to news sites that follow the subject. If you have educational videos or presentations, don't hesitate to embed them here as well.

   This group site in many ways resembles a resume—if you want to attract more people, you need to show knowledge and insight related to your specialization.
3. **Create a group blog.** Think of this as the cocktail party chatter. You can post your thoughts about news and trends around the theme of the group, and invite its members to share their own thoughts or questions. Keep your eye on the conversation, or employ a third party to manage the oversight of the discussion to ensure compliance. See Figure 29.2.

When news comes up that's related to your group, seize this opportunity to start a conversation about it. You can ask your members to share their

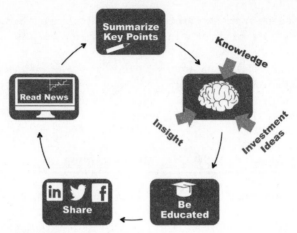

FIGURE 29.2 Write Articles

thoughts on this, or share your own ideas and see how they respond. This is the best way to listen to your members. Listening is an important step that can be ignored by social media marketers. It can help you get a better idea about your clients' minds and how a market is trending.[2]

Writing a quality blog can demonstrate your credibility, build your online influence, and finally attract clients to your business. As a financial professional, you usually have limited time in your day. Here are two important things to remember about blogging:

1. **Leverage your content.** You can do this by sharing your content on other social media channels and adding tags or keywords in the article to help search engines find what you write online.
2. **Keep a long-term focus.** As counterintuitive as it sounds, you don't write blogs to get clients. Blogging is part of a long-term strategy for business growth and branding. Concentrate on providing well-informed content with educational uses. Do this well, and the investors will follow.
   - **Invite people to participate.** Now it is time to invite folks to the party. Where are your audiences? You might already have a list of contacts, or you can find them in other social media channels or online forums.
   - **Build a library.** Today's investors are tech savvy and know how to research what they want to know before they seek advice from advisors. Consider building an online library at your site of content

---

[2]See Matthew Halloran, "Stop Guessing, Ask What Clients Want," *Financial Planning*, July 9, 2013, www.financial-planning.com/blogs/stop-guessing-ask-what-clients-want-2685709-1.html.

such as research reports, white papers, PowerPoint presentations, and videos.

PARTY VENUES: LINKEDIN, FACEBOOK, TWITTER

Just as with any cocktail party, the place you choose to set up your social media groups will color the dynamics of the gathering. Does your party take place at a swank restaurant or in the backyard of a lovely home? One setting is more formal than the other. Likewise, consider the elements of groups on various social platforms.

- **LinkedIn**—Groups on this site allow you to build your own community in an environment that attracts professionals like yourself. If you're an advisor, you can basically build your own local chamber of commerce where you're the president; the e-mails you dispatch to group members are five times more likely to be opened than those sent via regular e-mail. You can control who can post in your group. Some group owners are now even selling advertising into their group. LinkedIn offers special ad packages that can build and accelerate group growth. Creating a regional small business owners group allows you to circulate your own articles and posts and build your reputation as an expert; the group can also be used to promote your own workshops and other activities related to your business.
- **Facebook**—These groups are very topic-centric and tend to be better for more close-knit relationship building. People on Facebook tend to live on the site, so to speak, so it's more interactive than LinkedIn. You can produce a good Facebook group around your clients. For example, Matson Money, a Cincinnati registered investment advisor (RIA) with $5 billion in assets, created a Facebook presence and a private group for its internal advisors that calls itself the Wolfpack (280 advisors participate in this by-invitation-only group) to discuss issues and share advice. Got a question about the best way to handle the investment needs of a client with $1 million in assets? You can get more than a dozen replies quickly. Planning a trip to San Antonio and looking for folks to do a round of golf early? A short post to your own Wolfpack can help set that up. See Figure 29.3.
- **Twitter**—Creating lists on Twitter is another way to build social media groups. Many savvy users in the financial industry follow people according to different categories: journalists, firms, conferences, and so on. It's a way of keeping track of who you've met or who you want to meet. You don't even have to build your own list; you can follow other people's lists.

FIGURE 29.3 Matson Money Group on Facebook

For example, financial advisor and national blogger Michael Kitces has a list of financial advisors on Twitter, so it's easy to follow his list and see what those advisors are saying. Remember that lists can be public or private; not all of them will be available for inspection. When you attend a conference, it helps to create a list of attendees and speakers by using the event's hashtag—and then begin engaging with them. It's especially effective if you begin Tweeting with them prior to the conference.

As niche become the name of the game, online communities grow in importance. European-based Unience provides an investor's social network where asset managers such as Fidelity Spain, BBVA, and Bestinver create groups to engage with clients, build their audience, or connect internally with employees. Financial advisors use the platform to engage more efficiently with clients who may be dispersed over a broad geographic range; asset managers use it to get feedback on a new product, engage in an online conversation, or watch live discussions featuring portfolio managers via online video. See Figure 29.4.

FIGURE 29.4 Bestinver's Asset Management Group on the European-Based Unience Platform

BEST PRACTICES WITH GROUPS

With such a broad range of choices on group formation, it helps to keep a few tips in mind before you start:

- **Name It Correctly**—One of the biggest mistakes is calling the group by your company name. Only do that for groups of clients. Otherwise, create group names that reflect the topics around which they're built.
- **Open or Closed**—Specific groups should serve specific purposes:
  - Financial firms can create closed groups of financial advisors or portfolio managers at their company when private discussions are valued.
  - Open groups work around broad topics such as investment, personal finance, or business themes.
- **Consider the Capabilities**—Can you control who else can post? Can you share some of the group's content with other social channels or with the public? Does your platform have recordkeeping and other features needed for compliance?
- **Promote and Share**—Let the world know about your groups:
  - E-mail links to prospective members inviting them to join.
  - Include the link in content you create and distribute.
  - Encourage current members to invite others.

If your group is public or you want to recruit new members, be sure both the group and content it generates can be found in search engines. And remember the 80/20 rule—typically 20 percent of group members will account for 80 percent of the activity within the group.

CHAPTER 30

How Do We Prevent Competitors from Poaching Our Clients on Social Media?

Knotty compliance issues can serve as a disincentive to financial advisors weighing their involvement with social media, but often there's another matter in the back of their minds that drives their discomfort with social media even deeper.

Over the years, I've had numerous conversations with advisors at brokerages and registered investment advisors (RIAs) who feared operating in an open social network where other advisors could connect with retail investors. The reason? "Other advisors might take my clients!" The open and networked quality of social platforms appeared in their minds as a double-edged sword—their ability to strengthen relationships with their customers meant that their competitors could do the same. They were even afraid of outside firms recruiting other advisors on their staff.

This concern, of course, ignores a glaring truth—poaching can happen anyway. Just as we've noted that customers who have bad things to say will find a way to say them—whether you're involved in their social media world or not—so too can your clients or staff jump ship if they so desire. What it all comes down to is this: Are you doing right by your customers? Because if you are, they won't want to go elsewhere. If you aren't, well then, yes, you may have something to worry about. And it should be more than just this new thing called social media getting you to focus on *that* issue.

THREE WAYS TO PROTECT YOURSELF FROM POACHING

It's obvious that no one wants to spend time building valuable client relationships only to wake up one day and discover they've vanished. Sure, social media may open your professional world to advisor foxes who want to raid your client henhouse, but social media isn't the reason you lose them. The fault, Brutus, isn't in your social stars—it's in yourself.

Marie Swift, founder and CEO of Impact Communications, says the key to avoid being a victim of poachers is to know your clients and stay engaged with them. She shares the example of a California-based advisory firm whose clients frequent Facebook instead of advisor-preferred LinkedIn. So the firm's employees and leaders make a point of interacting with clients by making the experience fun and visual.

"Their strategy is to feature lots of photos of community interaction like client appreciation events or sharing milestones," says Swift. "So keep your clients engaged with the people in the firm to demonstrate not only your expertise but your humanity."

Here are three more key ways you can protect yourself and maintain your client relationships amid the growing competition:

1. **Define and enforce social media ownership.** While almost no agreement can offer foolproof legal protection, if you're careful to update your agreements frequently and make them well known, it will certainly make things more difficult for an ex-employee to walk away with your client list. Clearly outline who owns your company social media accounts—the company or the individual. To cover all your bases, be sure to outline ownership of account management in everything from the job description to the offer letter.

2. **Tighten your social media security.** In today's business environment, it's nearly impossible for advisors and the firms that employ them to continue flourishing without building strong social media bridges. That said, if the competition is intense and you're too permissive with your social media settings, you could be dangling your clients out there like bait for the circling sharks. Thankfully, most of the social networking sites provide varying levels of privacy settings. Following a list of clients on Twitter? Consider making this list private. Or perhaps a former colleague is now working for a competitor. If you had connected with him in the past on LinkedIn, he may still have access to all of your connections—likely a handful of which are clients and prospects. Consider modifying your privacy settings to prevent connections from seeing your full list of connections.

3. **Know what your competition offers, and stay current.** Stay abreast of what other advisors or firms are doing to attract and keep lucrative clients and top talent. You need to ensure your compensation, benefits, bonuses, incentives, rewards, and so on, are in line with—or ideally, slightly better than—the packages competing firms may offer. Below are

some examples of social listening tools that you can use to monitor the competition:

- **Corporate Listening**—Radian6 (owned by Salesforce), Oracle, and Adobe all provide in-depth listening tools and are used most often in large enterprises.
- **Social PR**—Meltwater and Vocus are traditional PR tools that have added listening tools for social media.
- **Free Tools**—Google analytics and Social Mention provide great listening capabilities. The more targeting you can get, the better.
- **Network Analytics**—Facebook, Twitter, and LinkedIn all offer in-network analytics and tools for monitoring competitors.

CLUES TO TIP YOU OFF TO POACHERS

While the tools will help, keep in mind that ultimately a human being needs to be monitoring your social networks. This means assigning a social media or community manager the responsibility of watching, engaging, and moderating risk and opportunity.

Additionally, you can utilize social listening to be tipped off that a client is leaving you. Such signs could include:

- A client is liking and sharing a competitor's social media content.
- A client stops liking and engaging with your social media posts.
- A client stops following your company or disconnects with you on LinkedIn.

LEAVING ON GOOD TERMS—AND GETTING YOUR CLIENT BACK?

And don't forget: If you do lose a client, perhaps through no fault of your own, you want to part on good terms. That's because, in this social media world, "even if you don't bring them back, you need to be aware of how they speak about you," Swift points out. You can separate on good terms, just as you would with a doctor or any other relationship, says Swift, and offers some pointers:

- Provide copies of any reports or recent statements and offer to send them directly to the new firm. Your generosity might just surprise your client.
- Maintain your relationship. For example, follow them or like their Facebook posts. Keep them on your newsletter list.

■ Send a note on the anniversary of their departure with any valuable updates. For example: "We think of you and hope you think of us. We have a new client portal and our Facebook page now features real-time Q&A with our CEO every Friday."

Who knows—the poached client may just discover that the grass isn't really greener on the other side. The client may even refer others to you.

Today's social media-driven business culture leaves you with a choice: You can either be the advisor who takes advantage of these prospecting strategies, or you can be the advisor who loses his best clients to more industry-engaged, social media-savvy competitors. Be the advisor you promise to be and leave no gaps or room for interlopers to poach your clients.

Managing Social Media Compliantly

What Are the Investor-Protection Rules as They Relate to Social Media?

Regulators are responsible for overseeing the welfare of investors. That covers a broad range of issues, and increasingly the use of social media by financial professionals is coming under scrutiny. In June 2013, for example, the Financial Industry Regulatory Authority (FINRA) issued a so-called targeted examination letter (also known as a sweep letter) to a number of broker/dealers (see Figure 31.1). Among other things, the agency was seeking:

■ Explanations of how the firm and its brokers are using social media (specifically Facebook, LinkedIn, Twitter, and blogs) in the conduct of its business.
■ The firm's written supervisory procedures concerning production, approval, and distribution of social media posts and other types of engagement.
■ An accounting of how the firm oversees internal compliance with its social media policies.

Some of the requests were extremely specific. FINRA, for example, wanted a list of the top 20 producing representatives who used social media for business purposes to interact with retail investors between February 4 and May 4 of that year. ("Please identify the type of social media used by each individual for business purposes during this time period. Please include the individual's full name and CRD number as well as the dollar amount of sales made and commissions earned during the period.")

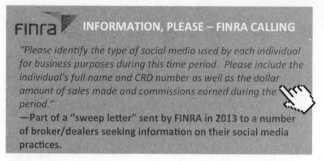

FIGURE 31.1   FINRA's Letter to Broker/Dealers on Social
Media Practices

FOUR SERVICES THAT DRAW SEC ATTENTION

It's much the same on the Securities and Exchange Commission (SEC) side of
the regulatory universe. When SEC examiners review how financial advisors
are using social media, they do so through the prism of the fundamental
protections for investors. These are outlined in the Investment Advisers Act of
1940, which establishes that advisors who fall under the act's jurisdiction owe
a fiduciary responsibility to their clients. This means acting in good faith,
providing full and fair disclosure of all material facts, and providing material
care to avoid misleading clients.

In practice, that means advisors need to offer the following:

- Disinterested and impartial advice. Clients should be assured that their
  advisors are recommending products and services with which the advisors have an arm's-length relationship.
- Recommendations that are suitable to the client's needs. For example,
  investors of advanced age often are poorly served by many annuity
  products, given that they may not live long enough to enjoy the products'
  full financial benefits.
- A high degree of care in ensuring that adequate and accurate representations and other information are presented to clients.
- A reasonable basis in fact for their representations.

To the extent that you establish an investment advisor relationship
through social media or other means of interaction, federal rules of due
care come into play. Social media can help start a conversation with a
potential client, but regulators don't see the legal guidelines come into
play until the advisor offers specific advice to a client and is paid for doing

so. On the other hand, if you say, "People over 60 should consider tax-free income, and here's why, and here's our latest report on options for planning tax free income," that's *not* investment advice because it's a thesis that doesn't relate to an individual.

Federal rules generally bar advisors from sitting on both sides of a transaction; you can't be an advisor where you're selling a security from one client to another, or where you're buying it from one client and selling to another client. The general rule is to require disclosure in these situations, so the clients give consent. Social media isn't likely to be a place where you effect transactions; there are electronic venues for trading that serve that purpose. But social media sometimes can be used by regulators for oversight purposes because advisors leave footprints in the social media world—you can see if someone is offering advice that's biased or unsuitable.

The SEC also generally prohibits advisors from charging performance fees except if the clients are relatively wealthy and can afford to negotiate for themselves. (They are typically people with $1 million to invest.) Again, social media can be used to identify clients interested in a performance fee structure and ready to start relationships, but by the time an investor is ready to commit funds to an advisor, those transactions move off the social platform and into more secure electronic environments. It's not unlike how client servicing is working in other realms of social media—people engage on Twitter, for example, then move to direct messages or telephones for more private conversations.

Financial professionals who are using social media, of course, need to keep these points topmost in their minds, as they would if they were using older forms of communication. Like FINRA, the SEC has posted guidance for financial professionals who are looking to use social media in their business. And like FINRA, the SEC is looking at advisor activity on social media with an eye on investor protection.

RECURRING PROBLEMS IN SEC EXAMINATIONS

As the agency reviews social media behavior among financial professionals, it has found a number of issues that surface in the course of its exams. Advisors who are involved with social media need to pay closer attention to these areas, since regulators have identified them as trouble spots:

- **Cherry-Picking Composites/Accounts**—Advisors who promote their performance need to avoid the selection of accounts with outsized performance records that would lead investors to assume such results are the norm. Likewise, avoid choosing beneficial time periods for reporting results or hiding important caveats in small print.

- **Comparing Performances to Inappropriate Indices**—Benchmark a growth fund with other growth funds, for example, instead of yield from a Treasury bond.
- **Representing Model or Back-tested Performances as Actual**—Disclosures that relate the distinction should be clearly displayed. Such data also should only be provided to sophisticated clients who understand the material.
- **Portability of Performance**—The ability of an investment advisor to cite as his own performance the performance of a predecessor firm or a firm at which the advisor's portfolio managers previously managed accounts is closely monitored. Be clear about what share of a particular measurement of performance can be attributed to your own effort.
- **Inaccurate Assets under Management**—Regulators frown on inflating the amount of investments managed by your practice.
- **False GIPS Claims**—Financial firms cannot misrepresent their results as complying with Global Investment Performance Standards (GIPS), created by the CFA Institute.
- **Not Presenting Net-of-Fees Performance Data**—Portfolio results that include only gross gains without subtracting what fees were charged to obtain the results are also frowned upon (especially if such results happen to be posted on websites).

In the wake of the financial crisis of 2008 and the Bernie Madoff scam that led to bankrupt retirements, both regulators and investors have sharpened their attention to investor protection issues. And the new digital world will likely present new opportunities to detect breaches in investor protection areas. So as firms and financial professionals venture into social media, remember to protect prospective clients in the same way you would want to be protected.

CHAPTER 32

How Can We Comply with Making Securities Recommendations Through Social Media?

Social media is often portrayed as a technological Wild West, where the conversation is no holds barred and everyone gives as good as they get. Indeed, the pervasive opinion hurling has some observers suggesting that social media may be contributing to a coarsening of the public dialogue—people are eager to share their opinions but not necessarily to help contribute to and structure a conversation on a given topic. There's an expression: "The biggest communication problem is we do not listen to understand. We listen to reply."

As it happens, the financial industry doesn't have the luxury of letting it all hang out on social media. And when it comes to discussions about investment advice, an advisor's blog is not a free-fire zone.

Securities recommendations must be suitable for the client for whom they are intended. In the social media world, this creates major difficulties—your audience can be hundreds or thousands of people. There's no way you can ensure that a particular recommendation you are making is sensible for everyone who's receiving your message.

THE TROUBLE WITH RECOMMENDATIONS

With a few exceptions, advisors generally are steering clear of making recommendations on social media, in chats, tweets, or even in static postings.

Remember, not every good idea is a good idea for everyone. Looked at differently, recommendations have to be suitable to the *specific person* to whom the recommendation is made. By and large, social media is a medium in which the people involved in a conversation may not know one another.

There also are limitations in the media itself. Take Twitter and chat rooms, for example. The problem of tweets and chats is that they are so short. It would be impossible to make a recommendation and disclose risk, conflicts of interest, the advisor's compensation, and the myriad of other things required of an advisor in the context of a tweet or chat.

Tweets and chats are the realm of teasers to get the reader to link to something deeper. That something might be a recommendation, if the problem of suitability can be overcome.

SOLVING THE SUITABILITY PROBLEM IN SOCIAL MEDIA

In some cases it's possible. Melissa Callison of Schwab says some advisors are setting up private groups, the suitability of whose invited members has already been assessed. An advisor might announce that he's hosting a seminar on technology stocks and feel comfortable with making recommendations to an audience that already has been vetted to receive such information. The vetting would follow know-your-customer processes—only potential investors that are known to the advisor by their risk profile, investment experience, and wealth would be invited into a group, in which recommendations suitable to their profile might be offered. A similar approach has been used in the context of offering private placements through a website to prescreened investors.

Some advisors may consider sharing content for broader audiences instead. Educational content is the base line focus for social media by most advisors today—and it is aimed at starting a conversation that leads to engagement on an individual basis, that can in turn lead to a relationship that results in a fee paid by that client. The goal of this use of social media is to create demand among individual investors for products or services that, historically, have been available over the phone.

Social media can be used to attract potential customers to sample research ideas that are offered on a subscription basis. The subscription service is fee-based, of course, so that the ultimate business model is based on access to a protected website or e-mail updates. The subscription model is not one that allows for recommendations tailored to a specific individual, but it can be tailored on a self-selected basis by category of investor.

Encouraging and facilitating conversations among clients about investment activities on blogs is an activity advisors need to think about. Those conversations help generate engagement between advisors and investors, engagement that can deepen relationships and broaden the pool of potential clients.

Advisors, however, still are liable for the activities on their blogs, and that includes inappropriate comments—endorsements of a stock pick, for example, or testimonials about an advisor's abilities. Advisors are responsible for these comments, even if the advisors aren't the ones making them.

AN ADVISOR'S RESPONSIBILITY FOR BLOG RECOMMENDATIONS

One of the reasons is the possibility that the advisor may appear to be implicitly endorsing their views by allowing them to appear on their blogs. Advisors are expected to be monitoring their sites, and if something shows up that's over the top, regulators look to advisors to do something about it.

The choices for dealing with a problematic post include deleting it or putting up a post of the advisor's own that makes it plain that the offending post is not a reflection of the advisor's own views. There's a clock ticking on this approach—comments on blogs can add up over time, and a response to a problem that's buried too far down on a chain may not be seen by advisors as useful. The longer the offending post is up, the greater the damage that regulators perceive it to cause.

And if the offense falls into the category of suspected criminal activity— say, a Ponzi scheme that the poster hopes to use the blog to facilitate— regulators expect advisors to act especially quickly. Don't drop a footnote into the blog; take the entire post down.

Mere disclaimers on the site won't afford an advisor absolute protection in the event that bad recommendations appear on the blog, since the advisor created the forum and is expected to be responsible for it. It's wise to create policies that outline what types of content are acceptable on the site and what others are not, and review such policies annually with an eye toward the experiences that have occurred. See Figure 32.1.

FIVE THINGS ADVISORS SHOULD KNOW WHEN MAKING RECOMMENDATIONS

Although the Investment Advisers Act of 1940 contains language that allows financial professionals to promote investment recommendations, the staff of the Securities and Exchange Commission (SEC) has taken the position that advisors may *not* provide a partial list of past recommendations, even if it's accompanied by an offer to provide a complete list.

FIGURE 32.1   Recommendations on Social Media

The advisor's choice now is either/or: Either you provide a complete list of your past recommendations, or you omit such recommendations entirely and offer instead to provide such a list.

When using social media to market past securities recommendations based on the best and worst performance, an advisor also is barred from showing the actual performances of such securities. Instead, the advisor may show only (1) the average weight of the best- and worst-performing holdings in a representative account during a specified period, and (2) the impact of those holdings on the representative account's return overall.

Advisors also may use social media to promote non-performance-based past recommendations provided:

- Recommendations are selected by objective, non-performance-based criteria.
- The same selection criteria is used for each quarter cited by the advisor.
- There is no direct or indirect reference to any realized or unrealized profit or loss on the named securities.
- The advisor maintains supporting records that present, among other things, the complete list of securities recommended by the advisor in the preceding year for the specific investment category covered, as well as the criteria used to select the specific recommendations listed.
- The advisor includes a cautionary disclaimer, such as, "The securities identified and described do not represent all of the securities purchased,

sold, or recommended for client accounts. The reader should not assume that an investment in the securities identified was or will be profitable."

Finally, advisors who use charts and formulas in their social media material may not claim that they will give investors certain results or help a person select securities, unless the limitations of the materials are prominently disclosed. Any assertion that a service or product is free must mean that it is free without any limitations or obligations.

CHAPTER 33

How Can We Pre-Approve Content?

You know what it's like when you eat plain vanilla ice cream—the basics are there, but it lacks any pizzazz.

Pre-approved content—articles, blog posts, and other material suitable for use by financial professionals on social media—generally comes in two flavors. One is an archive of material that's ready for the advisors' immediate use because its accuracy and context has already been vetted. The other alternative is letting professionals write the content themselves and establish a process in which their content is vetted before the authors share it in the social media world.

While it does the job and might be viewed as keeping you in compliance and reducing risk, guess what?

The industry appears to be moving beyond old-fashioned, plain vanilla pre-approved content.

Pre-approved content was all the rage two to three years ago as a one-size-fits-all solution to the problem of participating compliantly on social media channels. It was the baby step for those leading the way into social media. Today, we're beginning to see more education and training of employees up front as firms shift away from pre-approved content.

WHAT'S DRIVING THE SHIFT AWAY FROM PRE-APPROVED CONTENT?

Social media is a dialogue—not a one-way, static distribution of content.

Suppose you went to a cocktail party and the person standing next to you asked, "What do you do for a living?"

And you replied: "*Wait, let me go ask my BD what I can say and I'll be back.*" (As soon as I can track him down.)

The other guest wouldn't wait. He'd be off to the next live conversation—engaging, building a relationship, and who knows, maybe making a deal.

People clearly don't communicate with pre-approvals in the real world, and it's not considered effective in the social media world either.

That recognition is just one reason we're seeing a shift—albeit in its early stages—away from pre-approved content to education and training that allows professionals to provide information in real-time conversations online.

Other factors are also driving this change:

- Increasing adoption of social media by firms
- Recognition by regulators that it's here to stay
- Greater awareness by financial leaders of what social media communication is and how it needs to be executed effectively

THE RISKS OF PRE-APPROVING CONTENT

Okay, so maybe you're still thinking you want to pre-approve content.

There are some downsides, including:

- **Unreal-time**—The online conversation may have to be paused if an approval of content is needed first. Like the cocktail party example above —and perhaps your own experience when you're kept on hold— how would it make you feel about the firm or advisor if you asked a question and didn't get an answer right away? Would you want to reach out again? Would it affect your trust in them?
- **Impersonal**—How do you react when you see, "We're sorry for the inconvenience"? Content developed and essentially cut and pasted can come across as canned and generic. It lacks authenticity.
- **Degrees of Separation**—If content is created by folks who aren't close to the customer—an outside consultant, perhaps—this can also create issues; for example, an inability to give specific answers. There can be several degrees of separation between the author and the customer—and too many can just lead to a bad customer experience.

A STEPPING STONE: THE PROS OF PRE-APPROVING

Still, for a variety of reasons, pre-approving content might make sense. Perhaps you're a large bank with multiple employees in several divisions using social media, or a wealth division with hundreds or thousands of advisors. Pre-approval can allow you to group content by categories and give you a greater sense of control as you venture into social media.

For small firms, pre-approvals are uncommon since advisors generally serve as their own chief compliance officers (CCOs). But even those who have small staffs may want to pre-approve as employees get up to speed.

Pre-approval generally takes two forms:

1. **Employee-Driven Content**—Employees or advisors create the content, and then it goes into a queue for vetting. Once approved, it can be scheduled for posting.
2. **Company-Driven Content**—The firm provides content without employee input. However, the company could hold a monthly content meeting to provide employees the opportunity to share what they think.

Bottom line, pre-approving can make perfect sense for companies who have not yet engaged in social media. Using this gradual approach to more real-time engagement can:

- Help establish systems
- Increase confidence by the compliance department
- Develop a writing style and voice for social media

RAYMOND JAMES' SOCIAL EVOLUTION

Financial pros who are tempted by pre-approved content may want to consider the experience of Raymond James Financial. The firm, which works with more than 6,000 advisors serving about 2.5 million accounts, has discovered something valuable as its social efforts have evolved.

"Seventy percent of the content is pre-approved and 30 percent is original by the advisor," says Chief Marketing Officer Michael White, "but the advisor-created content gets four times the engagement as the pre-approved content."

Four times the engagement! If that's not reason enough to make social media training and personalized content a priority, I'm not sure what is. Clearly the advisor who is crafting his or her own messages grows to become adept at the process, a process that their brokerage or registered investment advisor (RIA) can accelerate by extending their own educational efforts.

FIGURE 33.1   Raymond James' Content Portal Provides Content and Workflow

Raymond James has given the subject some thought. The platform they use today features four primary components (see Figure 33.1):

- **Compliant, Approved Content**—Advisors can access a portal with pre-approved content and then choose which social platform he/she wants to use to share it.
- **Advisor-Created Content**—Advisors can submit a photo or link or post through a workflow at the brokerage. The content is sent to compliance for approval and, once approved, is posted. This happens within a few hours, White says.
- **Metrics**—The advisor can see the number of connections through the different social platforms, changes from the prior week, social listening, and engagement.
- **Marketing**—Last but perhaps most important is social listening. For example, advisors can get tipped off to key events in the lives of friends or others in their social networks—who might have changed jobs, moved,

or had a baby. For these important life events, if the advisor is connected, he or she can congratulate them and then suggest a 401(k) rollover or a 529 college account.

APPROACHES TO PRE-APPROVED CONTENT

Thinking that maybe the write-it-yourself option isn't for you? Financial businesses have multiple ways to provide their advisors with content that has already been vetted. Let's look at a few ways that they do it:

- **Pre-Approved Content Library**—Firms that create a robust library of pre-approved content over a broad range of topics—retirement planning, college savings, Social Security strategies—can solve their advisors' problem of finding compliant content for their social media needs.
- **Pre-Approved Scenario Content**—This is a subset of the previous option. Here, a firm creates a library of content approved by the compliance department based on various customer scenarios—complaints, a tech or service issue, or even compliments. A firm could easily have as many as 30 tweets or updates that could apply toward different scenarios. The goal is to have pre-approved content that can be used in real-time so the conversation continues without a pause or interruption.
- **Event-Related**—You could also develop content for upcoming events. If your CEO is speaking at a national conference, you could write material in advance that's related to the subject he's covering, and have your compliance people look it over.
- **Company Profiles**—If your company has a presence on Facebook or LinkedIn representing your brand or products and services, updates there could also be pre-approved.

Since advisors who write their own content appear to be more successful in engagement, however, let's consider the subject of firms that seek to make that happen.

A NEXT STEP: EDUCATION

Companies are now beginning to move to education and training to teach advisors and others about how to best utilize social media. This also includes ways to frame content and share it through the different social media. For example, firms that provide pre-approved content may still need to educate advisors on other aspects of preparing social media content, such as how to properly create status updates for their various social networks.

Education should include all employees, whether they're posting on behalf of the company or not. It should cover the purpose of using social media, the firm's approach and policy, governance, privacy considerations, and risks at different employee levels from CEO to manager.

Those employees executing the firm's social media efforts require more detailed training that should generally cover:

- **Social Media Best Practices**—Using social media to build a relationship rather than a tool to advertise.
- **Dos and Don'ts of Social Media**—Sample content and appropriate and inappropriate behaviors.
- **Personal versus Business**—The differences between personal and professional accounts, content, and representations.
- **Oversight**—This includes spot-checking and perhaps regular meetings at which the compliance officer would share examples from the archives of content. The discussion should cover what was questionable and why, and the suggested modification.
- **Internal Governance**—Identify key stakeholders and the process for modifying the firm's social media policy, plus related education.

Writing is often seen as a solitary exercise; indeed, the feeling of isolation it sometimes engenders can make the use of pre-approved content all the more tempting. In the end, however, managing content for the best results on social media is really a collaboration between the firm and the advisor. The company that helps its staff master social Web skills creates an environment where both sides benefit.

CHAPTER 34

How Can We Comply with Rules Related to Testimonials, Endorsements, and Advertising?

I t is one of the foundations of social media—the like button.

What quicker way is there to share how you feel about someone's post, photo, or video on Facebook than simply tapping the thumbs-up icon on the page? Likes have become a form of currency in the social universe, since bigger numbers equate with greater popularity.

And yet in the world of financial advisory, regulators don't like likes.

HATING THE LIKE BUTTON

Testimonials and endorsements are all part of one continuum. Unlike virtually any other product, where consumers look for references or endorsements, the Securities and Exchange Commission (SEC) took the view that testimonials are inherently misleading. That is, having the rich and famous state in an advertisement that an advisor made them so is just flat-out prohibited.

The SEC's abhorrence of testimonials extends to the like function of Facebook and to endorsements on LinkedIn (see Figure 34.1). This seems entirely at odds with the intention and original purpose of the testimonial rule—after all, testimonials are statements made by an individual, who is typically paid. They are not the voluntary acts of members of a crowd. Nonetheless, the SEC has drawn a line in the sand, using its anti-fraud powers, powers that extend to registered and unregistered advisors.

Faced with the SEC's clear statements against like/endorsement functions, advisors are finding ways to disable this functionality on social media.

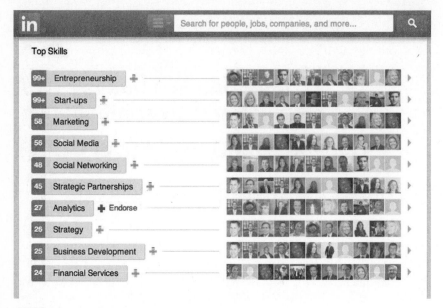

FIGURE 34.1   LinkedIn Endorsements

Still, there are other ways of promoting your practice via social media, ways that remain within regulatory boundaries.

Just remember, whether you're a registered representative supervised by the Financial Industry Regulatory Authority (FINRA) or a registered investment advisor (RIA) overseen by the SEC, those agencies have an interest in what's being said by your firm on social media.

OVERSEEING WHAT'S SAID ON SOCIAL MEDIA

Such content can sometimes mislead investors, something regulators want to avoid. As a result, advisors may be obliged in some cases to let their overseers know what's being said on their sites.

FINRA has taken the view that comments made by advisors in electronic chat rooms and similar forums are considered public appearances, and are governed by the same rules. There are no filing requirements for such conversations, although content standards are the same. (Of course, the advisor's firm is entitled to have stricter standards and may limit such activity on the Web or prohibit it entirely.)

The SEC is more hands on. Federal rules bar investment companies from circulating sales literature aimed at investors in a broad range of forms unless

the material is first filed with the agency. Ads that cover company performance are also required to be filed with the SEC unless they have already been
filed with FINRA.

The requirements on filing have led many advisors in the SEC universe to
feel a degree of insecurity about what they have to report to the agency
concerning their conversations on social media. In March 2013, the SEC
sought to assuage such fears by releasing detailed guidance concerning what
must be filed and what need not be.

FIVE CONVERSATIONS THAT DON'T REQUIRE FILING

In doing so, the SEC left some doors open for itself. Regulators say the need to
file depends on the content, context, and presentation of the online communications, with an eye on the substantive information being provided to social
media users. That being said, they specifically cited five cases in which
advisors would not have to file with the agency:

1. An incidental mention of a specific investment company or family of
   funds not related to a discussion of the investment merits of the fund—
   Examples include comments like, "Fund X Family of Funds invites you to
   their annual benefit for XYZ Charity." Or, "More than 100 Fund
   X employees volunteered for our Annual Day of Caring!"
2. The incidental use of the word *performance* in connection with a
   discussion of an investment company or family of funds, without specific
   mention of some or all of the elements of a fund's return (e.g., 1-, 5-, and
   10-year performance). Examples in this case include, "We update the
   performance of our funds every month and publish the results on Check
   entity here [firm's website URL]."
3. A factual introductory statement forwarding or including a hyperlink to
   a fund prospectus or to information that is filed pursuant to Section 24(b)
   or Rule 497. Examples they offered include: "We launched two new
   emerging market funds this week. More info about them is available here
   [website URL]," and, "John Doe is the new portfolio manager for ABC
   fund. [website URL]"
4. An introductory statement not related to a discussion of the investment
   merits of a fund that forwards or includes a hyperlink to general financial
   and investment information such as discussions of basic investment
   concepts or commentaries on economic, political, or market conditions.
   Examples include: "The 'low volatility anomaly' is explained in our
   latest white paper: [website URL]," and "The election is over, what is

next for our economy? See our report analyzing the elections. [website URL]"

5. A response to an inquiry by a social media user that provides discrete factual information that is not related to a discussion of the investment merits of the fund. The response may direct the social media user to the fund prospectus or to access information filed with FINRA, or to contact the issuer through a different medium such as telephone or e-mail. Such examples include:

- Inquiry: "Why are your funds such a large investor in ABC Manufacturer's stock?"

  Fund's posted response: "We respect your thoughts. As you know, ABC Manufacturer is found in many broad-market indices that our index funds are obligated to track, so some of our index funds hold those shares as a result."

- Inquiry: "What is a better investment, buying real estate or buying a REIT?"

  Fund's posted response: "There are a lot of things to consider when choosing between the two options. The answer depends on your goals and risk tolerance and whether you want to invest in a REIT, a fund that invests in REITs, or real property. While we can't talk about specific funds on [social media] please give us a call at 1-800-***-**** and we'll be happy to talk to you in more detail about this."

TWO CONVERSATION TOPICS THAT ADVISORS MUST FILE

The SEC also added some specific examples of social media communication that it expects advisors to file with the agency:

- A discussion of fund performance that provides specific mention of some or all of the elements of a fund's return (e.g., 1-, 5-, and 10-year performance) or promotes a fund's returns. Examples include, "Our quarter-end returns have exceeded our expectations!" And, "Please keep in mind the fund's high double-digit returns were primarily achieved during favorable market conditions."

- A communication initiated by the issuer that discusses the investment merits of the fund. Examples include "Looking for dividends? Think global and consider our new Global Equity Fund. [website URL]" and "What's your favorite technology to invest in? Read our portfolio manager's views regarding Fund X as an investment opportunity in this space. [website URL]"

Work collaboratively with your compliance experts as you cast your various messages for social media. Getting it right is important, but don't let uncertainties about what is compliant keep you from becoming more involved on social Web networks.

CHAPTER 35

How Can We Spot-Check Employee Behavior on Social Media?

As social media changes the way people interact, it's also recasting the relationship between financial advisors and their employers. Some professionals may feel that the life they live on social media is a private matter that doesn't concern their firm, but in fact the things that they say on the Web can draw regulators' notice.

So it's important for chief compliance officers to know what accounts their employees have on social media and what they're saying on those accounts. Even on Yelp, the online business review site that covers everything from restaurants to cardiologists, if an advisor in any way is representing his firm, the things he says can be deemed to be official and must attend to rules set by the Financial Industry Regulatory Authority (FINRA) and the Securities and Exchange Commission (SEC). Those comments also must be archived according to regulators' rules.

BUSINESS USE OF PERSONAL WEBSITES

The personal can easily turn into the professional where social media is concerned. Take LinkedIn. This network for professionals is a place where communications almost always matter for regulatory purposes, since the individual is representing his or her firm through their profile on the site. After all, current employment is the first thing people look at on the site.

On Facebook, however, this may not be the case. An advisor may be using it just to comment on family activities or the performance of his favorite

FIGURE 35.1 Spot-Checks Move from the Paper World to the Online World

baseball team. But if he uses the site to promote investment opportunities, his firm may be held accountable for such conduct.

Regulators expect firms to have systems for monitoring employee behavior on social media, so compliance experts recommend that firms outline internal practices for doing so (Figure 35.1). As part of an annual compliance review, employers can require their advisors to disclose the sites on which they're active—the employee, for instance, would say, "The sites I use in social media are the following, and I don't refer to the firm in my personal accounts, except on LinkedIn, where I've listed that I'm an employee of the firm." Many advisors already disclose their personal brokerage accounts to a firm, so a social media disclosure would not be a novel exercise.

It's a good idea to track what your advisors are doing on social media. In the first place, regulators expect firms to know if their financial reps are offering a webinar or representing the firm in a certain fashion or talking about investment products—any behaviors being done outside of the supervised social networking sites that the firm's chief compliance officer (CCO) is monitoring. (The SEC put out an advisory on this in January 2012.[1]) The practice of reviewing employee behavior on social media is sometimes called creeping, and it could be considered a form of snooping if not for the regulatory necessity of doing so. (And remember, the social sites under review are already open to the public. The firm is only interested in seeing what anyone else can see on an advisor's site.)

---

[1]SEC, "Investment Adviser Use of Social Media," National Examination Risk Alert, January 4, 2012, https://www.sec.gov/about/offices/ocie/riskalert-socialmedia.pdf.

THE REGULATORS ARE SEARCHING ON SOCIAL MEDIA

Keep in mind that regulators themselves are monitoring social behavior. It's not clear how often spot-checking of web postings occurs, but in almost every social community there is a regulator present—at LinkedIn, Facebook, and even at major financial firms such as Schwab and Fidelity.

The Office of Compliance Inspections and Examinations at the SEC says it looks at social media practices when its auditors visit financial practices. Audits focus on practices that are newly registered and that have not been examined before. For new firms, it's not likely to take place until your third anniversary. The OCIE solicits tips from the public over the Web asking for reports of misbehavior on social media.

So if a financial practice wants to avoid a conflict when examiners come to visit, the best thing to do is establish procedures and certification by the advisors that they are not, for example, using their Facebook account for business purposes. The good news is there are third-party firms that can provide platforms that allow CCOs to monitor employees' personal and business accounts. Again, the first step in the process is requiring employees to disclose whether or not they have social media accounts; then the firms certify whether the activities on those accounts comply with its policies. An ounce of policy protection is worth a pound of audit unpleasantness.

CHAPTER 36

What Cybersecurity Mistakes Should Advisors Avoid?

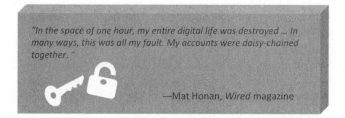

"In the space of one hour, my entire digital life was destroyed ... In many ways, this was all my fault. My accounts were daisy-chained together."

—Mat Honan, *Wired* magazine

We've all heard the story of Target, in which 40 million retail customers had their credit card and personal information compromised. And we know how easy it is for bad actors to lie their way through in the offline world. Bernie Madoff made that clear.

Whether it's the Target data breach, concern over Facebook's privacy settings, or the growing trend of financial firms to move customers online, all are raising concerns about the protection of personal data.

Indeed, cybersecurity has become a buzzword, and it's serious business in financial services.

"Levels of cyber-risk that might be fine if you're selling dish soap can create enormous headaches for the financial services sector," says Ed McNicholas, partner at Sidley Austin and co-leader of the law firm's privacy, data security, and information law practice.

The term *cybersecurity* has been in our lexicon since the 1990s.[1] As advisors and firms move to social channels, mobile devices, and iPads as a key method of handling all communications, security takes on a whole new level of importance.

---

[1]Cybersecurity—definition and first mention, *Merriam-Webster*. www.merriam-webster .com/dictionary/cybersecurity.

WHAT CRIMINALS GAIN AND CONSUMERS LOSE

Cybercrime is the illegal collection or use of data for financial gain. Data provides access to bank, credit card, and other financial account information that can be re-sold or used for identity theft purposes. I'm reminded of my friend MaryAnne, whose entire identity—including her Social Security number—was stolen and used to charge purchases to her accounts and access funds in her bank.

For other criminals, it might just be an attention-getting move to demonstrate one's powerful hacking skills. These are called *hacktivists*, doing it either to disrupt a business or to audition for some greater crime in which they can participate.

"Originally they attacked through e-mail and networks directly," says Blane Warrene, a technology expert and co-founder of the social media archiving service Arkovi. "But, now with so many digital channels, being able to insert malware quietly offers them opportunities to create, in essence, a tunnel to ferret out this data."

And it's not just data at risk. How about your brand? That's right. A wave of attacks can disrupt your business and tarnish your brand publicly. "These can be very costly incidents as well," Warrene notes.

We've seen many cases of social engineering to compromise individuals and firms. The clearest explanation for how social engineering works is to read the story of Mat Honan, a technologist and *Wired* writer.[2]

"The very four digits that Amazon considers unimportant enough to display in the clear on the Web are precisely the same ones that Apple considers secure enough to perform identity verification," Honan writes.

Honan admits that the security failures that plagued him were his own fault.

Had he just taken a few basic steps—from using two-factor authentication to backing up his computer, he wouldn't have lost his entire digital life—from his kid's photos to e-mails.

PricewaterhouseCoopers found that the industry is spending 50 percent more in 2014 on cybersecurity.[3] Likewise, Deloitte estimates that U.S.

---

[2]Mat Honan, "How Apple and Amazon Security Flaws Led to My Epic Hacking," *Wired*, August 6, 2012, www.wired.com/2012/08/apple-amazon-mat-honan-hacking.
[3]"PwC's 6th Annual Digital IQ Survey," PricewaterhouseCoopers, 2014, www.pwc.com/us/en/advisory/digital-iq-survey/financial-services.jhtml. Accessed June 8, 2014.

financial services firms lost on average $23.6 million from cybersecurity breaches in 2013—the highest average loss across all industries the consulting firm tracks.[4]

IMPLICATIONS FOR ADVISORS AND ORGANIZATIONS

With that overview, now let's look at it from a financial advisor's perspective. "Bad actors or hackers often look to individual's devices—from computers to smartphones and tablets—as a way into larger networks," Warrene points out.

While a social media account can be hacked, of greater concern is the way the breach may potentially provide access to the device—smartphone, laptop, tablet—that is used by its owner to enter and use the social media account. Access to the device can possibly lead to hacks into business networks, causing the leak of confidential data or, worse, infect many other systems on that network.

For an individual responding to an attack, it is essential to not only recover your account through the procedures available at the social network in question but to also have your device(s) analyzed to ensure there are not any remnants of an attack sitting dormant and waiting for later use.

Not only do individuals need to consider cyberdefense, so do institutions. From an organizational perspective, firms need to consider:

- How they will provide access to social networks.
- How they will manage the publishing workflow and handle engagement to those posts.
- Detailed procedures for securing networks and individual devices, including the heuristic approach to sniffing out possible unpublished malware and attacks.
- Recovery procedures for handling widespread compromise.

A CLOSER LOOK AT THE RISKS

McNicholas says, "Professionals have a duty to use robust security against both insider and outsider threats."

---

[4]"Transforming Cybersecurity—New Approaches for an Evolving Threat Landscape," Deloitte, February 11, 2014. www.deloitte.com/assets/Dcom-UnitedStates/Local Assets/Documents/FSI/us_fsi_Transformingcybersecurity_021114.pdf.

As an example, when social media profiles reveal too much information, it can be used for social engineering or, worse, compromise client data. And the reverse can happen: An employee venting on Facebook that he must cancel his weekend plans because the "big deal" in the office must close by Tuesday can be devastating when The Street gets wind of it.

The Federal Financial Institutions Examination Council places the potential risks into three general categories: compliance and legal risks, reputation risks, and operational risks.[5] Here's what the agency says:

- **Compliance and Legal Risks**
  Compliance and legal risks are the possibility of enforcement actions and/ or civil lawsuits arising out of a financial institution's use of social media. Most regulations, consumer financial protection rules, and other laws do not provide exemptions where social media is used.
- **Reputation Risk**
  There's also the reputational risk arising from negative public opinion in connection with the use of social media.
  - **Fraud and Brand Identity Risks**—Financial institutions should consider using social media monitoring tools and methods to identify and respond to reputation risks that may arise. "Spoofs of institution communications, man-in-the-middle attacks, or other hacks that allow fraudsters to masquerade as the institution pose real risk," says McNicholas.
  - **Privacy Risks**—A financial institution should have procedures in place to address risks from other social media users posting confidential or sensitive information on a financial institution's social media site or page.
  - **Consumer Complaints and Inquiry Risks**—Monitoring procedures should alert financial institutions to statements or complaints posted on social media sites.
  - **Employee Use of Social Media Risks**—Employee use of social media, both personally and at business, should be addressed through policies and training.
  - **Third-Party Risks**—An institution is directly responsible for monitoring its social media site, even if the functions are outsourced to a third party.
- **Operational Risk**
  Operational risk is defined as risk of loss from inadequate or failed processes, people, or systems, which can arise from a financial institution's use of information technology, including social media. Social

---

[5]Federal Financial Institutions Examination Council. www.ffiec.gov.

media use makes firms particularly vulnerable to malware and account takeover, and it needs to be included in the firm's security incident response procedures.

WHAT FINRA AND THE SEC SAY

Both the Securities and Exchange Commission (SEC) and the Financial Industry Regulatory Authority (FINRA) released cybersecurity guidance in 2014, setting the tone for examinations and how advisors and firms should set their priorities. At a higher level, the regulators are looking at:

- The security of devices (computers, phones, and tablets) and networks
- How client data is handled and protected
- The validity of written supervisory procedures to include focus on handling incidents
- How business continuity will provide a recovery path from a security incident
- Are firms acquiring cyber-specific insurance coverage

FINRA, through its January 2014 Examination Letter, says it's attempting to understand:[6]

- The types of threats
- Where vulnerabilities may exist within firms
- Firms' existing approaches to cybersecurity risks
- Ways to share observations and findings with firms

In April 2014, the SEC held a Cybersecurity Roundtable in which Chairwoman Mary Jo White underscored the "compelling need for stronger partnerships between the government and private sector" to maintain the integrity of the markets and protect customer data.

The SEC also announced it would be conducting examinations of 50 broker/dealers and RIAs to further understand, among other things[7]:

- An entity's cybersecurity governance
- Assessment of risks
- Protection of networks and information

---

[6]SEC's Office of Compliance Inspections and Examinations, Cybersecurity Initiative, www.sec.gov/ocie/announcement/Cybersecurity+Risk+Alert++%2526+Appendix+-+4.15.14.pdf.
[7]Blane Warrene, "Running WordPress Securely," *Investment News*, April 29, 2014. www.investmentnews.com/article/20140429/BLOG02/140429895.

In short, regulators are trying to understand where the gaps are and how to address them going forward.

NOT HIP TO HACKERS? THREE RISKS FOR ADVISORS

The growing sophistication of technology is accompanied by the danger that tech poses when it's in the hands of sophisticated and unscrupulous people. What are the kinds of cybersecurity risks advisors might face when operating in the social media world?

Warrene says that attacks break down into three basic groupings, from obvious to subtle:

1. *The Malware Link* —You've probably gotten a direct message from a friend on Twitter. It says: "Check this out!" And you're wondering: "What is this?" This is a malware link—a link that, if you follow it, is tied to something malicious such as a virus that can surreptitiously load onto your device. Often the goal is meant to remain un-discovered, instead of destroying something on your device. Other times it's more sinister: Innocent people have these bots running in the background of their computers, either to collect information or access other computers.
2. *The Alluring Follower* —Let's say you discover a follower who appears to have huge influence through the follower's own sizable number of followers, millions. The follower offers a catchy message and link. You think, "Oh my gosh, I've arrived on Twitter!" Yet common sense dictates that only a fraction of people have that kind of following on Twitter. These followers' links are efforts to infect your devices.
3. *Direct Hacks*—An effort to directly hack your system is usually done by what is called a brute force attack. This is where the hacker uses software to try many variations of logins to eventually guess the right way in. The attacks often employ stolen credentials of the victims.

Common sense will keep attackers at bay in the first two cases. In the third case, direct hacks of your social accounts can be defended against through two-factor authentication and using a unique password on each account—a hard habit to develop, but one that provides peace of mind. The two-factor authentication—available in the settings function of nearly all social media platforms—adds an additional step to logging in and hampers remote hacks. Generally, once you've entered your username and password, a text message is sent to a mobile device of your choice and that code is required to finish the login. Take note that, in order for this effort to be effective, your mobile phone also needs to be secured (password to unlock); if you lose your phone, this defense is defeated.

KEY MOVES TO WARD OFF RISKS

The bottom line is, if hackers find devices that are unprotected, then they have a path to ultimately get to valuable information that can access client accounts.

So, how do you or your firms protect against it? Surprisingly, experts agree that even some of the most fundamental moves to protect you, your firm, or your clients are not in place at the firm or individual level. Here are some steps that Warrene suggests firms take:

- *Do the Basics*—These include:
  - *Lock and Encrypt Computers*—Both the SEC and FINRA are examining cybersecurity techniques. On a Mac, you can turn on FileVault so that it encrypts data. On a PC, you can use PGP Encryption from Symantec, among others. For smaller advisors, BitLocker is included in Windows 8 for free. With all of these tools, you're protected when your computer is off and at rest. So, if you're at Starbucks grabbing a cup of coffee and someone walks off with your computer, chances are, they'll close the computer and put it under their arm, triggering the encryption. They'll get the computer but not your data.
  - *Enable Anti-Virus Software*—Use an anti-virus software enabled for automatic updating and automatic scanning as well as automatic quarantine.
  - *Use a Password Manager*—A password manager, such as 1Password, LastPass, or RoboForm, should be a requirement. These provide centralized management of usernames and passwords and allow individuals to securely sync passwords across devices. Avoid keeping password notebooks or Excel files.
  - *Mix Passwords*—As noted above, use unique passwords on each of the social media sites. While this might be painful, the peace of mind may be worth it. Also consider changing your passwords twice a year.
- *Create a Customer Feedback Loop*—It's surprising the number of financial firms that do not have an easy way for customers to communicate online about some issue or breach. Consider a message in statements or online directing consumers to alert leaders to possible cybersecurity threats.

■ *Protect Smart Phones and Tablets*—These devices also need clear protection including:
  - ■ Passwords on phones and tablets to make them operable
  - ■ Required use of a VPN service (Cloak, VPN1Click) to encrypt your WiFi connection when on public networks or at all times. An individual can go to Cloak and, for $1.99 a month, encrypt his connection to the Internet.
  - ■ Activation of the "FindMe" capability, which allows you to locate that lost or stolen phone, and possibly destroy the data to keep it out of the hands of thieves. Apple provides this natively. Android and iOS users can leverage Lookout for this purpose. Windows Mobile users can leverage the locator service feature offered by cell phone carriers' insurance provider (Assurion being the dominant player).

OTHER SOCIAL MEDIA PROTECTION TIPS

■ *Posting on Your Website*——Web publishing is a straightforward process. The key is in the tools you use to post content. For example, if using WordPress, secure that platform to better protect yourself and prevent the uploading of files that could infect your site or your visitors.[8] Another key risk is related to attempts to access your site's admin login. (This is especially the case with WordPress because it uses a common username—admin—for all admin accounts initially set up.) The same goes for other DIY platforms, such as SquareSpace. If you're not hosting your own website, an industry provider such as Advisor Websites or Broadridge can assist with your security efforts to make publishing more efficient.

■ *Third-Party Posting on Your Website*—Critical here is ensuring that third-party publishing is moderated. Never allow others to upload files without first scanning them for potential risks. If you are using a content management system, such as WordPress, you can mitigate this risk by having third-parties login as a contributor, which limits them to typing in their content for your moderation and publication. This is an effective way to use guest writers, which is also a powerful marketing tool. Alternatively, a simple copy and paste—a method you can use on LinkedIn and other platforms—is also considered safe.

---

[8]Blane Warrene, "Running WordPress Securely," *Investment News*, April 29, 2014. http://www.investmentnews.com/article/20140429/BLOG02/140429895

■ *Facebook, Twitter, LinkedIn, Google*—Here is where using two-factor authentication is essential. It prevents most, if not all, hacks of social accounts. And what about comments on these profiles? Let's say someone hacks your Facebook account and posts something unsavory, such as pornography. You'll need to remove the content, secure your account (changing password, etc.), recover it so you can delete any content, and turn on two-factor authentication to avoid it happening again. On Twitter, if someone posts something offensive about you, block them from being connected to your account and report them as spam. (The networks are pretty good about following up on this.)

THE FUTURE OF CYBERSECURITY

With the increased use of social media and the focus on cybersecurity by regulators, what's next? Among the biggest shifts—and debated issues—is the move to the cloud.

While many in the financial industry view data and website hosting in the cloud as risky, others say the old-fashioned methods pose more risk.

"We are extraordinarily cautious about client data," a tech exec at a $25 billion San Francisco-based investment firm told me. "We don't want even one small piece of information leaked. For now, everything needs to be hosted internally."

But even in my own experience, some of the largest companies in America were delighted to hear of services hosted in the cloud.

"Amazon (cloud hosting) is safer than any hosting we could do ourselves," says Nicolas Oriol, an MIT graduate and founder of Unience, the European social media site for financial professionals.

At some point, says Warrene, "even large institutions won't have full control of all aspects of what they are responsible for, and security risks will be tiered—from individual devices, to corporate networks, and ultimately to the cloud—which means Apple, Amazon, Google, Microsoft, as well as players like Oracle."

As biometrics emerge, rules and regulations will evolve. For example, passwords are considered protected speech while fingerprints are not. What are the implications if, ultimately, all client data is secured by fingerprint?

As we shift from computers to tablets to potentially wearable and interactive computing for business, what risks and liabilities will emerge? If we authenticate through, say, a retinal scan, and a criminal compromises that method, will they have deeper access than ever before?

With social media still in its infancy, cybersecurity challenges will only increase. "The growth of nation-state cybersecurity threats focused on intellectual property theft, market disruption, and competitive intelligence gathering pose tremendous threats to social media platforms," says McNicholas.

Regulators will need to evolve new guidance that adapts the basic protections for customers and consumers to new technologies. That, in turn, will require an increased use of new technologies to monitor new technologies, and a continuing dialogue with industry.

For firms and financial professionals, it calls for flexibility. Speed is the new normal, and firms will need to be flexible both internally and externally as they continue to engage with regulators.

CHAPTER 37

How Does the JOBS Act Impact Social Media and Hedge Funds?

When the federal Jumpstart Our Business Startups (JOBS) Act went into effect in 2013, supporters hailed it as a milestone for the financial industry and investors alike.

One of the things the law did was loosen longstanding rules that restricted the ability of hedge funds and other investment companies to promote their private placements to the public. Advertising such investments to the general public had been barred before JOBS.

Now hedgies can market these securities across a broad range of advertising channels, including social media. The rules restricting participation in such placements to qualified investors still stand, with the funds required to take reasonable steps to verify the investors' qualifications. The criteria are defined as follows:

- An individual net worth or joint net worth with a spouse that exceeds $1 million at the time of the purchase, excluding the value (and any related indebtedness) of a primary residence.
- An individual annual income that exceeded $200,000 in each of the two most recent years or a joint annual income with a spouse exceeding $300,000 for those years, and a reasonable expectation of the same income level in the current year.

WHO WANTS TO BUY A PLACEMENT?

What, you say? You haven't seen pro football players on television commercials lately plugging placements as they would SUVs or fast food? And you haven't gotten pitches for the same investments via social media?

Estimated Capital Raised 2012		
Registered Offerings	$1.2 trillion	
	Operating Companies	**Pooled Investment Funds**
Rule 506	$173 billion	$725 billion
Rule 144A	$636 billion	$4 billion
Total	$1.5 trillion	

FIGURE 37.1   Private Placement Data from SEC
Source: SEC

Don't be surprised. Industry insiders say it could take some time before
financial professionals have digested the rules enough to feel comfortable
with promoting securities in a new way. There already are complaints that
some of the new regulations conflict with others that have been on the books
for some time and have been enforced by other government agencies. See
Figure 37.1.

And there's also the natural tendency of firms to not stick their necks out,
but wait for others to jump into the placement promotion pool and see how
cold the water really is.

Some hedge funds already are moving. TopTurn Capital produced a
nearly three-minute ad in 2013 promoting its services.[1] Meanwhile, ff
Venture Capital is among the first companies in its channel to use general
solicitation of investors post-JOBS Act; the firm already has more than 5,000
followers on Twitter.[2]

One thing people in the business agree upon is that social media is a
channel they want to participate in to a greater degree, if for no other reason
than their clients are using social media themselves.

Daniel Schreck, head of marketing at Equinox Partners, which manages
$1.5 billion, says it's "a great disappointment" that it can't advertise or do
general solicitation despite the JOBS Act. Schreck says there are solicitation
rule conflicts between the Commodities Futures Trading Commission

---

[1]Mariah Summers, "Here's The First Ever Hedge Fund Ad, Complete With A Professional Surfer," Buzzfeed, December 13, 2013, www.buzzfeed.com/mariahsummers/
heres-the-first-ever-hedge-fund-ad.
[2]John Frankel, "Pioneering a New Frontier for Venture Capital," ff Venture Capital,
October 11, 2013, http://ffvc.com/blog/2013/10/11/pioneering-new-frontier-venture-
capital.

(Equinox trades commodities) and the SEC, which rewrote its rules to conform with JOBS mandates.

Schreck had hoped, among other things, to do a public website and some targeted advertising, but has put those plans on the shelf for now until the dust settles over what his firm will be allowed to do. The hedge fund industry is moving slowly as well, for similar reasons, he adds. It's nothing new; even in Europe regulators can make it difficult for companies outside the continent to invest within its borders.

Equinox's goal was to have a comprehensive public website where it could have its investors all share links to the firm's videos or newsletters with friends and colleagues, and effectively serve as marketers of the company. "That's how every other company works," Schreck says. Still, Equinox's target audience is deeply niched; with a $5 million minimum investment, its securities are a luxury product, "so we try to be very selective, concise, and engaging in the communication we put out," he says.

Schreck looks forward to a day when he can do more on social media. "With the JOBS act and changes to marketing, we want to be a first mover and pioneer," he says. "We have a good product, we know the audience, and now we want a more robust and creative distribution channel. Moreover, people will develop innovative online tools to reach a broader target market."

A TECH UPGRADE FOR PRIVATE INVESTMENT

Some other firms already are exploring ways to use social media to bring investors and hedge funds together. Artivest links fund managers with investors who are looking for ways to enter the alternatives and private fund spaces. Chief Investment Officer David A. Levine sees the company as responding to a need that's not being met in an industry that's hidebound over technology. See Figure 37.2.

Levine knows from personal experience. A Twitter user since 2007 (@davealevine), Levine noticed that the private funds industry wasn't using technology the same way he was. Artivest employs social media in its outreach to clients and potential investors. It pushes out ideas about investing opportunities via a blog and uses Twitter, LinkedIn, and Facebook to promote and share the content.

"Every other industry has gone through a technology upgrade, and we think it's time for private investing," Levine says. With the approval of the JOBS Act, "We think there's a perfect storm of change . . . tech changes, economic changes, and regulatory changes."

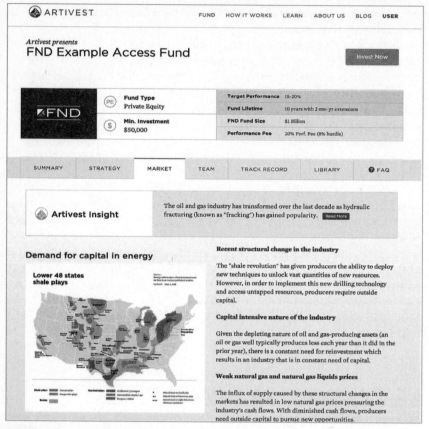

FIGURE 37.2   Investing With Artivest

Yet adoption still lags. Levine sees three drivers that would help pick up the pace:

1. **Clarification of Regulatory Changes**—This will take time, he says; syncing action across regulatory bodies can make it easier.
2. **Tech Adoption**—Even though people are using smartphones every day, it takes time for them to adopt and become comfortable with tech changes in their businesses.
3. **Industry Pioneers**—Some financial gurus have taken advantage of changes in the industry to promote their ideas, such as hedge fund manager Cliff Asness and activist investor Carl Icahn pushing out tweets.

"One thing that allows the best firms in the industry to stay ahead is that they do think about ways to improve their business," Levine says. "Using proven technologies that exist and are used in other industries is such an obvious thing, and upgrading the process of investing is a natural next step."

There's an inevitability to the process, he adds, predicting that discovering, evaluating, and participating in investment options will be much easier. "Does that mean that parts of your business that are outward-facing use those technologies? I think so. It means you can engage from any location to a broad base of sophisticated investors."

CHAPTER 38

How Will Social Media Change the Role of the CCO in the Years Ahead?

It's no secret that the financial industry has grown more complicated in the recent past, given the development of derivatives and other increasingly exotic securities—coupled with the 2008 market crash. And it's likely that matters will grow more complex still in the years ahead, as the industry grapples with heavier regulation under the Dodd-Frank regimen and the implications of social media and other rapidly evolving technology.

So how does this change the lives of chief compliance officers (CCOs) at brokerages, banks, registered investment advisors (RIAs), and other financial practices? Clearly, demands on the CCO will grow apace, and industry observers say that employers will need to adapt.

"Today, you have the CFTC, the Fed, the SEC, FINRA," Melissa Callison, vice president, communications compliance at Charles Schwab, tells me. "So if you're planning on behalf of your firm, because of the complexity in products and in regulations, you have to invest in that infrastructure."

Compliance officers, you might say, have a new job description: crystal ball reader (see Figure 38.1).

"The key is that they have to be more *risk identifiers* than ever," says Barbara Stettner, managing partner at the international law firm of Allen & Overy. "The expectation is that CCOs will have to look around the corner for the organization—Where is tech taking us, and what are the global risks the firm will be facing given the business line they're engaged in? They can't just be putting fires out anymore; now, it's about thinking ahead. I have this new tech, or a new generation that can't get off iPads, so how does that impact compliance and my role?"

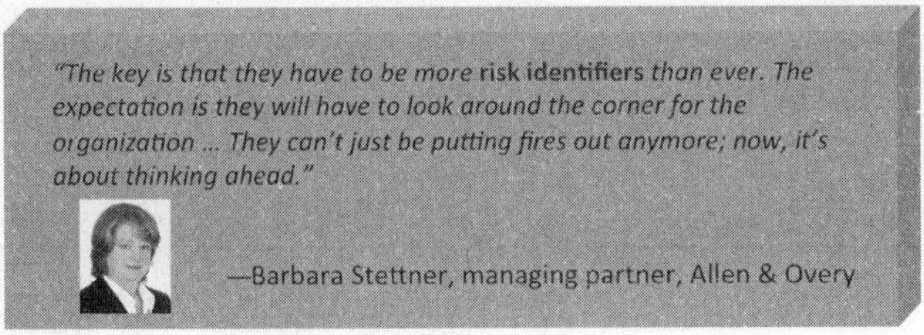

> "The key is that they have to be more risk identifiers than ever. The expectation is they will have to look around the corner for the organization ... They can't just be putting fires out anymore; now, it's about thinking ahead."
>
> —Barbara Stettner, managing partner, Allen & Overy

FIGURE 38.1   CCO's New Job Description: Futurist

THREE AREAS OF CHANGE FOR CCOs

Knowing the fundamentals of compliance will still remain core to the CCO's mission, but three other areas will increasingly demand the manager's attention in the next decade:

1. **Technology Management**—As the firm updates the technology it uses, the CCO will need to understand it well enough to ensure that it is being used in an appropriate and compliant manner.
2. **Cybersecurity**—As firms become more reliant on online resources to conduct their activities, the challenge of ensuring that its data is secure will become even more daunting.
3. **New Investment Products and Markets**—The almost limitless ingenuity of capital markets has created new financing vehicles. At the same time, investment markets grow increasingly internationalized—and drawing in nations with underdeveloped legal systems and infrastructure. CCOs must assess the new risks and ensure the integrity of the valuation process for such assets and the documentation of investment due diligence.

Social media platforms are evolving along with technology, and that can complicate the life of the CCO. The old marketing and advertising rules won't change much, but the forums—Twitter, LinkedIn, and so on—will continue to develop and pose significant challenges to the industry.

Compliance officers won't be able to rest on their laurels in such an environment, experts say.

"CCOs must become aware of how the younger investment managers use technology in the normal course of a business," says Tina Petruzziello, founder and compliance principal at Boston Compliance Associates. "Identifying the risks and potential compliance issues will force the CCOs to continuously learn about and keep abreast of new ways of communicating with the public. The ability to use new technology and social media platforms must be incorporated in a robust compliance program."

Her colleague, David Rozenson, counsel and senior consultant at Boston Compliance, sees an inherent compliance conflict looming.

"As the social media platforms become more complex, the best approach for CCOs may be to keep it simple—to establish basic principles and prohibitions regarding employees' use of social media and stressing that they apply to all communications outside of the work environment," he says.

Compliance training for employees must explain the specific risks associated with the careless use of social and other communications media, he adds. It helps to offer samples of both appropriate posts and ways to respond to social contacts from current and prospective clients.

A RISING TIDE OF COSTS

Don't look for compliance costs to fall in this environment. Regulators are expecting more from financial professionals in the areas of surveillance and recordkeeping, and the technology that firms will need to deploy isn't cheap. Tradeoffs result from the tension.

"So as technology increases, that could reduce the overall costs, but you'll have to make an investment in other areas like hiring new staff with diverse skills—maybe coders, or ex-FBI working on counterterrorism, or ensuring you have cybersecurity protections in place," Schwab's Callison says. Expect more pressure to find return on investment (ROI) on the higher mechanisms required for compliance, and more struggles between CCOs and CEOs on the subject.

Petruzziello says that more regulations and guidance around social media will inevitably boost costs. There is no way around that without restricting use of social media by employees.

"The downside of such restriction is missed exposure and opportunities," she says. "Balancing risks and costs remains the old but new problem for CCOs and their investment managers."

Also driving the pressure on the compliance bottom line: regulatory risk from outside the American borders. Firms aren't staying in one nation anymore. And some countries in Asia and Europe are developing an American taste for litigation, perhaps following the examples of attorneys general in many U.S. states.

"Every AG knows that if they find a scandal in the industry, it's a trip to the governor's mansion," Stettner says. "So there's a lot of pressure on the regulators to not sit back on their heels."

She stops short of recommending to advisors that they avoid social media in their practices, however—it's still a basic tool that the next generation of investors uses to communicate.

Unfortunately, the CCO struggle with the regulatory landscape is likely to continue. Regulators tend to react to issues as they emerge in the financial industry, rather than set proactive parameters. CCOs grapple with the nuts and bolts of compliance matters every day and can see pitfalls coming more quickly. But it's hard to enforce a best practice in an industry without a mandate from government overseers.

"Even if everyone wants to 'do the right thing' when the revenue upside is seemingly unlimited, the compliance function has a difficult task ahead," Petruzziello says.

A CHANGING ROLE FOR CCOs

So as the industry changes, expect the demands on the CCO to grow in kind. The job is likely to see broader responsibilities—more matters subject to compliance, and regulators seeking to have an individual in the organization who can be held accountable. The job is likely to have more supervisory tasks, and CCOs will need to be able to do more than just grasp the nuances of the Investment Advisers Act—they also will need to be savvy practitioners of C-suite politics as they rub elbows with the top brass. The goal is to be respected and to influence a culture of compliance at the firm.

Don't look to outsourcing compliance as a way of significantly containing costs. Some minor responsibilities can be farmed out, but core compliance functions are always the obligation of the company itself. FINRA offers rules on what can be outsourced; the SEC already is balking at some oversight going overseas, where records could be out of their reach. The good news: Tech solutions can help lessen the burden of chores such as documenting client communications.

At the same time, the CCO must be true to his or her mission. It is the responsibility of the compliance officer to ensure that compliance violations be disclosed, even those that damage the firm's reputation. Bad investment performance can hurt the firm's brand, but a CCO must make certain that it is reported accurately and not in a misleading manner.

Sample Social Media Policy

Here is a model social media policy prepared by Stuart Fross, partner at Foley & Lardner LLC. © Foley & Lardner, LLC 2014.

Use of Social Media
Policies and Procedures

1. Statement of Policy

The Advisor's use of social media is governed by this policy. *Social Media* is defined as Facebook, Twitter, YouTube, LinkedIn, as well as Internet blogs and other interactive forums.

Any use of social media by the Advisor:

- Must be accurate and not fraudulent, deceptive, manipulative, or misleading,
- Must not omit to state material information,
- Must comply with all internal guidelines and applicable rules associated with advertising,
- Must comply with this policy, and
- Must be reviewed prior to use by the Chief Compliance Officer (CCO) or his/her designee.

The Advisor's use of social media shall be governed by and employees shall comply with the following compliance policies and procedures:

A. Advisor Accounts. The Advisor may establish its own social media accounts with the prior approval of the CCO. The approved social media sites are as set forth in Exhibit 1.

The Advisor will allow only the individuals specified in Exhibit 2 to post information on its behalf to social media.

B. Personal Sites Prohibited from Business Uses. No personal social media account or web page may be maintained by an individual employee for any business use. A *business use* will be inferred from any reference to the Advisor, to any fund or investment strategy, except that an employee may list the Advisor as the employee's place of employment and contact details on a personal site (such as LinkedIn).

This restriction does not apply to the maintenance of social media accounts or web pages for personal use outside the scope of employment that do not involve any business use.

C. *Type of information that can be posted.* Any information posted on a social media website must be general in nature and must be informational in nature.

D. *Type of information that cannot be posted.* The Advisor will not post recommendations for the purchase or sale of any investment: Posted content must not be targeted to a specific individual or group of individuals, and may not contain any recommendation or call to action. Posted content may not consist of investment advice.

E. *Product-specific information.* Information about a product offered by the Advisor may be posted only as *static content*. All static content must be reviewed and approved prior to use in accordance with the procedures set forth below.

F. *Static content* for the purposes of this social media policy is content which, once posted, cannot be altered, commented on within the page on which it is posted, or modified in any way by anyone other than the author. Specifically, this will include material posted on the physical portion of a social media website that does not allow for interactive, real-time communications, including comments or messaging. All static content is considered to be *advertising* and must be pre-approved by in accordance with the Advisor's advertising review policy.

G. *Interactive social media.* The Advisor may participate in the real-time interactive portion of social media websites if supported by

  i. an approved access control mechanism,
 ii. a comprehensive recordkeeping capability,
iii. a compliance review system,
 iv. capacity for the CCO to control who can delete postings,
  v. capacity for the CCO to delete postings, and
 vi. capacity to include appropriate disclaimers.

Product-specific information may not be posted on the interactive portion of a social media website.

H. *Third-Party Postings.* If the Advisor maintains a social networking website that allows for real-time interactive communications, the CCO (and each person listed on Exhibit 2) must monitor third-party postings for possible client complaints (daily/weekly).

   a. *Complaints.* If the Advisor (or any personnel of the Advisor) detects a customer complaint through monitoring, the Advisor must follow its usual complaint procedures.
   b. *Red Flags.* If the third-party content contains red flags that suggest that the third-party content is misleading, or if the posting appears offensive or inappropriate, the content shall be removed. Each person listed on Exhibit 2 shall monitor third-party postings at least weekly and shall alert the CCO to red flags. The CCO (or an officer of the Advisor working at the CCO's direction) shall monitor the site for complaints and red flags as noted above.
   c. *Adoption or Endorsement of Third-Party Postings Prohibited.* The Advisor does not permit any activity by its employees that would amount to adopting third-party content or endorsing it. The following specific activities are prohibited by any employee:
       i. assisting in the preparation of content for any third party;
       ii. requesting a third party to post content;
       iii. paying for the production or posting of content;
       iv. endorsing the content through other posts (e.g., liking the content);
       v. endorsing the content of a third party by including it in one of the employee's posts;
       vi. forwarding or re-posting third-party content; and,
       vii. incorporating third-party content into the Advisor's content.

2. Who is Responsible for Implementing this Policy?

The CCO is responsible for implementing and monitoring this policy and for reviewing and approving all materials to be utilized in social media to ensure the materials are consistent with the Advisor's internal guidelines and applicable regulatory requirements. The [insert name] (the "Department") is responsible for maintaining, as part of the Advisor's books and records, copies of all social media materials including all backup documentation and a record of reviews and approvals in accordance with the Advisor's Record-keeping Policy.

3. Procedures to Implement this Policy

Social media materials and communications will generally be prepared by or under the supervision of the Department. The key elements of the procedures are summarized below:

- All advertisements and promotional materials must be reviewed and approved by the CCO prior to use.

- Each employee that is authorized to post information on a social media site on behalf of the Advisor is responsible for ensuring that the CCO has expressly approved any static social media material used in writing. Any modification to previously approved materials must be re-submitted to the CCO for re-approval.
- The Department is responsible for maintaining copies of any social media materials, including backup documentation and any reviews and approvals, for at least six years following the last time any material is disseminated.
- The CCO shall maintain, as Exhibit 2 to this policy, a list of those individuals that are permitted to post information to social media websites on behalf of the Advisor. This list shall be approved and dated by the CCO. This list shall also designate the individuals that are permitted to participate in any interactive portions of social media websites on behalf of the Advisor.

4. Pre-approval Process for Static Content Social

Prior to disseminating any social media materials the CCO or his/her designee should review them in accordance with the following guidelines. The CCO or his/her designee may consult with the Advisor's outside counsel to resolve any uncertainty or novel issues about the application of these requirements to new social media materials.

The CCO or his/her designee shall take the following steps:

- Assure that a copy of the social media material is maintained, along with any supporting records. The Advisor should maintain the advertising records in a manner so that they are readily available to the regulatory inspection staff.
- Review all materials for any false, misleading, or promissory statements or any omissions that make a statement misleading in the context in which made.
- Review materials for accuracy and to eliminate any prohibited content, including recommendations.
- Review materials relating to any product or service to determine if there is any required disclosure.
- Review the accuracy of any calculation of any performance data that is proposed to be submitted to the static portion of a social media website and confirm that the format and content of the performance data complies with the Advisor's advertising policies, including the policy on past specific recommendations.

5. Employees Authorized to Post Interactive Content

- Each employee that is authorized to post interactive content shall have previously submitted advertising material for review by the CCO.
- The employee shall have complied with all advertising policies of the advisor.
- The employee shall not have been (warned or) sanctioned under the Advisor's compliance policies or procedures, including the Code of Ethics.
- The employee shall have met with the CCO and demonstrated familiarity with (i) this policy and (ii) the SEC's advertising rules.
- The employee shall have submitted proposed posts for review by the CCO which posts have met with the CCO's approval. The employee shall pre-clear his/her blog posts with the CCO until the CCO grants permission to cease pre-clearance.

6. Monitoring Interactive Content
The CCO or his/her designee shall take the following steps:

- The CCO will institute a program of ongoing monitoring of the Advisor's social media postings, including any third-party responses to the Advisor's postings, by reviewing interactive content on the sites listed on Exhibit 1 at least weekly.
- The CCO will institute a program of periodic monitoring of employee social media sites for compliance with this policy.
- The Advisor may utilize the services of a third-party to monitor its social media postings and any third-party responses thereto. If the Advisor utilizes the services of a third party for monitoring purposes, the Advisor shall obtain a periodic certification attesting that the firm has conducted ongoing monitoring of the Advisor's use of social media and any third-party content posted in response thereto, for compliance with this policy and any findings of non-compliance.
- In response to any third-party postings (including Likes) in response to the Advisor's social media content, the CCO shall review the third-party postings to determine whether, in the opinion of the Advisor, such third-party postings might be considered a testimonial of the Advisor's social media content. If the Advisor determines that the third-party posting may contain testimonial material, the Advisor will remove the third-party posting and, if necessary, related Advisor content. The Advisor shall document all determinations taken in response to third-party postings.
- The Advisor shall obtain periodic certifications from all employees attesting that they did not post any information that is related to the Advisor or the Advisor's business to any website or in any interactive media.

I have read the Advisor's Use of Social Media Policy and understand the foregoing. I agree to abide by the restrictions on the use of social media by employees the Advisor as set forth in this Policy and understand that a violation of this Policy by me may lead to disciplinary action, up to and including monetary penalties, and termination of employment.

Print name _____

Signature_____

Date _____

Exhibit 1

List of Permitted Social Media Sites

1. Twitter
2. LinkedIn

CCO Approved: _____

Print Name: _____

Date: _____

Exhibit 2

List of Approved Persons

1. [insert name]Will monitor third-party content on [insert name of site] (Approved/Not Approved to Post Interactive Content)

CCO Approved: _____

Print Name: _____

Date: _____

Regulatory Notice   11-39

Social Media Websites and the Use of Personal Devices for Business Communications

Guidance on Social Networking Websites and Business Communications

Executive Summary

In January 2010, FINRA issued *Regulatory Notice 10-06*, providing guidance on the application of FINRA rules governing communications with the public to social media sites and reminding firms of the recordkeeping, suitability, supervision and content requirements for such communications. Since its publication, firms have raised additional questions regarding the application of the rules. This *Notice* responds to these questions by providing further clarification concerning application of the rules to new technologies. It is not intended to alter the principles or the guidance provided in *Regulatory Notice 10-06*.

Questions concerning this *Notice* may be directed to:

► Joseph E. Price, Senior Vice President, Advertising Regulation/Corporate Financing, at (240) 386-4623;

► Thomas A. Pappas, Vice President, Advertising Regulation, at (240) 386-4553; or

► Amy Sochard, Director, Advertising Regulation, at (240) 386-4508.

August 2011

Notice type:
► Guidance

Suggested Routing
► Advertising
► Compliance
► Legal
► Operations
► Registered Representative
► Senior Management

Key Topics
► Communications With the Public
► Personal Electronic Devices
► Recordkeeping
► Social Networking Websites
► Supervision

Referenced Rules & Notices
► NASD Rule 2210
► NASD Rule 2211
► NASD Rule 3010
► FINRA Rule 4511
► NTM 05-48
► Regulatory Notice 08-77
► Regulatory Notice 10-06
► Regulatory Notice 11-14
► SEA Rule 17a-3
► SEA Rule 17a-4

FINRA
Financial Industry Regulatory Authority

1

Background

1. Recordkeeping

The obligations of a firm to keep records of communications made through social media depend on whether the content of the communication constitutes a business communication. Rule 17a-4(b) under the Securities Exchange Act of 1934 (SEA) requires broker-dealers to preserve certain records for a period of not less than three years, the first two in an easily accessible place.[1] Among these records, pursuant to SEA Rule 17a-4(b)(4), are "[o]riginals of all communications received and copies of all communications sent (and any approvals thereof) by the member, broker or dealer (including inter-office memoranda and communications) relating to its business as such, including all communications which are subject to rules of a self-regulatory organization of which the member, broker or dealer is a member regarding communications with the public."[2] The SEC has stated that the content of an electronic communication determines whether it must be preserved.[3]

2. Supervision

NASD Rule 3010 requires each firm to establish and maintain a system to supervise the activities of each associated person that is reasonably designed to achieve compliance with applicable federal securities laws and FINRA rules. As part of this responsibility, a registered principal must review prior to use any social media site that an associated person intends to employ for a business purpose. The registered principal may approve use of the site for a business purpose only if the registered principal has determined that the associated person can and will comply with all applicable FINRA rules, the federal securities laws, including recordkeeping requirements, and any additional requirements established by the firm.

The registered principal must review an associated person's proposed social media site in the form in which it will be "launched." Some firms require a registered principal to review the first posting by an associated person on an interactive forum within the site. This approach can help to ensure that the registered principal will be reviewing not only the initial communication, but the social media site itself in its completed design.

FINRA considers unscripted participation in an interactive electronic forum to come within the definition of "public appearance" under NASD Rule 2210. Public appearances do not require prior approval by a registered principal. Firms may adopt risk-based supervisory procedures utilizing post-use review, including sampling and lexicon-based search methodologies, of unscripted participation in an interactive electronic forum. The procedures a firm adopts must be reasonably designed to ensure that interactive electronic communications do not violate FINRA or SEC rules, including the content requirements of NASD Rule 2210, such as the prohibition on misleading statements or claims and the requirement that communications be fair and balanced. A static posting is deemed an "advertisement" under NASD Rule 2210 and therefore requires a registered principal to approve the posting prior to use.[4]

3. Links to Third-Party Sites

Firms may not establish a link to any third-party site that the firm knows or has reason to know contains false or misleading content. A firm should not include a link on its website if there are any red flags that indicate the linked site contains false or misleading content. Additionally, a firm is responsible under NASD Rule 2210 for content on a linked third-party site if the firm has adopted or has become entangled with its content. For example, a firm may be deemed to have "adopted" third-party content if it indicates on its site that it endorses the content on the third-party site. A firm could be deemed to have become "entangled" with a third-party site if, for example, it participates in the development of the content on the third-party site.

4. Data Feeds

Firms must adopt procedures to manage data feeds into their own websites. FINRA is aware of situations in which firms have received data feeds that were inaccurate. Firms must be familiar with the proficiency of the vendor of the data and its ability to provide data that is accurate as of the time it is presented on the firm's website. Firms also must understand the criteria followed by vendors in gathering or calculating the types of data that the firm intends to feed into its website, in order to determine whether the vendor is performing this function in a reasonable manner.[5] Firms also should regularly review aspects of these data feeds for any red flags that indicate that the data may not be accurate, and should promptly take necessary measures to correct any inaccurate data.

Questions & Answers

Recordkeeping

Q1: Does determining whether a communication is subject to the recordkeeping requirements of SEA Rule 17a-4(b)(4) depend on whether an associated person uses a personal device or technology to make the communication?

A1: SEA Rule 17a-4(b)(4) requires a firm to retain records of communications that relate to its "business as such." Whether a particular communication is related to the business of the firm depends upon the facts and circumstances. This analysis does not depend upon the type of device or technology used to transmit the communication, nor does it depend upon whether it is a firm-issued or personal device of the individual; rather, the content of the communication is determinative. For instance, the requirement would apply if the electronic communication was received or sent by an associated person through a third-party's platform or system. A firm's policies and procedures must include training and education of its associated persons regarding the differences between business and non-business communications and the measures required to ensure that any business communication made by associated persons is retained, retrievable and supervised.

Q2: When an associated person posts autobiographical information, such as place of employment or job responsibilities, does this information constitute a business communication?

A2: As discussed in question 1 above, firms must develop policies and procedures that include training regarding the difference between business and non-business communications to enable appropriate compliance. In certain contexts, such as sending a resume to a potential employer, the communication could be viewed as not relevant to the business of the firm. In other contexts, such as posting a list of products or services offered by the firm, the communication likely will be viewed as a business communication.

Q3: May a firm or associated person sponsor a social media site or use a communication device that includes technology which automatically erases or deletes the content?

A3: No. Technology that automatically erases or deletes the content of an electronic communication would preclude the ability of the firm to retain the communications in compliance with their obligations under SEA Rule 17a-4. Accordingly, firms and associated persons may not sponsor such sites or use such devices.

Q4: Do the recordkeeping requirements apply to third-party posts to a firm or an associated person's social media sites if the firm or the individual has not adopted or become entangled with the post?

A4: *Regulatory Notice 10-06* addresses the application of NASD Rule 2210 to third-party posts on a social media site established by a firm or its associated persons. Unless the firm or its associated persons have adopted or become entangled with the post, FINRA generally does not treat third-party posts as the firm's or its associated persons' communications under the rule. The recordkeeping requirements, however, require retention of the records of all communications received by a firm or its associated persons relating to its business as such.

Q5: Do the recordkeeping requirements differ for static and interactive communications?

A5: They do not—the recordkeeping requirements are governed by the content of the communication. As noted above, the FINRA *supervision* requirements differ for static and interactive communications.

Supervision

Q6: Can interactive content become static?

A6: Yes. For example, interactive content could be copied or forwarded and posted in a static forum, such as a blog or static area of a Web page, in a manner that renders it static content. It then would constitute an advertisement under NASD Rule 2210, requiring prior approval by a registered principal of the firm.

Q7: What measures should a firm adopt to monitor compliance with its social media policies?

A7: A firm must conduct appropriate training and education concerning its policies, including those relating to social media. Firms must follow up on "red flags" that may indicate that an associated person is not complying with firm policies. Some firms require each associated person to certify on an annual or more frequent basis that the associated person is acting in a manner consistent with such policies. When feasible, some firms also have chosen to randomly spot check websites to help them monitor compliance with firm policies.

Q8: Must material changes to static content posted by a firm or its associated persons on a social media site that contains business communications receive prior approval by a registered principal?

A8: NASD Rule 2210(1)(b) requires a registered principal to approve each advertisement and item of sales literature before the earlier of its use or filing with FINRA's Advertising Regulation Department. NASD Rule 2210(c)(8) excludes from the filing requirements any advertisement or sales literature that previously had been filed and that is to be used "without material change." Firms are expected to adopt procedures requiring prior registered principal approval of any advertisement or sales literature that has been materially changed, even if it had been previously approved in an earlier version. For example, changes in the description of the advantages of investing in the advertised product or of its risks would typically require registered principal prior approval. Since static content posted by a firm or its associated persons on a social media site that contains business communications is considered to be an advertisement, these procedures must apply to such static content.

Third-Party Posts, Third-Party Links and Websites

Q9: If a third party posts a business-related communication, such as a question about a security, on an associated person's personal social media site, may the associated person respond to the communication?

A9: Yes, provided that the response does not violate the firm's policies concerning participation on a personal social media site. If a firm has a policy that associated persons may not use a personal social media site for business purposes, then a substantive response by the associated person would violate this policy.[6] Some firms permit a non-substantive response, and pre-approve statements that their associated persons may make to respond to such posts and that direct the third party to other firm-approved communication media, such as the firm's email system.

Q10: To what extent is a firm responsible for any third-party website that the firm or its associated person "co-brands"?

A10: Under NASD Rule 2210, a firm that co-brands any part of a third-party site, such as by placing the firm's logo prominently on the site, is responsible for the content of the entire site. Under these circumstances, FINRA considers the firm to have adopted the content on that site. A firm is responsible under NASD Rule 2210 for content on a linked third-party site if the firm has adopted or become entangled with its content. *Regulatory Notice 10-06* describes the "adoption" and "entanglement" theories as they apply to third-party posts on a firm's social media sites. FINRA considers a firm to have adopted content in a third-party post if the firm or its personnel explicitly or implicitly endorse or approve the post.

Q11: When is a firm *not* responsible for the content on a third-party site to which it links?

A11: A firm may establish a link to the site of an independent third party without assuming responsibility for the content of that site under NASD Rule 2210 if:

▶ the firm does not "adopt" or become "entangled" with the content of the third-party site; and

▶ the firm does not know or have reason to know that the site contains false or misleading information.

Q12: If firm policy requires deletion of inappropriate third-party content, will the firm be considered to have adopted any third-party posts that are not deleted?

A12: No. The fact that the firm has a policy of routinely blocking or deleting certain types of content in order to ensure the content is appropriate would not mean that the firm had adopted the content of the posts left on the site. For example, most firms using social media sites block or screen offensive material. Such a policy would not indicate that the firm has adopted the remaining third-party content.

Q13: Does NASD Rule 2210 require firms to approve or maintain records of statistical information that the firm has regularly updated on its website?

A13: NASD Rule 2210(b)(1) requires that a registered principal approve each advertisement and item of sales literature prior to use or filing with FINRA's Advertising Regulation Department. NASD Rule 2210(b)(2) requires firms to maintain all advertisements and sales literature, including the names of the persons who prepared them or approved their use, for a period beginning on the date of first use and ending three years from the date of last use.

Statistical information that is posted on a firm's website would be considered an "advertisement" subject to the approval and recordkeeping requirements of NASD Rules 2210(b)(1) and (2). However, some firms establish templates for the presentation of this data, and subject these templates to those provisions. The data that is fed into the website in accordance with such a template would not be subject to the requirements of NASD Rules 2210(b)(1) and (2). The firm must have procedures reasonably designed to ensure that the data can be verified to ensure that it is timely and accurate, and that the firm can promptly correct data that is erroneous when posted or becomes inaccurate over time.

Accessing Social Media Sites From Personal Devices

Q14: May associated persons use personal communication devices and other equipment, such as a smart phone or tablet computer, to access firm business applications and perform business activity if the firm employs technology that enables the firm to keep records and supervise the activity?

A14: Yes. Firms may permit their associated persons to use any personal communication device, whether it is owned by the associated person or the firm, for business communications. FINRA recognizes that the development of new technologies can facilitate the ability of associated persons to perform their responsibilities and, in the case of registered representatives, to serve their clients. Of course, the firm must be able to retain, retrieve and supervise business communications regardless of whether they are conducted from a device owned by the firm or by the associated person.

In order to ensure that the business communications are readily retrievable without necessitating the capture of personal communications made on the same device, firms should have the ability to separate business and personal communications, such as by requiring that the associated persons use a separately identifiable application on the device for their business communications. If possible, this application should provide a secure portal into the firm's own communication system, particularly if confidential customer information may be shared. If the firm has the ability to separate business and personal communications, and has adequate electronic communications policies and procedures regarding usage, then the firm is not required to supervise the personal emails made on these devices. Of course, firms also are free to treat all communications made through the personal communication device as business communications.

Endnotes

1. SEA Rule 17a-4(f) permits broker-dealers to maintain and preserve these records on "micrographic media" or by means of "electronic storage media," as defined in the rule and subject to a number of conditions.

2. *See also* NASD Rule 2210(b)(2) (requiring the retention of all advertisements, sales literature and independently prepared reprints), NASD Rule 2211(b)(2) (requiring the retention of institutional sales material) and NASD Rule 3010(d)(3) (requiring the retention of correspondence of registered representatives).

3. *See* Reporting Requirements for Brokers or Dealers under the Securities Exchange Act of 1934, SEC Rel. No. 34-38245 (Feb. 5, 1997).

4. FINRA has filed with the SEC a proposed rule change that would replace most of the NASD and NYSE rules governing communications with the public with a series of new FINRA rules. *See* SR-FINRA-2011-035. Among other changes, the term "advertisement" would be subsumed within a new communication category, "retail communication."

5. *Cf. Regulatory Notice 08-77* (Dec. 2008) (Customer Account Statements) (discussion of "data vendors"). *See also Notice to Members (NTM) 05-48* (July 2005) (Members' Responsibilities When Outsourcing Activities to Third-Party Service Providers); *Regulatory Notice 11-14* (March 2011) (FINRA Requests Comment on Proposed New FINRA Rule 3190 to Clarify the Scope of a Firm's Obligations and Supervisory Responsibilities for Functions or Activities Outsourced to a Third-Party Service Provider).

6. Of course, if the firm permits business-related communications on a personal social media site, then the firm must supervise that site for compliance with applicable rules and the federal securities laws.

Regulatory Notice 10-06

Social Media Web Sites

Guidance on Blogs and Social Networking Web Sites

Executive Summary

Americans are increasingly using social media Web sites, such as blogs and social networking sites, for business and personal communications. Firms have asked FINRA staff how the FINRA rules governing communications with the public apply to social media sites that are sponsored by a firm or its registered representatives. This *Notice* provides guidance to firms regarding these issues.

Questions concerning this *Notice* may be directed to:

➤ Joseph E. Price, Senior Vice President, Advertising Regulation/ Corporate Financing, at (240) 386-4623; or

➤ Thomas A. Pappas, Vice President and Director, Advertising Regulation, at (240) 386-4500.

Background

According to a recent report by the Pew Internet and American Life Project, 46 percent of American adults who use the Internet logged onto a social networking site in 2009, which is up from 8 percent in 2005.[1] Other studies have shown that use of social media sites by businesses to communicate with customers and the public has grown significantly in the past few years.[2]

FINRA has provided guidance concerning particular applications of the communications rules to interactive Web sites in the past. For example, in March 1999, FINRA stated that a registered representative's participation in an Internet chat room is subject to the same requirements as a presentation in person before a group of investors.[3] This guidance was codified in 2003, when FINRA defined the term "public appearance" in NASD Rule 2210 to include participation in an interactive electronic forum.[4]

January 2010

Notice Type
➤ Guidance

Suggested Routing
➤ Advertising
➤ Compliance
➤ Legal
➤ Operations
➤ Registered Representative
➤ Senior Management

Key Topics
➤ Blogs
➤ Communications with the Public
➤ Recordkeeping
➤ Social Networking Web Sites
➤ Supervision

Referenced Rules & Notices
➤ ICA Section 24(b)
➤ NASD Rule 2210
➤ NASD Rule 2310
➤ NASD Rule 2711
➤ NASD Rule 3010
➤ NASD Rule 3070
➤ NASD Rule 3110
➤ NYSE Rule 351
➤ NYSE Rule 401A
➤ NYSE Rule 410
➤ NYSE Rule 472
➤ NTM 01-23
➤ NTM 03-33
➤ Regulatory Notice 07-59
➤ Regulatory Notice 09-55
➤ SEA Rule 17a-3
➤ SEA Rule 17a-4
➤ Securities Act Rule 482

FINra

Financial Industry Regulatory Authority

1

FINRA also has provided guidance regarding the application of the communication rules in its *Guide to the Internet for Registered Representatives*,[5] and has released podcasts on these issues to help educate firms and their personnel.[6] Nevertheless, FINRA staff has continued to receive numerous inquiries from firms and others concerning how the FINRA rules governing communications with the public apply to the use of social media sites by firms and their registered representatives. Firms also have inquired regarding their recordkeeping responsibilities for communications posted on social media sites.

In September 2009, FINRA organized a Social Networking Task Force composed of FINRA staff and industry representatives to discuss how firms and their registered representatives could use social media sites for legitimate business purposes in a manner that ensures investor protection. Based on input from the Task Force and others, and further staff consideration of these issues, FINRA is issuing this *Notice* to guide firms on applying the communications rules to social media sites, such as blogs and social networking sites. The goal of this *Notice* is to ensure that—as the use of social media sites increases over time—investors are protected from false or mislead-ing claims and representations, and firms are able to effectively and appropriately supervise their associated persons' participation in these sites. At the same time, FINRA is seeking to interpret its rules in a flexible manner to allow firms to communicate with clients and investors using this new technology.

While many firms may find that the guidance in this *Notice* is useful when establishing their own procedures, each firm must develop policies and procedures that are best designed to ensure that the firm and its personnel comply with all applicable requirements. Every firm should consider the guidance provided by this *Notice* in the context of its own business and its compliance and supervisory programs.

This *Notice* only addresses the use by a firm or its personnel of social media sites for business purposes. The *Notice* does not purport to address the use by individuals of social media sites for purely personal reasons.

Questions & Answers

Recordkeeping Responsibilities

Q1: Are firms required to retain records of communications related to the broker-dealer's business that are made through social media sites?

A1: Yes. Every firm that intends to communicate, or permit its associated persons to communicate, through social media sites must first ensure that it can retain records of those communications as required by Rules 17a-3 and 17a-4 under the Securities Exchange Act of 1934 and NASD Rule 3110. SEC and FINRA rules require that for record retention purposes, the content of the communication is determinative and a broker-dealer must retain those electronic communications that relate to its "business as such."[7]

FINRA is aware that some technology providers are developing systems that are intended to enable firms to retain records of communications made through social media sites. Some systems might interface with a firm's network to capture social media participation and feed it into existing systems for the review and retention of email. Other providers are developing technology that might permit a registered representative working off-site to elect to access social media through platforms that will retain the communications on behalf of the firm.

Of course, it is up to each firm to determine whether any particular technology, system or program provides the retention and retrieval functions necessary to comply with the books and records rules. FINRA does not endorse any particular technology necessary to keep such records, nor is it certain that adequate technology currently exists.

Suitability Responsibilities

Q2: If a firm or its personnel recommends a security through a social media site, does this trigger the requirements of NASD Rule 2310 regarding suitability?

A2: Yes. Whether a particular communication constitutes a "recommendation" for purposes of Rule 2310 will depend on the facts and circumstances of the communication. Firms should consult *Notice to Members (NTM) 01-23* (Online Suitability) for additional guidance concerning when an online communication falls within the definition of "recommendation" under Rule 2310.

Various social media sites include functions that make their content widely available or that limit access to one or more individuals. Rule 2310 requires a broker-dealer to determine that a recommendation is suitable for every investor to whom it is made.

Q3: What factors should firms consider when developing procedures for supervising interactive electronic communications on a social media site that recommend specific investment products?

A3: Communications that recommend specific investment products often present greater challenges for a firm's compliance program than other communications. As discussed above, they may trigger the FINRA suitability rule, thus creating possible substantive liability for the firm or a registered representative. These communications must often include additional disclosure in order to provide the customer with a sound basis for evaluating the facts with respect to the product. They also might trigger other requirements under the federal securities laws.[8] FINRA has brought disciplinary actions regarding interactive electronic communications that contained misleading statements about investment products that the communications recommended.[9]

For these reasons, firms must adopt policies and procedures reasonably designed to address communications that recommend specific investment products. As a best practice, firms should consider prohibiting all interactive electronic communications that recommend a specific investment product and any link to such a recommendation unless a registered principal has previously approved the content.

Alternatively, many firms maintain databases of previously approved communications and provide their personnel with routine access to these templates. Firms might consider prohibiting communications that recommend a specific investment product unless the communication conforms to a pre-approved template and the specific recommendation has been approved by a registered principal. Firms also should consider adopting policies and procedures governing communications that promote specific investment products, even if these communications might not constitute a "recommendation" for purposes of our suitability rule or otherwise.

Types of Interactive Electronic Forums

The definition of "public appearance" in NASD Rule 2210 includes unscripted participation in an interactive electronic forum such as a chat room or online seminar. Rule 2210 does not require firms to have a registered principal approve in advance the extemporaneous remarks of personnel who participate in public appearances. However, these interactive electronic forums are subject to other supervisory requirements and to the content requirements of FINRA's communications rule.

Q4: Does a blog constitute an "interactive electronic forum" for purposes of Rule 2210?

A4: The treatment of a blog under Rule 2210 depends on the manner and purposes for which the blog has been constructed. Merriam-Webster's Online Dictionary defines "blog" as "a Web site that contains an online personal journal with reflections, comments, and often hyperlinks provided by the writer."[10] Historically, some blogs have consisted of static content posted by the blogger. FINRA considers static postings to constitute "advertisements" under Rule 2210. If a firm or its registered representative sponsors such a blog, it must obtain prior principal approval of any such posting. Today, however, many blogs enable users to engage in real-time interactive communications. If the blog is used to engage in real-time interactive communications, FINRA would consider the blog to be an interactive electronic forum that does not require prior principal approval; however, such communications must be supervised, as discussed below.[11]

Q5: Social networking sites, such as Facebook, Twitter and LinkedIn, typically include both static content and interactive functions. Are these sites interactive electronic forums for purposes of Rule 2210?

A5: Social networking sites typically contain both static and interactive content. The static content remains posted until it is changed by the firm or individual who established the account on the site. Generally, static content is accessible to all visitors to the site.

Examples of static content typically available through social networking sites include profile, background or wall information. As with other Web-based communications such as banner advertisements, a registered principal of the firm must approve all static content on a page of a social networking site established by the firm or a registered representative before it is posted.[12] Firms may use an electronic system to document these approvals.

Social networking sites also contain non-static, real-time communications, such as interactive posts on sites such as Twitter and Facebook. The portion of a social networking site that provides for these interactive communications constitutes an interactive electronic forum, and firms are not required to have a registered principal approve these communications prior to use. Of course, firms still must supervise these communications, as discussed below.

10-06   January 2010

Supervision of Social Media Sites

Q6: How must firms supervise interactive electronic communications by the firm or its registered representatives using blogs or social networking sites?

A6: The content provisions of FINRA's communications rules apply to interactive electronic communications that the firm or its personnel send through a social media site. While prior principal approval is not required under Rule 2210 for interactive electronic forums, firms must supervise these interactive electronic communications under NASD Rule 3010 in a manner reasonably designed to ensure that they do not violate the content requirements of FINRA's communications rules.[13]

Firms may adopt supervisory procedures similar to those outlined for electronic correspondence in *Regulatory Notice 07-59* (FINRA Guidance Regarding Review and Supervision of Electronic Communications). As set forth in that *Notice*, firms may employ risk-based principles to determine the extent to which the review of incoming, outgoing and internal electronic communications is necessary for the proper supervision of their business.

For example, firms may adopt procedures that require principal review of some or all interactive electronic communications prior to use or may adopt various methods of post-use review, including sampling and lexicon-based search methodologies as discussed in *Regulatory Notice 07-59*. We are aware that technology providers are developing or may have developed systems that are intended to address both the books and records rules and supervisory procedures for social media sites that are similar or equivalent to those currently in use for emails and other electronic communications. FINRA does not endorse any particular technology. Whatever procedures firms adopt, however, must be reasonably designed to ensure that interactive electronic communications do not violate FINRA or SEC rules.

Firms are also reminded that they must have policies and procedures, as described in *Regulatory Notice 07-59*, for the review by a supervisor of employees' incoming, outgoing and internal electronic communications that are of a specific subject matter that require review under FINRA rules and federal securities laws, including:

➤ NASD Rule 2711(b)(3)(A) and NYSE Rule 472(b)(3), which require that a firm's legal and compliance department be copied on communications between non-research and research departments concerning the content of a research report;

➤ NASD Rule 3070(c) and NYSE Rule 351(d), which require the identification and reporting of customer complaints; NYSE Rule 401A requires that the receipt of each complaint be acknowledged by the firm to the customer within 15 business days; and

> ➤ NASD Rule 3110(j) and NYSE Rule 410, which require the identification and prior written approval of every order error and other account designation change.

Q7: What restrictions should firms place on which personnel may establish an account with a social media site?

A7: Firms must adopt policies and procedures reasonably designed to ensure that their associated persons who participate in social media sites for business purposes are appropriately supervised, have the necessary training and background to engage in such activities, and do not present undue risks to investors. Firms must have a general policy prohibiting any associated person from engaging in business communications in a social media site that is not subject to the firm's supervision. Firms also must require that only those associated persons who have received appropriate training on the firm's policies and procedures regarding interactive electronic communications may engage in such communications.

As firms develop their policies, they should consider prohibiting or placing restrictions on any associated person who has presented compliance risks in the past, particularly compliance risks concerning sales practices, from establishing accounts for business purposes with a social media site. In its supervision of social networking sites, each firm must monitor the extent to which associated persons are complying with the firm's policies and procedures governing the use of these sites. Firms also should consider policies that address associated persons' continued use of such sites if the firm's supervisory systems demonstrate compliance risks. Firms should take disciplinary action if the firm's policies are violated.

Third-Party Posts

Q8: If a customer or other third party posts content on a social media site established by the firm or its personnel, does FINRA consider the third-party content to be the firm's communication with the public under Rule 2210?

A8: As a general matter, FINRA does not treat posts by customers or other third parties as the firm's communication with the public subject to Rule 2210. Thus, the prior principal approval, content and filing requirements of Rule 2210 do not apply to these posts.

Under certain circumstances, however, third-party posts may become attributable to the firm. Whether third-party content is attributable to a firm depends on whether the firm has (1) involved itself in the preparation of the content or (2) explicitly or implicitly endorsed or approved the content.

The SEC has referred to circumstance (1) above as the "entanglement" theory (*i.e.*, the firm or its personnel is entangled with the preparation of the third-party post) and (2) as the "adoption" theory (*i.e.*, the firm or its personnel has adopted its content).[14] Although the SEC has employed these theories as a basis for a company's responsibility for third-party information that is hyperlinked to its Web site, a similar analysis would apply to third-party posts on a social media site established by the firm or its personnel.

For example, FINRA would consider such a third-party post to be a communication with the public by the firm or its personnel under the entanglement theory if the firm or its personnel paid for or otherwise was involved with the preparation of the content prior to posting. FINRA also would consider a third-party post to be a communication with the public by the firm or its personnel under the adoption theory if, after the content is posted, the firm or its personnel explicitly or implicitly endorses or approves the post.[15]

Q9: Must a firm also use a disclaimer to inform customers that third-party posts do not reflect the views of the firm and have not been reviewed by the firm for completeness or accuracy?

A9: Assuming the disclaimer was sufficiently prominent to inform investors of the firm's position, such a disclaimer would be part of the facts and circumstances that FINRA would consider in an analysis of whether a firm had adopted or become entangled with a posting.

Q10: Must a firm monitor third-party posts?

A10: FINRA does not consider a third-party post to be a firm communication with the public unless the firm or its personnel either is entangled with the preparation of the third-party post or has adopted its content. Nevertheless, FINRA has found through its discussions with members of the Social Networking Task Force and others that many firms monitor third-party posts on firm Web sites. For example, some firms monitor third-party posts to mitigate the perception that the firm is adopting a third-party post, to address copyright issues or to assist compliance with the "Good Samaritan" safe harbor for blocking and screening offensive material under the Communications Decency Act.[16]

Some of the other best practices adopted by Task Force members include:

➤ establishing appropriate usage guidelines for customers and other third parties that are permitted to post on firm-sponsored Web sites;

➤ establishing processes for screening third-party content based on the expected usage and frequency of third-party posts; and

➤ disclosing firm policies regarding its responsibility for third-party posts.

January 2010   10-06

Endnotes

1   *See* Amanda Lenhart, Pew Internet and American Life Project, *The Democratization of Online Social Networks* (Oct. 8, 2009), *http://fe01.pewinternet.org/Presentations/2009/41--The-Democratization-of-Online-Social-Networks.aspx.*

2   Sharon Gaudin, *Business Use of Facebook, Twitter Exploding,* Computerworld (Nov. 9, 2009), at *www.computerworld.com/s/article/9140579/Business_use_of_Twitter_Facebook_exploding.*

3   *See* "Ask the Analyst – Electronic Communications," NASD Regulation, *Regulatory & Compliance Alert* (Mar. 1999) ("March 1999 Ask the Analyst").

4   *See* NASD Rule 2210(a)(5).

5   *See Guide to the Internet for Registered Representatives,* at *www.finra.org/Industry/Issues/Advertising/p006118.*

6   *See* "Electronic Communications: Blogs, Bulletin Boards and Chat Rooms" (Feb. 23, 2009), and "Electronic Communications: Social Networking Web Sites" (Mar. 10, 2009) at *www.finra.org/ podcasts.*

    FINRA is also hosting webinars on compliance considerations for social networking sites on February 3 and March 17, 2010. Find more information at *www.finra.org/webinars.*

7   *See,* SEC Rel. No. 34-37182 (May 9, 1996), 61 Fed. Reg. 24644 (May 15, 1996); SEC Rel. No. 34-38245 (Feb. 5, 1997), 62 Fed. Reg. 6469 (Feb. 12, 1997); *Notice to Members 03-33* (July 2003).

8   For example, even if FINRA considers a communication made through an interactive electronic forum to be a public appearance, the SEC staff could still conclude that Rule 482 under the Securities Act of 1933 and the filing requirements of Section 24(b) of the Investment Company Act of 1940 apply to the communication. Accordingly, firms must consider these requirements in determining whether to permit interactive electronic communications that discuss registered investment companies.

9   For example, in a Default Decision dated November 23, 2009, FINRA fined and suspended a registered principal who held put options for himself and issued unapproved bulletin board messages that urged investors to sell the underlying stock. The bulletin board messages omitted material disclosure regarding his interest in the stock.

10 Merriam-Webster's Online Dictionary, definition of "blog," at *http://www.merriam-webster.com/dictionary/BLOG.*

11 The key to this distinction between whether a blog is considered an advertisement versus an interactive electronic forum is whether it is used to engage in real-time interactive communications with third parties. Thus, the mere updating of a non-interactive blog (or any other firm Web page) does not cause it to become an interactive electronic forum, even if the updating occurs frequently.

12 Currently, NASD Rule 2210(b) requires that a registered principal of a firm approve all advertisements and sales literature prior to use either electronically or in writing. FINRA has proposed amendments to this rule. These amendments would retain this prior to use principal approval requirement for "retail communications" as defined in the proposal. *See Regulatory Notice 09-55* (Sept. 2009).

Endnotes Continued

13 *See, e.g.,* March 1999 Ask the Analyst, *supra*
note 3.

14 *See Commission Guidance on the Use of*
Company Web Sites, SEC Rel. No. 34-58288
(Aug. 1, 2008), 73 Fed. Reg. 45862, 45870 (Aug.
7, 2008) ("2008 SEC Release"); *Use of Electronic*
Media, SEC Rel. No. 33-7856 (April 28, 2000), 65
Fed. Reg. 25843, 25848-25849 (May 4, 2000).

15 *See* 2008 SEC Release, *supra* note 14, 65 Fed.
Reg. 45870 n.78.

16 *See* 47 U.S.C. § 230(c).

Guide to the Internet for Registered Representatives

Introduction

NASD has developed this page to make registered representatives (RRs) aware of the compliance requirements and potential liabilities when using the Internet and electronic communications.

This page addresses some general compliance requirements that apply to electronic communications. It also discusses specific considerations relating to the use of e-mail, group e-mail, and Web sites including chat rooms and instant messaging. We have based the information on published rules, interpretations and notices. Wherever possible, a link to the actual text of the rule or interpretation is provided.

An RR's compliance responsibilities when communicating via the Internet or other electronic media are the same as in face-to-face discussions or in written communications with the public. In addition, RRs must be aware of internal firm policies and procedures that may limit, prohibit, or restrict the use of electronic communications.

General Compliance Requirements

Electronic communications may fall under any one of the following categories of communications. They may be considered as correspondence, public appearances, advertisements, sales literature, reprints and institutional sales material. These methods of communication are covered under the NASD Conduct Rules and also explained on the Advertising Regulation Web page. In general:

- Publicly available Web sites are considered **advertisements**.

- E-mail to 25 or more prospective retail customers is considered **sales literature**.

- E-mail to either a single customer (prospective or existing) or to an unlimited number of existing retail customers and/or less than 25 prospective retail customers (firm-wide) within a 30 day period is considered **correspondence**.

Communications with the public must:

- be based on principles of fair dealing and not omit material information, particularly risk disclosure;

- not make exaggerated, unwarranted, or misleading claims;

- give the investor a sound basis for making an investment decision; and

- not contain predictions or projections of investment results.

NASD would give close scrutiny to circumstances where an RR personally buys shares of a thinly traded stock and then publicly makes a buy recommendation, or promotes the stock in a chat room.

Suitability - RRs must have a reasonable basis for believing that each recommendation to a customer is suitable based on the information provided by the customer.

Conflicts of Interest - RRs must avoid any conflicts of interest in transactions with customers. Conduct Rule 2711, IM-2210-1 (6)(C) and Notices to Members 02-39 and 04-18 cover conflict of interest issues regarding research reports and stock recommendations.

Use of Current Information - RRs who communicate electronically must understand the importance of using current information. Outdated information runs a high risk of being inaccurate and misleading to investors.

Supervision - Conduct Rule 3010 requires member firms to supervise the activities of each RR. The supervisory responsibility of the member firm covers the use of e-mail, bulletin boards, chat rooms, and Web sites when it relates to the firm's business.

State Registration Requirements Apply - Each state has separate registration requirements for individuals doing business in that state. Use of e-mail, group e-mail, bulletin boards, chat rooms, and Web sites may be a solicitation of business. Generally, the solicitation of business in a state triggers the requirement for registration. RRs are advised to rely on their individual firms for guidance regarding state registration issues.

Use of E-Mail and Instant Messaging

Whether from the office or home, e-mail and instant messaging to the public falls under NASD jurisdiction. Frequently, RRs mistakenly believe that if they correspond with clients via e-mail or instant messaging from home the communication is not under the purview of their firm or regulators. The use of e-mail or instant messaging to communicate with individual clients may be considered correspondence or sales literature subject to NASD Conduct Rules.

Member firms are required to supervise and review business-related e-mail and instant messaging sent by RRs, whether from home or the office.

- NASD Conduct Rule 3010 - **Supervision** -- This NASD Rule addresses the review of an RR's electronic messages by a member firm. The Rule requires members to establish, maintain and enforce written procedures for advertisements, sales literature and correspondence, to ensure compliance with all applicable securities laws and rules. Therefore, RRs must know their firm's supervisory and review policies and comply with them, even if they are more restrictive than what is allowed under NASD rules. Many members restrict the use of e-mail communications with customers because of the difficulties of supervision and review. Some members prohibit the use of instant messaging altogether because of perceived difficulties in adequately supervising this activity. In fact, NASD Notice to Members 03-33 indicates that if a member is unable to establish an adequate supervisory program, the member must prohibit the use of instant messaging in customer communications. Members that permit instant messaging must use a platform that enables the member to monitor, archive, and retrieve message traffic. **Failure to follow the firm's supervisory**

    and review procedures and regulations in general may subject an RR to either internal and/or regulatory disciplinary action.
- <u>Notice to Members 99-03</u> provides a full discussion of how Rule 3010 applies to electronic communications.
- <u>NASD Conduct Rule 3110</u> - **Books and Records** -- This NASD Rule requires that correspondence (both written and electronic) with public customers be maintained in compliance with applicable NASD rules and with SEC Rules 17a-3 and 17a-4. This means that an RR's e-mail or instant messaging to the public relating to the firm's business generated at the office or at home, is subject to these provisions. RRs should know and comply with their firm's policies in this area.

E-mail or instant messaging to the public from the office or home falls under NASD jurisdiction.

Prior written approval is required for all group e-mail not considered correspondence as defined.

Group e-mail or instant messaging is an identical electronic mail message sent to multiple individuals. This type of electronic message is generally considered sales literature. Whether it is considered sales literature or correspondence mainly depends on whether it is going to existing or prospective customers and the number of customers involved. Under Conduct Rule 2210, group e-mail or instant messaging to 25 or more prospective retail customers would be considered sales literature. The Rule requires that sales literature receive prior written approval by a registered principal. Depending upon the content, sales literature may also require filing with NASD's Advertising Regulation Department. RRs are required to work within their firm's policies and procedures to avoid compliance problems and potential liability.

Group e-mail or instant messaging categorized as sales literature must be approved prior to use by a registered principal of the member firm.

<u>NASD Rule 2211</u> addresses the compliance requirements for institutional sales material, including electronic mail messages. The content compliance standards and supervisory obligations are generally the same for retail and institutional communications. However, e-mail communications that meet the definition of "institutional sales material" do not need to be filed with <u>NASD's Advertising Regulation Department</u>.
- <u>NASD Conduct Rule 2210(b)</u> - **Approval and Recordkeeping**. This NASD Rule requires that sales literature, both written and electronic, be maintained as part of the firm's records. Therefore, e-mails with the public relating to the firm's business are subject to these provisions. RRs must know what their firm's policies and procedures are in order to comply with these rules.

Electronic Chat Rooms

Chat room participation by RRs is considered a public appearance and subject to the same guidelines.

Therefore, RRs must follow the same requirements for participating in a chat room that they would if they were speaking in person before a group of investors. There are no filing requirements, but RRs are accountable under NASD Conduct Rules and the federal securities laws for what they say regarding securities or services. Also, member firms are responsible for supervising the business-related activities of RRs including chat room participation. Remember, these rules apply regardless of whether an RR is in the office or at home.

Because chat rooms contain live, unprepared communications, RRs are not required to get their comments approved in advance, unless their firm requires them to do so. In addition, chat room communications are not subject to the filing requirements of NASD Conduct Rule 2210(c). However, the content standards under Rule 2210(d) and IM-2210-1 do apply. RRs must check their firm's policy to see if they are allowed to participate in investment-related chat rooms and to seek permission from their firms to participate prior to doing so.

The fact that an individual is registered subjects him/her to a higher standard than members of the general public. Given the fast-paced environment of chat rooms, casual or off-handed statements have the potential of crossing the line between being a reasonable opinion and an exaggerated or unwarranted claim. Because of the difficulties of supervision and the potential liabilities from participating in chat rooms, many firms limit or prohibit participation altogether.

The content standards of Rule 2210(d) and related IM-2210-1 apply to public appearances, including chat room participation.

Web Sites

Web sites are advertisements and are subject to all requirements of NASD Conduct Rule 2210.

There are no separate rules or guidelines for use in preparing advertising material for the Internet. Web sites are subject to the same standards as other forms of advertisements. All Web sites used in connection with a securities business must be approved prior to use by a registered principal and must comply with Rule 2210.

Following are two examples of Web site usage by RRs:

1. **Personal Web sites (not securities/investment related)** may contain a short biography or profile describing the individual as being an RR, provided securities or investment activities are not the focus of the information on the site. Such sites are not considered advertisements under NASD rules.

2. An RR's **personal profile** on a member firm's Web site is subject to NASD rules. In this case, the RR would be responsible for having such pages approved internally by a registered principal. These pages may be individually designed, or use the firm's pre-approved templates. Some firms provide templates for RRs to use, while others allow for more customization of the information.

Points to remember:

Member firm name required - Web sites must clearly and prominently include the name of the member firm (or a legal fictional name) by which the firm is commonly recognized or name required by any state or jurisdiction) so that investors know the firm with which they are doing business.

State registration may be required - Since Web sites can be viewed from anywhere, state registration/licensing requirements may apply. Be sure to check with your firm to ensure compliance with such requirements.

Research reports require approval - Research reports require approval, in writing, by a registered principal before they are posted on a Web site. Conduct Rule 2711, IM-2210-1 (6)(C) and Notices to Members 02-39 and 04-18 cover the rule prohibitions and the conflict of interest disclosures that must be made by a research analyst or included in a research report.

Use current information - Outdated information runs a high risk of being inaccurate and may mislead investors.

Disclose risk factors - Both the content of the risk disclosure and its location are important. Risk disclosure should clearly and accurately describe the risks involved. Disclosures should be included in the appropriate locations within the Web site and in the related material. This is important because visitors may jump from one Web page to another, or come to the site from different entry points. Investors should see the disclosures regardless of their entry point into the site.

Day Trading Rules - NASD Rules 2360 and 2361 apply to member firms that promote day trading strategies. Firms are required to furnish a risk disclosure statement to a non-institutional customer prior to opening an account for the customer. In addition, the firm will either have to (1) approve the customer's account for a day trading strategy, or (2) obtain from the customer a written agreement that the customer does not intend to use the account for day-trading purposes. As part of the account approval process, the firm is required to make a threshold determination that day trading is appropriate for the customer. Notice to Members 00-62, provides more information on these day-trading rules.

Speed & Reliability Claims - Communications that refer to the speed and reliability of a firm's electronic trading systems must not exaggerate the firm's capabilities. Notice to Members 99-11 provides guidance about disclosures that firms provide to customers to educate them about the effects of market volatility and volume.

Linking to other Web Sites

Linking to other sites raises concerns because these sites may contain misleading or incorrect information. An RR's Web site should not have a link to a site that he/she knows or has reason to know contains false or misleading information about products or services. RRs should exercise the same care in choosing links as they would in referring customers to any outside source of information.

Linking to NASD Web Sites. A Web site may link to NASD Web sites provided:

- the link must be a text-only link clearly marked "NASD";

- the appearance, position, and other aspects of the link may not be such as to damage or dilute the goodwill associated with NASD's name and trademarks;

- the appearance, position, and other aspects of the link may not create the false appearance that an entity is associated with or sponsored by NASD;

- the link, when activated by a user, must display these sites full-screen and not within a "frame" on the linked Web site.

Pertinent Links:
- Broker Guidance & Information
- Registered Representatives & Other Securities Industry Professionals
- Disciplinary Information

IM Guidance Update

March 2014 | No. 2014-4

GUIDANCE ON THE TESTIMONIAL RULE AND SOCIAL MEDIA

From time to time, we have been asked questions concerning the nature, scope and application of the rule that prohibits investment advisers from using testimonials in their advertisements. In addition, in the past several years, we have been asked a number of questions concerning investment advisers' use of social media. We are now providing this guidance concerning registered investment advisers' use of social media and their publication[1] of advertisements that feature public commentary about them that appears on independent, third-party social media sites.[2]

We understand that use of social media has increased the demand by consumers for independent, third-party commentary or review of any manner of service providers, including investment advisers. We recognize that social media has facilitated consumers' ability to research and conduct their own due diligence on current or prospective service providers. Through this guidance, we seek to clarify application of the testimonial rule as it relates to the dissemination of genuine third-party commentary that could be useful to consumers.

Specifically, we seek through this guidance to assist firms in applying section 206(4) of the Investment Advisers Act of 1940 ("Advisers Act") and rule 206(4)-1(a)(1) thereunder ("testimonial rule") to their use of social media.[3] The guidance, in the form of questions and answers, also seeks to assist investment advisers in developing compliance policies and procedures reasonably designed to address participation in this evolving technology, specifically with respect to the publication of any public commentary that is a testimonial.

Consistent with previous staff guidance, we believe that in certain circumstances, as described below, an investment adviser's or investment advisory representative's ("IAR's") publication of all of the testimonials about the investment adviser or IAR from an independent social media site on the investment adviser's or IAR's own social media site or website would not implicate the concern underlying the testimonial rule.[4]

US Securities and Exchange Commission
Division of Investment Management

BACKGROUND

Section 206(4) generally prohibits any investment adviser from engaging in any act, practice or course of business that the Commission, by rule, defines as fraudulent, deceptive or manipulative. In particular, rule 206(4)-1(a)(1) states that:

> *[i]t shall constitute a fraudulent, deceptive, or manipulative act, practice, or course of business . . . for any investment adviser registered or required to be registered under [the Advisers Act], directly or indirectly, to publish, circulate, or distribute any advertisement which refers, directly or indirectly, to any testimonial of any kind concerning the investment adviser or concerning any advice, analysis, report or other service rendered by such investment adviser.*

Rule 206(4)-1(a)(1) was designed to address the nature of testimonials when used in investment advisory advertisements. When it adopted the rule, the Commission stated that, in the context of investment advisers, it found ". . . such advertisements are misleading; by their very nature they emphasize the comments and activities favorable to the investment adviser and ignore those which are unfavorable."[5] The staff has stated that the rule forbids the use of a testimonial by an investment adviser in advertisements "because the testimonial may give rise to a fraudulent or deceptive implication, or mistaken inference, that the experience of the person giving the testimonial is typical of the experience of the adviser's clients."[6]

Whether public commentary on a social media site is a testimonial depends upon all of the facts and circumstances relating to the statement. The term "testimonial" is not defined in the rule, but the staff has consistently interpreted that term to include a "statement of a client's experience with, or endorsement of, an investment adviser."[7] Depending on the facts and circumstances, public commentary made directly by a client about his or her own experience with, or endorsement of, an investment adviser or a statement made by a third party about a client's experience with, or endorsement of, an investment adviser may be a testimonial.[8]

The staff also has stated that an investment adviser's publication of an article by an unbiased third party regarding the adviser's investment performance is not a testimonial, unless it includes a statement of a client's experience with or endorsement of the adviser.[9] The staff also has stated that an adviser's advertisement that includes a partial client list that does no more than identify certain clients of the adviser cannot be viewed either as a statement of a client's experience with, or endorsement of, the adviser and therefore is not a testimonial.[10] Such an advertisement could nonetheless violate section 206(4) and rule 206(4)-1(a)(5) if the advertisement is false or misleading.[11]

The staff no longer takes the position, as it did a number of years ago, that an advertisement that contains non-investment related commentary regarding an IAR, such as regarding an IAR's religious affiliation or community service, may be deemed a testimonial violative of rule 206(4)-1(a)(1).[12]

The following questions and answers are intended to provide more guidance.

Third-party commentary

Q1. *May an investment adviser or IAR publish public commentary that is an explicit or implicit statement of a client's experience with or endorsement of the investment adviser or IAR on the investment adviser's or IAR's social media site?*

A1. Generally, staff believes that such public commentary would be a testimonial within the meaning of rule 206(4)-1(a)(1) and its use in an advertisement by an investment adviser or IAR would therefore be prohibited.

- For example, if an investment adviser or IAR invited clients to post such public commentary directly on the investment adviser's own internet site, blog or social media site that served as an advertisement for the investment adviser or IAR's advisory services, such testimonials would not be permissible.

Q2. *May an investment adviser or IAR publish the same public commentary on its own internet or social media site if it comes from an independent social media site?*

A2. When an investment adviser or IAR has no ability to affect which public commentary is included or how the public commentary is presented on an independent social media site; where the commentators' ability to include the public commentary is not restricted;[13] and where the independent social media site allows for the viewing of <u>all</u> public commentary and updating of new commentary on a real-time basis, the concerns underlying the testimonial prohibition may not be implicated.

As described in more depth below, publication of public commentary from an independent social media site would not raise any of the dangers that rule 206(4)-1(a)(1) was designed to prevent if:

- the independent social media site provides content that is independent of the investment adviser or IAR;

- there is no material connection between the independent social media site and the investment adviser or IAR that would call into question the independence of the independent social media site or commentary; and

- the investment adviser or IAR publishes <u>all</u> of the unedited comments appearing on the independent social media site regarding the investment adviser or IAR.[14]

Under these circumstances, an investment adviser or IAR may include such public commentary in an advertisement without implicating the concerns underlying the testimonial rule.

If, however, the investment adviser or IAR drafts or submits commentary that is included on the independent social media site, the testimonial rule generally would be implicated. Also, if the investment adviser or IAR is allowed to suppress the publication of all or a portion of the commentary, edit the commentary or is able to organize or prioritize the order in which the commentary is presented, the testimonial rule generally would be implicated.

Q3. *What content is not independent of an investment adviser or IAR and what is a material connection that would call into question the independence of a site or commentary?*

A3. Commentary would not be independent of an investment adviser or IAR if the investment adviser or IAR directly or indirectly authored the commentary on the independent social media site, whether in their own name, a third party's name, or an alias, assumed or screen name.

An investment adviser or IAR would have a material connection with a site or commentary that would call into question the independence of the site or commentary if, for example, the investment adviser or IAR: (1) compensated a social media user for authoring the commentary, including with any product or service of value; or (2) prioritized, removed or edited the commentary.[15]

- For example, an investment adviser could not have a supervised person submit testimonials about the investment adviser on an independent social media site and use such testimonials in advertisements without implicating the testimonial rule.

- An investment adviser or IAR could not compensate a client or prospective client (including with discounts or offers of free services) to post commentary on an independent social media site and use such testimonials in advertisements without implicating the testimonial rule.

Q4. *May an investment adviser or IAR publish testimonials from an independent social media site in a way that allows social media users to sort the criteria?*

A4. An investment adviser or IAR's publication of testimonials from an independent social media site that directly or indirectly emphasizes commentary favorable to the investment adviser or IAR or de-emphasizes commentary unfavorable to the investment adviser or IAR would implicate the prohibition on testimonials. The investment adviser may publish only the totality of the testimonials from an independent social media site and may not highlight or give prominence to a subset of the testimonials.

- Investment adviser or IAR sites may publish the testimonials from an independent social media site in a content-neutral manner, such as by chronological or alphabetical order, which presents positive and negative commentary with equal prominence.

- Social media users, however, are free to personally display the commentary and sort by any criteria, including by the lowest or highest rating. Investment adviser and IAR sites may facilitate a user's viewing of the commentary by providing a sorting mechanism as long as the investment adviser or IAR site does not itself sort the commentary.

Q5. *May an investment adviser or IAR publish testimonials from an independent social media site that includes a mathematical average of the public commentary?*

A5. Publication by an investment adviser or IAR of such testimonials from an independent social media site would not raise any of the dangers that rule 206(4)-1(a)(1) was designed to prevent if the independent social media site were designed to make it equally easy for the public to provide negative or positive commentary about an investment adviser or IAR.

- Investment advisers or IARs could publish testimonials from an independent social media site that include a mathematical average of the commentary provided that commenters themselves rate the investment advisers or IARs based on a ratings system that is not designed to elicit any pre-determined results that could benefit any investment adviser or IAR.

- The independent social media site, the investment adviser and the IAR may not provide a subjective analysis of the commentary.[16]

Inclusion of Investment Adviser Advertisements on Independent Social Media Site

Q6. *May an investment adviser or IAR publish public commentary from an independent site if that site also features the investment adviser or IAR's advertising?*

A6. The existence of an investment adviser or IAR's advertisement within the architecture of an independent site that also contains independent public commentary does not, in combination, create a prohibited testimonial or otherwise make the advertisement false or misleading, provided that the investment adviser complies with the material connection and independence factors described above and provided that the advertisement is easily recognizable to the public as a sponsored statement.

- In other words, an advertisement would not cause the investment adviser or IAR's publication of the independent social media site's commentary to violate rule 206(4)-1 where (1) it would be readily apparent to a reader that the investment adviser or IAR's advertisement is separate from the public commentary featured on the independent social media site and (2) the receipt or non-receipt of advertising revenue did not in any way influence which public commentary is included or excluded from the independent social media site.

Reference to Independent Social Media Site Commentary Investment Adviser Non-Social Media Advertisements

Q7. *May an investment adviser or IAR refer to public commentary from an independent social media site on non-social media advertisements (e.g., newspaper, radio, television)?*

A7. An investment adviser or IAR could reference the fact that public commentary regarding the investment adviser or IAR may be found on an independent social media site, and may include the logo of the independent social media site on its non-social media advertisements, without implicating the testimonial rule.

- For example, an IAR could state in its newspaper ad "see us on [independent social media site]," to signal to clients and prospective clients that they can research public commentary about the investment adviser or IAR on an independent social media site.

- In contrast, an investment adviser or IAR may not publish any testimonials from the independent social media site on the newspaper ad without implicating the testimonial rule.[17]

Client lists

Q8. Would a list or photographs of "friends" "or "contacts" on an investment adviser or IAR's social media site that is viewable by the general public be considered a testimonial or otherwise violate section 206(4) or rule 206(4)-1?

A8. It is common on social media sites to include a communal listing of contacts or friends. The staff has stated that an advertisement that contains a partial client list that does no more than identify certain clients of the adviser cannot be viewed either as a statement of a client's experience with, or endorsement of, the investment adviser, and therefore is not a testimonial.[16] Such an advertisement, however, could be false or misleading under rule 206(4)-1(a)(5) depending on the facts and circumstances.

- If the contacts or friends are not grouped or listed so as to be identified as current or past clients of an IAR, but are simply listed by the social media site as accepted contacts or friends of the IAR in the ordinary course, such a listing of contacts or friends generally would not be considered to be in violation of rule 206(4)-1(a)(1).

- However, if an IAR attempts to create the inference that the contacts or friends have experienced favorable results from the IAR's investment advisory services, the advertisement could be considered to be in violation of section 206(4) and rule 206(4)-1.

Fan/Community Pages

Q9. Individuals unconnected with a particular investment adviser or IAR may establish "community" or "fan" or other third-party sites where the public may comment on a myriad of investment topics, along with commentary regarding an investment adviser firm or individual IARs. Do such sites raise concerns under rule 206(4)-1?

A9. In the ordinary course, a third party's creation and operation of unconnected community or fan pages generally would not implicate rule 206(4)-1. We strongly caution investment advisers and supervised persons when publishing content from or driving user traffic to such sites (including through hyperlinks to such sites), particularly if the site does not meet the material connection and independence conditions described above. The Commission has stated that:

> Any SEC-registered investment adviser (or investment adviser that is required to be SEC registered) that includes, in its web site or in other electronic communications, a hyperlink to postings on third-party web sites, should carefully consider the applicability of the advertising provisions of the [Advisers Act]. Under the Advisers Act, it is a fraudulent act for an investment adviser to, among other things, refer to testimonials in its advertisements.[19]

Endnotes

1   For purposes of this guidance, "publication" refers to any form of real-time broad-
     cast through social media or the Internet whether by hyperlinking, posting, live-
     streaming, tweeting, or forwarding or any similar public dissemination and, does not
     relate to advertisements on non-Internet or non-social media sites, such as paper,
     television or radio. Social media allows for instantaneous updating of posted com-
     mentary and concurrent viewing of *all of* the comment history; in contrast, paper,
     television and radio are static media that reflect public commentary at a particular
     point in time and are limited media that would typically not reproduce all of the
     available public commentary simultaneously (often due to cost, space and other
     considerations).

2   As used herein, "independent social media sites" refers specifically to third-party
     social media sites that predominantly host user opinions, beliefs, findings or experi-
     ences about service providers, including investment advisory representatives or
     investment advisers (*e.g.*, Angie's List). An investment adviser's or IAR's own social
     media profile or account that is used for business purposes is not an "independent
     social media site."

3   This *IM Guidance Update* only addresses the use by a firm or IARs of social media
     sites for business purposes. This Update does not address the use by individuals of
     social media sites for purely personal reasons. This Update does not seek to address
     any obligations under state law of social media for business use. In addition, this
     guidance does not seek to address the use of social media sites by broker-dealers.

4   Any such advertisements also must comply with rule 206(4)-1(a)(5).

5   Investment Advisers Act Rel. No. 121 (Nov. 2, 1961) (adopting rule 206(4)-1).

6   *See* Richard Silverman, Staff No-Action Letter (pub. avail. March 27, 1985).

7   *See* Cambiar Investors, Inc., Staff No-Action Letter (pub. avail. Aug. 28, 1997)
     ("Cambiar").

8   *See* DALBAR, Inc., Staff No-Action letter (pub. avail. March 24, 1998) ("DALBAR").

9   *See* New York Investors Group, Inc., Staff No-Action Letter (pub. avail. Sept. 7, 1982);
     Stalker Advisory Services, Staff No-Action Letter (pub. avail. Feb. 14, 1994). *See also*
     Kurtz Capital Management, Staff No-Action Letter (pub. avail. Jan. 22, 1988).

10   *See* Cambiar, supra note 7.

11   *Id.* ("For example, the inclusion of a partial client list in an adviser's advertisement
     has the potential to mislead investors if the clients on the list are selected on the
     basis of performance and this selection bias is not adequately disclosed. A list that
     includes only advisory clients who have experienced above-average performance
     could lead an investor who contacts the clients for references to infer something
     about the adviser's competence or about the possibility of enjoying a similar invest-
     ment experience that the investor might not have inferred if criteria unrelated to the
     client's performance had been used to select the clients on the list or if the selec-
     tion bias was fully and fairly disclosed.").

12 *See* Dan Gallagher, Staff No-Action Letter (pub. avail. July 10, 1995). Advisers that publish advertisements regarding non-investment related commentary remain subject to the fiduciary responsibilities imposed by section 206(1) and (2) of the Advisers Act. Thus an adviser cannot use social media to perpetrate affinity frauds, which are investment scams that prey upon members of identifiable groups, such as religious or ethnic communities, the elderly, or professional groups. Affinity frauds can target any group of people who take pride in their shared characteristics, whether they are religious, ethnic, or professional. *See* http://www.sec.gov/investor/pubs/affinity.htm.

13 Some independent social media sites may have member fees or subscriptions payable by users. An investment adviser or IAR's publication of public commentary from a site that charges member or subscription fees to public users would not call into question the independence of the independent social media site for purposes of our views herein.

14 Independent social media sites may have editorial policies that edit or remove public commentary violative of the site's own published content guidelines (*e.g.*, prohibiting defamatory statements; threatening language; materials that infringe on intellectual property rights; materials that contain viruses, spam or other harmful components; racially offensive statements or profanity). An investment adviser or IAR's publication of public commentary that has been edited according to such an editorial policy would not call into question the independence of the independent social media site for purposes of the staff's views herein.

15 As explained in Q6 below, any arrangement whereby the investment adviser or IAR compensated the independent social media site, including with advertising or other revenue, in order to publish or suppress the publication of anything less than the totality of the public commentary submitted could render any use by the IAR or investment adviser on its social media site violative of the prohibition on testimonials.

16 *See* DALBAR, supra note 8.

17 *See* supra note 1.

18 *See Cambiar, supra* note 7.

19 *See* Commission Guidance on the Use of Company Websites at note 83, Investment Company Act Rel. No. 28351 (Aug. 1, 2008). *See also SEC Interpretation: Use of Electronic Media*, Investment Company Act Rel. No. 24426 (May 4, 2000).

The Investment Management Division works to:

▲ protect investors

▲ promote informed investment decisions and

▲ facilitate appropriate innovation in investment products and services

through regulating the asset management industry.

If you have any questions about this IM Guidance Update, please contact:
Catherine Courtney Gordon
Chief Counsel's Office/Public Inquiry
Phone: 202.551.6825
Email: IMOCC@sec.gov

National Examination Risk Alert

By the Office of Compliance Inspections and Examinations[1]

In this Alert:

Topic: Observations related to the use of social media by registered investment advisers.

Key Takeaways:

Investment advisers that use or permit the use of social media by their representatives, solicitors and/or third parties should consider periodically evaluating the effectiveness of their compliance program as it relates to social media. Factors that might be considered include usage guidelines, content standards, sufficient monitoring, approval of content, training, etc. Particular attention should be paid to third party content (if permitted) and recordkeeping responsibilities.

Volume II, Issue 1   January 4, 2012

Investment Adviser Use of Social Media

I.   Introduction

Social media[2] is landscape-shifting. It converts the traditional two-party, adviser-to-client communication into an interactive, multi-party dialogue among advisers, clients, and prospects, within an open architecture accessible to third-party observers. It also converts a static medium, such as a website, where viewers passively receive content, into a medium where users actively create content.

The use of social media by the financial services industry is rapidly accelerating. In growing numbers, registered investment advisers ("RIAs" or "firms") are using social media to communicate with existing and potential clients, promote services, educate investors and recruit new employees. Pursuant to Advisers Act Rule 206(4)-7,[3] firms using social media should adopt, and periodically review the effectiveness of, policies and

---

[1]   The Securities and Exchange Commission ("SEC"), as a matter of policy, disclaims responsibility for any private publication or statement by any of its employees. The views expressed herein are those of the staff of the Office of Compliance Inspections and Examinations, in coordination with other SEC staff, including in the Division of Enforcement's Asset Management Unit and the Division of Investment Management, and do not necessarily reflect the views of the Commission or the other staff members of the SEC. The staff of the Financial Industry Regulatory Authority ("FINRA") was also consulted in the preparation of this Risk Alert. This document was prepared by the SEC staff and is not legal advice.

[2]   "Social media" is an umbrella term that encompasses various activities that integrate technology, social interaction and content creation. Social media may use many technologies, including, but not limited to, blogs, microblogs, wikis, photos and video sharing, podcasts, social networking, and virtual worlds. The terms "social media," "social media sites," "sites" and "social networking sites" are used interchangeably in this communication.

[3]   17 C.F.R. §206(4)-7.

procedures regarding social media in the face of rapidly changing technology.[4]

Firms' use of social media must comply with various provisions of the federal securities laws, including, but not limited to, the antifraud provisions,[5] compliance provisions,[6] and recordkeeping provisions.[7]

RIAs' use of social media has been a matter of interest to the staff, which recently identified registered investment advisers of varying sizes and strategies that were using social media to evaluate whether their use complied with the federal securities laws.[8] Below are some observations from that review, as well as factors that the staff believes a firm that permits the use of social media may want to consider in complying with its obligations under the federal securities laws.

II.   Staff Observations

A.   Compliance Program Related to the Use of Social Media

Many firms have policies and procedures within their compliance programs that specifically apply to the use of social media by the firm and its IARs; however, the staff observed variation in the form and substance of the policies and procedures. The staff noted that many firms have multiple overlapping procedures that apply to advertisements, client communications or electronic communications generally, which may or may not specifically include social media use. Such lack of specificity may cause confusion as to what procedures or standards apply to social media use. Many procedures were also not specific as to which types of social networking activity are permitted or prohibited by the firm and many did not address the use of social media by solicitors.

---

[4]   This Alert is not intended as a comprehensive summary of all compliance matters pertaining to the use of social media by RIAs. Rather, it discusses measures that may assist RIAs in designing reasonable procedures designed to prevent violations of the Advisers Act and other federal securities laws with respect to firm, investment advisory representative ("IAR") and solicitor (employees or third parties that solicit or "find" new advisory clients) use of social media.

[5]   *See, e.g.*, Section 17(a) of the Securities Act of 1933 ("Securities Act"), 15 U.S.C. §77q(a), Section 10(b) of the Securities Exchange Act of 1934 ("Exchange Act"), 15 U.S.C. §78j(b), and Rule 10b-5 thereunder, 17 C.F.R. §240.10b-5, and Sections 206(1), 206(2), and 206(4) of the Advisers Act, 15 U.S.C. §§806-6(2), 806-6(4), and Rule 206(4)-1 thereunder, 17 C.F.R. §206(4)-1.

[6]   *See, e.g.*, Section 206(4) of the Advisers Act, 15 U.S.C. § 806-6(4), and Rule 206(4)-7 thereunder, 17 C.F.R. §206(4)-7.

[7]   *See, e.g.*, Section 204 of the Advisers Act, 15 U.S.C. § 804, and Rule 204(2) thereunder, 17 C.F.R. §204(2).

[8]   To the extent that a firm provides both brokerage and investment advisory services ("dual registrant"), it is required to adhere to both the federal securities laws and FINRA applicable rules, including but not limited to, depending on the circumstances, Rule 17a-4(b) (recordkeeping) under the Exchange Act, 17 C.F.R §240.17a-4(b), and NASD Rules 2210 and 3010. FINRA has issued guidance regarding the application of the federal securities laws and its rules to the use of social media by broker-dealers or their representatives. *See* FINRA Regulatory Notice 11-39 (Aug. 2011); FINRA Regulatory Notice 10-06 (Jan. 2010).

When evaluating its controls and compliance program, a firm should first identify conflicts and other compliance factors currently creating risk exposure for the firm and its clients in light of the firm's particular operations, and then test whether its existing policies and procedures effectively address those risks.[9]

Below is a non-exhaustive list of factors[10] that an investment adviser[11] may want to consider when evaluating the effectiveness of its compliance program with respect to firm, IAR or solicitor use of social media:

- **Usage Guidelines**. A firm may consider whether to create firm usage guidelines that provide guidance to IARs and solicitors on the appropriate and inappropriate use of social media. A firm may also consider addressing appropriate restrictions and prohibitions regarding the use of social media sites based on the firm's analysis of the risk to the firm and its clients. For example, a firm may choose to provide an exclusive list of approved social media networking sites for IARs' use or prohibit the use of specific functionalities on a site.

- **Content Standards**. A firm may consider the risks that content created by the firm or its IARs or solicitors implicates its fiduciary duty or other regulatory issues (*e.g.*, such as content that contains investment recommendations, information on specific investment services or investment performance). A firm may also consider whether to articulate clear guidelines with respect to such content, and whether to prohibit specific content or impose other content restrictions.[12]

- **Monitoring**. A firm may consider how to effectively monitor the firm's social media sites or firm use of third-party sites, taking into account that many third-party sites may not provide complete access to a supervisor or compliance personnel.

- **Frequency of Monitoring**. A firm may consider the frequency with which it monitors IAR or solicitor activity on a social media site. For example, using a risk-based approach, a firm may conclude that periodic, daily or real-time monitoring of the postings on a site is appropriate. This determination could depend on the volume and pace of communications posted on a site or the nature of, and the probability to

---

[9]   *See* Rule 206(4)-7. *See generally* Compliance Programs of Investment Companies and Investment Advisers, 68 FR 74714, 74716 (Dec. 24, 2003)("Compliance Release").

[10]   Firms are encouraged to consider the factors described herein in assessing the effectiveness of their compliance program and implementing improvements that will best protect their clients. Firms are cautioned that these factors and suggestions are neither exhaustive nor will they constitute a safe harbor nor a "checklist" for SEC examiners. Other factors besides those highlighted here may also be appropriate. While some of the factors discussed herein reflect existing regulatory requirements, the adequacy of a compliance program can be determined only with reference to the profile of the specific firm and the specific facts and circumstances.

[11]   Dual registrants may also want to consider these factors, although they do not modify or displace firms' obligations under the federal securities laws, FINRA or other rules relevant to social media, or FINRA guidance in this area, as referenced in footnote 7 *supra*.

[12]   A majority of the advisers we observed prohibited the posting of recommendations or information on specific products or services on their social media sites.

mislead contained in, the subject matter discussed in particular conversation streams. The after-the-fact review of violative content days after it was posted on a firm's social networking site, depending on the circumstances, may not be reasonable, particularly where social media content can be rapidly and broadly disseminated to investors and the markets.

- **Approval of Content.** A firm may want to consider the appropriateness of pre-approval requirements (as opposed to after-the-fact review, as discussed above).[13]

- **Firm Resources**. A firm may consider whether it has dedicated sufficient compliance resources to adequately monitor IAR or solicitor activity on social media sites, including the ability to monitor the activity of numerous IARs or solicitors. A firm may also consider employing conversation monitoring or similar services from outside vendors, if, for example, the firm has many IARs or solicitors who use social media sites. A firm may consider using sampling, spot checking, or lexicon-based or other search methodologies, or a combination of methodologies, to monitor social media use and content.[14]

- **Criteria for Approving Participation**. In analyzing the risk exposure for a firm and its clients due to the use of a social networking site, the firm's compliance procedures may consider, without limitation, the reputation of the site, the site's privacy policy, the ability to remove third-party posts, controls on anonymous posting and the advertising practices of any social media site that the firm, or its IARs or solicitors use to conduct business.

- **Training**. In establishing or reviewing any training requirements for its IARs, a firm may consider implementing training related to social media that seeks to promote compliance and to prevent potential violations of the federal securities laws and the firm's internal policies.

- **Certification**. A firm may consider whether to require a certification by IARs and advisory solicitors confirming that those individuals understand and are complying with the firm's social media policies and procedures.

- **Functionality**. A firm may consider the functionality of each social media site approved for use, including the continuing obligation to address any upgrades or modifications to the functionality that affect the risk exposure for the firm or its clients. Such consideration is particularly significant given the rapidly evolving nature of this new media. For example, a firm that chooses to host social media on a site that includes a functionality or engages in a practice that exposes a client-user's

---

[13] The pre-approval of postings on a social media site is presently only required for broker-dealers in certain circumstances. *See* NASD Rule 2210.

[14] While the firm may use third-party services for this purpose, the firm is ultimately responsible for its IARs' or solicitors' use of social media.

4

privacy, which practice or policy cannot be disabled or modified, may need to consider whether the firm's participation is appropriate.

- **Personal/Professional Sites**. A firm may consider whether to adopt policies and procedures to address an IAR or solicitor conducting firm business on personal (non-business) or third-party social media sites. For example, a firm may choose to specify what types of firm communications or content are permitted on a site that is not operated, supervised or sponsored by the firm. While a firm may determine that it is appropriate to permit business card information on a specific personal site or third-party site, it may choose to prohibit conducting firm business on that site.

- **Information Security**. A firm may consider whether permitting its IARs to have access to social media sites poses any information security risks. Protecting information and information systems from unauthorized access, use, disclosure, disruption, modification, perusal, inspection, recording or destruction is an important risk faced by all firms. Although hacking and other breaches of information security can be posed in multiple ways, use of social media, especially third party social media sites, may pose elevated risks. Firms may consider adopting compliance policies and procedures to create appropriate firewalls between sensitive customer information, as well as the firm's own proprietary information, and any social media site to the extent that the firm permits access to such sites by its IARs.

- **Enterprise Wide Sites**. An RIA that is part of a larger financial services or other corporate enterprise may consider whether to create usage guidelines reasonably designed to prevent the advertising practices of a firm-wide social media site from violations of the Advisers Act

B.   Third-Party Content

Most firms allow third parties to make postings on their social media sites, but the policies and procedures governing such third-party postings vary in what types of postings are permissible. Some firms allow third parties to post messages, forward links, and post articles on the firms' social media sites, while other firms have explicit policies limiting third-party use to "one way postings," where the firms' IARs or solicitors post on the firms' social media sites but do not interact with third parties or respond to third-party postings. More conservatively, some firms limit third-party postings to authorized users and prohibit postings by the general public. Many firms post disclaimers directly on their site stating that they do not approve or endorse any third-party communications posted on their site in an attempt to avoid having a third-party posting attributed to the firm.

Firms that allow for third-party postings on their social media sites may consider having policies and procedures concerning third-party postings, including the posting of testimonials about the firm or its IARs as well as reasonable safeguards in place to avoid any violation of the federal securities laws.

- **Testimonials.** Whether a third-party statement is a testimonial[15] depends upon all of the facts and circumstances relating to the statement. The term "testimonial" is not defined in Rule 206(4)-1(a)(1), but SEC staff consistently interprets that term to include a statement of a client's experience with, or endorsement of, an investment adviser. Therefore, the staff believes that, depending on the facts and circumstances, the use of "social plug-ins" such as the "like" button could be a testimonial under the Advisers Act.[16] Third-party use of the "like" feature on an investment adviser's social media site could be deemed to be a testimonial if it is an explicit or implicit statement of a client's or clients' experience with an investment adviser or IAR. If, for example, the public is invited to "like" an IAR's biography posted on a social media site, that election could be viewed as a type of testimonial prohibited by rule 206(4)-1(a)(1).

C.   Recordkeeping Responsibilities

The Advisers Act sets forth the recordkeeping obligations of registered investment advisers.[17] The recordkeeping obligation does not differentiate between various media, including paper and electronic communications, such as e-mails, instant messages and other Internet communications that relate to the advisers' recommendations or advice. RIAs that communicate through social media must retain records of those communications if they contain information that satisfies an investment adviser's recordkeeping obligations under the Advisers Act.[18] In the staff's view the content of the communication is determinative. A firm that intends to communicate, or permit its IARs to communicate, through social media sites may wish to determine that it can retain all required records related to social media communications and make them available for inspection.

Social media offers multiple ways to communicate with existing or potential clients from status updates, discussion boards, emails, texting, direct messaging or chat rooms. RIAs should consider reviewing their document retention policies to ensure that any required records generated by social media communications are retained in compliance with the federal securities laws, including in a manner that is easily accessible for a period not less than five years. RIAs

---

[15]   Rule 206(4)-1(a)(1) states that:

[i]t shall constitute a fraudulent, deceptive, or manipulative act, practice, or course of business ... for any investment adviser registered or required to be registered under [the Advisers Act], directly or indirectly, to publish, circulate, or distribute any advertisement which refers, directly or indirectly, to any testimonial of any kind concerning the investment adviser or concerning any advice, analysis, report or other service rendered by such investment adviser.

[16]   Some social media sites do not permit an investment adviser to disable the "like" or similar feature, which may require an investment adviser to develop a system to monitor and, if necessary, remove third-party postings.

[17]   Rule 204-2 requires investment advisers to make certain books and records relating to their advisory business ("required records") and to keep them for a specified period of time. In addition, the rule requires investment advisers that keep required records in an electronic format to keep them in a manner that allows the records to be arranged and indexed. *See* Section 204 of the Advisers Act and Rule 204-2 thereunder.

[18]   *See* Rule 204-2.

should consider whether their retention policies account for the volume of communication and unique communication channels available to each particular social media site. Investment advisers may consider adopting compliance policies and procedures that address (if relevant) the following factors, among others, relating to the recordkeeping and production requirements of required records generated by social media communications:

- Determining, among other things, (1) whether each social media communication used is a required record, and, if so, (2) the applicable retention period, and (3) the accessibility of the records.
- Maintaining social media communications in electronic or paper format (*e.g.*, screen print or pdf of social media page, if practicable).
- Conducting employee training programs to educate advisory personnel about recordkeeping provisions.
- Arranging and indexing social media communications that are required records and kept in an electronic format to promote easy location, access and retrieval of a particular record.
- Periodic test checking (using key word searches or otherwise) to ascertain whether employees are complying with the compliance policies and procedures (*e.g.*, whether employees are improperly destroying required records).
- Using third parties to keep records consistent with the recordkeeping requirements.

IV. Conclusion

While many RIAs are eager to leverage social media to market and communicate with existing clients, and to promote general visibility, RIAs should ensure that they are in compliance with all of the regulatory requirements and be aware of the risks associated with using various forms of social media. The staff hopes that sharing observations from its recent review of RIAs' use of social media as well as its suggestions regarding factors that firms may wish to consider is helpful to firms in strengthening their compliance and risk management programs. The staff also welcomes comments and suggestions about how the Commission's examination program can better fulfill its mission to promote compliance, prevent fraud, monitor risk, and inform SEC policy. If you suspect or observe activity that may violate the federal securities laws or otherwise operates to harm investors, please notify us at http://www.sec.gov/complaint/info_tipscomplaint.shtml.

About the Author

A nationally known leader in wealth management and consumer advocacy, Jennifer Openshaw has observed first-hand how technology is rapidly changing the financial industry. She has advised Fortune 500 firms, including Microsoft, on technology, social media, and communications, and writes a column on consumer investing and tech tools for *Dow Jones' MarketWatch* and the LinkedIn Influencer program. She was named among the 25 Rising Stars of the Internet for her work as founder and CEO of Women's Financial Network, a pioneer in serving women investors online, and later sold the business to Wall Street legend Muriel Siebert. Jennifer started her career in the California State Treasurer's Office and has also held top positions at Bank of America, Wilshire Associates, and BankOne before serving as an executive of several consumer and wealth advisor social media platforms. Jennifer has appeared on *Oprah*, *Dr. Phil*, CNN, and Fox. She speaks nationwide to financial services companies, universities, and government agencies and also chairs Consumer Action's Corporate Advisory Board. Jennifer's previous book, *The Millionaire Zone* (Hyperion), is based on research about how the wealthy use their social networks to achieve financial success. Jennifer lives in Connecticut with her husband and two daughters. Follow her on Twitter at @jopenshaw and on LinkedIn at LinkedIn/in/jenopenshaw.

You may also contact her directly at info@sociallysavvyadvisor.com.

About the Contributors

Stuart Fross is a partner at Foley & Lardner. He specializes in securities laws and regulations, with special expertise in social media, investment managers, and pooled investment vehicles. He previously served as general counsel and senior vice president for Strategic Initiatives with Fidelity Management & Research Company as well as general counsel for Fidelity International, where he oversaw compliance in Europe, Asia, and Bermuda. Mr. Fross is the co-author of several books and articles, including *The Uneasy Chaperone* (Management Practice) and "Alternative Investment Fund Managers Directive—The Registered Investment Advisers Implementation Checklist" (*The Investment Lawyer*).

Author, speaker, and entrepreneur **Amy McIlwain** is president and founder of Financial Social Media, a full-service social media management and digital marketing agency specific to the financial service space. With over 15 years' experience in interactive media, Amy has appeared on FOX, CBS, ABC, and NBC affiliates as a social media expert and delivers keynote presentations to financial service organizations around the world. She is a regular contributor to *InvestmentNews* and in 2014 was named by LifeHealthPro as one of the 24 Most Creative People in Insurance. Amy can be reached on Twitter at @amymcilwain.

About the Companion Website

This book has a companion website, which can be found at www.wiley .com/go/financialsocial (password: savvy123). This website contains the following assets:

Video Links

Resources:
- 5 Reasons Social Media Matters to Financial Advisors
- Model Social Media Policy for Financial Institutions by Stuart Fross
- 2014 Individual Investors Social Media Behavior Report

Compliance References:
- 2013 FFICE Guidance on Social Media
- FINRA Regulatory Notice 10-06
- FINRA Regulatory Notice 11-39
- NASD Guide to the Internet for Registered Representatives
- SEC Guidance on the Testimonial Rule and Social Media, March 2014
- SEC IM Guidance Update, March 2013
- SEC National Examination Risk Alert

Contact the Author